The Arts in the Economic Life of the City

**A study by Urban Innovations Group
School of Architecture and Urban Planning
University of California, Los Angeles**

Harvey S. Perloff, Director

American Council for the Arts
570 Seventh Avenue
New York, NY 10018

© **1979 American Council for the Arts**
Additional copies may be obtained from:
ACA Publications
570 Seventh Avenue
New York, NY 10018

Library of Congress card catalog
number: 79–29764

ISBN 0-915400-16-2 (casebound)
ISBN: 0-915400-17-0 (paperbound)

Design: Kidokoro, Greenboam & Casey

This publication was made possible by generous contributions from the Shell Companies Foundation and the National Endowment for the Arts.

About the American Council for the Arts

The American Council for the Arts (ACA) is the only national organization representing and serving the entire arts constituency. With membership from every state and nearly every art form, ACA speaks on behalf of all the arts; its services are available to all artists and arts organizations.

All of ACA's activities fall into one or more of the following categories:

Management Training ACA helps the arts help themselves. It helps groups improve their effectiveness and efficiency. It helps them make optimum use of resources. It helps them market their product and respond to community needs.

Information Through its research, publications, and conferences, ACA provides the mechanism for the development and exchange of information on all the arts, for all the arts.

Advocacy/Promotion ACA is the only organization speaking for all the arts on a national level. It not only promotes the arts and demonstrates their importance, it also helps formulate arts policy. By seeking to increase support for the arts from all segments of the public and private sectors, ACA is trying to stablize the arts support base and make sure that no one segment bears a disproportionate share of the burden.

In short, the mission of ACA is to be the national resource center and service organization for all the arts.

ACA Officers
Chairman
Louis Harris
President
Anne Bartley
Vice Chairmen
Theodore Bikel
Edward M. Block
Mrs. Edward Marcus
Secretary-Treasurer
John Kilpatrick
Special Counsel for National Policy
Jack G. Duncan
Director
W. Grant Brownrigg

Board Members
Jane Alexander
Gerald Bartell
John Bitterman
Donald G. Conrad
Gilbert M. Denman, Jr.
Eugene Dorsey
Richard Dreyfuss
Enrique Duran
Arthur Gelber
Kitty Carlisle Hart
Richard Hunt
Mrs. B. T. Hurley, Jr.
George M. Irwin
Mayor Maynard Jackson
Mrs. Fred Lazarus, III
Governor William G. Milliken

Michael Newton
Alwin Nikolais
Milton Rhodes
Lloyd Rigler
David Rockefeller, Jr.
Rodney Rood
William Ruder
Robert Sakowitz
Frank Saunders
Edward L. Saxe
Homer E. Sayad
Stephen Stamas
Norton Stevens
Wesley C. Uhlman
Esther Wachtell
Mrs. Gerald H. Westby
Charles Yates

Preface

As the decade of the seventies closes out we see many signs of a new way of thinking about the arts in urban planning. Cities such as Dallas, Los Angeles, Hartford and San Antonio have demonstrated far more than a token recognition of the arts among civic priorities. A momentum has begun toward integrating the arts more sensitively and more deeply into city revitalization programs.

To build on this momentum, the American Council for the Arts is offering this new publication, *The Arts in the Economic Life of the City,* an analysis of how cultural activities can be an integrated part of the economic development of large central cities. The study was conducted by UCLA's Urban Innovations Group under the direction of Harvey S. Perloff, dean, School of Architecture and Urban Planning. Dr. Perloff has been a leading and influential proponent of the field of cultural planning. While the book gives a national overview of the many facets involved in cultural planning, it offers a special analysis of the strategies and developments that occurred in Los Angeles.

ACA has demonstrated its early and continued concern for the integral role of the arts in an urban environment through a number of books and conferences which explore this important topic. Most recently, ACA has published *Local Government and the Arts,* a comprehensive volume which explores the arts-government relationship, and in December 1979, conducted a major conference in San Antonio on *The Arts and City Planning*—a collaborative undertaking with key national arts organizations concerned with this issue, Partners for Livable Places, the American Planning Association, the U.S. Conference of Mayors and the National League of Cities.

The publication of this book would not have been possible without the most generous support of both the Shell Companies Foundation and the National Endowment for the Arts. We at ACA are deeply grateful to the Shell Companies Foundation and the NEA for their participation.

I want to express appreciation to Annette Covatta, ACA's director of programs, and to Robert Porter, manager of publications, for editing the manuscript and overseeing its production and printing.

As we move into the eighties, ACA will work closely with individuals, government agencies and organizations that are concerned about connecting the physical city, economic growth and cultural opportunities in a more sensitive and integrated way so that our urban environment may reach full maturity.

W. Grant Brownrigg, Director
American Council for the Arts.

Foreword

The purpose of this study is to consider the ways in which the economic contribution of the arts to the larger central cities—most of which are facing economic difficulties—might be enhanced. Concentration on such central cities is particularly appropriate since they now contain the largest proportion of the urban poor and minority families, individuals who have the greatest difficulties in getting jobs. The economic contribution of the arts to the less advantaged, as to society at large, is therefore of special significance.

The study approaches the subject through three avenues: (1) the development of a "model" or framework to inventory and analyze arts activities and institutions and to evolve strategies to enhance the contribution of the arts to local economies (Part I); (2) an overview of the arts activities and institutions in one city, Los Angeles, to lay an in-depth foundation for the discussion of strategies and tactics of change, (Part II); and (3) the probing of strategies to improve the organization and financing of the arts "system" to strengthen its economic contribution (Part III).

The study has been a group effort, involving faculty, students and recent graduates from UCLA, particularly the School of Architecture and Urban Planning and the Management in the Arts Program of the Graduate School of Management. But group efforts are made up of individual contributions and these should be recognized. They are of four kinds: (1) the major contributors, those who were involved in every phase of the study, provided the materials for at least as much as one chapter, and reviewed the various drafts; (2) the supplementary contributors, those who provided materials for a single section of a chapter (mainly to the study of the arts in Los Angeles); (3) the editing and art work; and (4) the individuals in the arts and at the university who advised us, some of whom reviewed various drafts of the present volume. The specific contributions are as follows:

The Major Contributors to the Study

Harvey S. Perloff, Dean, School of Architecture and Urban Planning

Organized the study, directed the research, prepared the first and last chapters of the volume and sections throughout, as well as the "highlights."

Paul Bullock, Research Economist, Institute of Industrial Relations

Prepared the materials on community arts, the movie and record industries, CETA, as well as some miscellaneous materials.

Lee Cooper, Director, Management in the Arts Program, Graduate School of Management

Prepared the materials on financing the arts, crafts, and miscellaneous materials on the theater.

Simon Eisner, President, Urban Innovations Group (the practice arm of the School of Architecture and Urban Planning), which sponsored the study.

Prepared the materials on locational planning for the arts.

Hyman R. Faine, Professor, Management in the Arts Program, Graduate School of Management

Prepared materials on unions in the arts.

Roger Gomez, Student in the Urban Planning Program, School of Architecture and Urban Planning

Prepared materials on community arts, including their financing, on unions, and on governmental agencies in the arts.

Nan Halperin, Recent graduate of the Management in the Arts Program, Graduate School of Management

Prepared the materials on marketing (expanding audiences).

Barry Katz, Student in the Urban Planning Program, School of Architecture and Urban Planning

Prepared materials on urban redevelopment, cultural facilities and public financing of arts activities in Los Angeles.

Kathryn Lim, Recent graduate of the Architecture/Urban Design Program, School of Architecture and Urban Planning

Prepared materials on architecture and on the people-mover proposal.

Katherine Van Ness, Student in the Urban Planning Program, School of Arcitecture and Urban Planning

Prepared the materials on arts employment in Los Angeles.

Supplementary Contributions

Richard Rogers, Visiting Professor, Architecture/Urban Design Program, School of Architecture and Urban Planning
Prepared material for the proposal on the people-mover.

Manfred Schiedhelm, Professor, Architecture/Urban Design Program, School of Architecture and Urban Planning
Some materials on redevelopment in Los Angeles.

Laurel Dickranian, Student in the Management in the Arts Program, Graduate School of Management
The materials on orchestral music in Los Angeles.

Sherri Geldin and **Barbara Whitney,** Students in the Management in the Arts Program, Graduate School of Management
Materials on visual arts in Los Angeles.

Ellen K. Klarman, Student in the Management in the Arts Program Graduate School of Management
Materials on festivals and special events in Los Angeles.

Carl Kravitz, Student in the Management in the Arts Program, Graduate School of Management
Materials on the movie and recording industries in Los Angeles.

Kate Rosloff, Student in the Management in the Arts Program, Graduate School of Management
Materials on the dance in Los Angeles.

Damon Schwartz, Student in the Management in the Arts Program, Graduate School of Management
Some of the materials on the theater in Los Angeles.

Editing

Helen L. Horowitz, Post-Doctoral Fellow, School of Architecture and Urban Planning
Editing of the manuscript.

Reviews of Various Drafts and Advice

Lee Burns, Ron Filson, Don Shoup, Ed Soja, Professors in School of Architecture and Urban Planning (and Urban Innovations Group)
Celeste Anlauf, Executive Assistant, Los Angeles Shakespeare Festival
Warren Christiansen, Director, Garden Theater Festival
Patrick Ela, Administrative Director, Craft and Folk Art Museum
Eddy S. Feldman, Member of the Board, California Confederation of the Arts
J. Foster, Director, Music and Performing Arts Commission, County of Los Angeles
Calvin Hamilton, Director, Los Angeles City Planning Department
Edward N. Helfeld, Administrator, Community Redevelopment Agency
Claire Isaacs, Director, Junior Arts Center
C. Bernard Jackson, Director, Inner City Cultural Center
Adriana Kleinman, Principal Planner, City of New York Planning Department
Bee Lavery, Administrative Coordinator to the Mayor, City of Los Angeles
Barbara Perry, Director, Jobs-in-the-Arts
Rodney L. Punt, Acting Director, Municipal Arts Department
Don Rickles, President, American Federation of Theater and Radio Artists
Edward Weston, West Coast Executive Secretary, Actors' Equity
James Woods, Director, Studio Watts
Peg Yorkin, Managing Director, Free Public Theater Foundation
Vince Zariano, Director, Plaza de las Raza
Herbert Zipper, Projects Director, School of Performing Arts, USC

Manuscript

Jean King, Management Services Officer, School of Architecture and Urban Planning
Directed the typing and organization of the many drafts of the manuscript with remarkable skill.

As director of the study, I wish to extend my

warmest thanks to all of the above. They made participation in the enterprise a delightful experience for me. I also wish to thank the National Endowment for the Arts for its financial support and to express my gratitude to Robert McNulty for his help and guidance.

Harvey S. Perloff

The Arts in the Economic Life of the City

TABLE OF CONTENTS

	Preface	i
	Foreword	iii
PART 1	**A FRAMEWORK**	**1**
1-1	Introduction	3
PART 2	**THE ARTS IN ONE CITY (LOS ANGELES)**	**13**
2-2	Employment in the Arts in Los Angeles	16
2-3	The Arts Institutions: The Non-Profit Sector	22
2-4	The Arts Institutions: The "Mixed" and For-Profit Sectors	37
2-5	The Role of Festivals and Special Events	47
2-6	Government Support for the Arts	53
PART 3	**STRATEGIES FOR CHANGE**	**67**
3-7	Increasing Paying Audiences: Marketing Factors to Encourage Expansion of the Arts	74
3-8	Organizing the Finances of the Arts: An Overview	80
3-9	Federal Government Programs in the Arts, and Their Possible Expansion	88
3-10	Enhancement of Arts Employment Through the Cooperation of Trade Unions and Employers	94
3-11	Using the Arts to Beautify, Restore and Revitalize the City: The Enhancement of Employment and Income in Architecture and Building	99
3-12	City Revitalization Through the Redevelopment and Restoration Process: The Special Role of the Arts	107
3-13	Locational Planning for the Arts	115
3-14	Strengthening Neighborhood Arts	119
3-15	Organizing to Strengthen the Economic Role of the Arts	125
	Appendices	133

PART I
A FRAMEWORK
Highlights

Our society has dual objectives for the arts: the achievement of artistic excellence *and* contribution to the community. Increasingly, the latter encompasses the actual and potential contribution of the arts to the strengthening of local economies. This does not take anything away from the inherent value of the arts; it is simply a highly desirable PLUS.

The potential contribution of the arts to the economic life of the city is tied to the total arts "system" which extends to: (1) the artists and the many other participants, (2) the supportive institution, and (3) the community. The economic contribution of the arts depends upon how well these elements function together. There has been limited appreciation of the workings of the arts "system." This study uses the "systems" framework throughout.

In the future, central cities increasingly will be dependent on service activities for jobs and income, since manufacturing and even wholesale and retail trade is relocating to the suburbs and beyond. Among services, the arts have special importance for the central city because of their potential for employing workers who might otherwise have difficulty in getting jobs and because the arts can make a contribution to the attractiveness of the city and therefore to its economic viability.

The substantial unemployment in the arts is partly due to their great attraction to many people. Often, people working part time or full time in other activities declare themselves unemployed in the arts. The arts unions face a delicate balancing act in this predominantly unorganized industry between protecting the gains already made and helping to push the arts into new areas of potential economic growth.

The arts in the nonprofit sector fall within a category of services where the direct payments for the service make up only a part of the funds available to cover the cost of supplying the service. The remainder is covered by governmental and foundation grants and individual and corporate philanthropy. However, unlike more highly organized services such as medicine and education, the rationale for consistent and substantial support of the arts by private and public wealth is not yet fully developed or widely accepted. The future contribution of the arts to the economic life of the city will depend upon whether the desirability for a sustained high level of support, and particularly public support, is soon accepted. Increasing the size of audiences, and therefore the base of individual "purchases" of arts services, is equally important, since this narrows the "income gap" of arts institutions and enlarges the scope of independent support.

The current disorganization of the arts and their limited and uncertain support constrain the contribution of the arts to local jobs and incomes. This study, therefore, addresses these issues particularly. Factors that have largely been neglected are emphasized, with only brief references to the matters that have been much discussed in the past, such as the "income gap." Thus, we focus on the institutional requirements and community needs within the arts "system," as well as on the changes in the social and physical environment that are desirable if the arts and the cities are to flourish together in the future.

1.1 Introduction:
A Framework to Inventory and Analyze the Arts and Develop a Strategy for Improvements

One can imagine an arts enthusiast saying to the worried mayor of a large city suffering substantial unemployment:

> "I know of an 'industry' that can supply many jobs for the city's unemployed and strengthen its economy.
>
> "Oddly enough, this 'industry' itself suffers from high unemployment. It is largely unorganized; in fact, it is hardly an 'industry' in the usual economic meaning of the term. It is the *laissez-faire* economist's dream of an open labor market. Everyone can enter the industry and many, many do. The more job opportunities that appear, the more additional workers are attracted and declare themselves unemployed in it."

The question of strengthening the local economy would probably be of the greatest concern to the mayor if his was among the majority of large cities that was losing population and jobs to the suburbs, and suffering fiscal difficulties. Yet the mayor would probably think the arts advocate mad—unless the mayor himself was closely associated with the arts, in which case the whole thing would have a familiar ring.

It is not easy to comprehend the seeming contradictions when the economics of the arts are considered: How, indeed, can a field suffering high unemployment come to the aid of an economically troubled city? There is need for a "model" of the arts (essentially a systemic picture) that can explain where economics fits in, that can characterize the whole set of activities known as the arts and provide a framework for making cooperative and public plans and policies with regard to this set of activities. There are a number of elements that fit into such a "model" of the arts.

Dual Objectives

First and foremost is our society's dual objectives for the arts: the achievement of artistic excellence *and* contribution to the community. Not only are there *dual* objectives, but these encompass expanding concepts. The search for excellence extends not only to the traditional "high" arts, but to an ever-growing set of activities that reflects each generation's view of the arts. These activities include not only the traditional arts of symphony, opera, theater, ballet, literature, architecture, painting and sculpture, but also modern musical forms, movies, radio and TV, and a very wide spectrum of crafts and graphic activities from photography to silkscreening. Artistry is the common thread, and time and means to create are essentials. Just as the concept of artistry expands, so, too, does the concept of the contribution that the arts are expected to make to society. The arts have always been seen as the essence of culture, as well as a force which contributes to community and ethnic pride and therefore to social cohesion. More recently, people have begun to look to the arts as a means to educate "the whole person" and those defined as "hard-to-educate." They have been seen as potentially playing a role in neighborhood revitalization, a modern version of contributing to social and community cohesion. Further, the arts increasingly are being viewed as an actual and potential contributor to the strengthening of local economies, a relatively new and uncertain attribute of the arts' contribution to the community.

The full import of the wide range of disparate activities and continually expanding concepts comes to life when one tries to categorize "the arts." The census constantly gets itself in trouble in trying to report what is happening in the arts. While continuous change is an ingrained characteristic of the United States economy in general, nowhere does the census have more trouble recording the most basic statistics—reports on employment and unemployment and the life and death of enterprises—than in the arts. The arts categories differ totally among the various censuses of population, occupation, industry and business, and within these censuses, the categories and definitions differ substantially from decade to decade. Thus, the major occupational grouping is "Writers, Artists and Entertainers," the major industrial category is "Entertainment and Recreational Services," and the key categories in the *Survey of Current Business* are "Motion Pictures" and "Other Amusements." Clearly, all of these categories are inadequate to state what is happening in the arts.

The Arts "System"

It is hard to understand what is going on in the arts, or to grasp the arts' future potential in the economic life of the city, without examining the totality, or the arts "system" (or "network" or "industry" or whatever collective term is preferred). There are clearly many ways to categorize a substantial set of activities and institutions like "the arts," depending on the purpose at hand. For our own limited purposes, we can categorize the arts—largely to appreciate their breadth and to highlight areas for concern—as set out in Figure 1 and in Table 1.

Three main elements are identified: (1) the artists and other participants; (2) the supportive institutions; and (3) the community—or even broader, the encompassing social and physical environment. In the form of a matrix (as shown in Table 1), with the various arts activities shown on one side and the three major elements with their major components shown on the other, the full scope of the arts begins to emerge.

The *artists* (in the broadest sense of the term) are central to the whole "system," more so than the key people in almost any other set of activities in our nation. They make the arts system go and give life to it. The quality, as well as the quantity, of what they create says a great deal not only about their own excellence but about the effectiveness of the other participants and the supporting institutions. It is important to appreciate the essential roles that the *other participants* (the managers, agents, administrators, technicians, teachers and volunteers) and the *supporting institutions* (artistic, technical, financial and job-and-income support) play in both objectives set for the arts. While these categories are complicated, there is some appreciation of their roles and importance.

There is much less understanding and appreciation of the third category—*the community and the social and physical environment*. This category encompasses society as a whole and its physical setting, both very much involved with the arts. The role of the encompassing society, or community, is one of actual and potential audience, as well as a source of community, neighborhood, and governmental support arrangements and organizations. The physical environment includes public and private facilities that are or can be employed for the arts, and the arts setting—the part of the physical environment, such as parks or downtown areas, that is used for arts activities and public art. (See Table 1). These elements are discussed at some length in various parts of this volume.

At this point, we want only to note the many elements that make up the arts system. However, it should be evident by examining Table 1 that a full-fledged information system based on such a matrix, if one could be developed, would provide data about each of the arts activities, including: employed and unemployed; income earned; funds raised among the different supportive institutions; audiences attracted (or that might conceivably be attracted) and space available in different kinds of facilities. This would be solely inventory of course, but even simple inventory can be enormously helpful in developing an understanding of the arts and can provide the *raw material* for more sophisticated and dynamic models to be used in evolving public policy for the arts.

Enter the Dismal Science

The arts model that will help us to frame and understand the actual and potential contribution of the arts to the economic life of the city must inevitably use the language and concepts of economics. But here we discover something disturbing. The economic studies that have been carried out to date have been exceedingly limited in scope and, indeed, often tend to put the arts in a rather unfavorable light. Three kinds of studies have been dominant:

1. the income gap, or Baumol's disease (named after the economist who first highlighted the pervasiveness of an income gap in nonprofit arts organizations);[1]
2. the high unemployment in the arts; and
3. the economic impact of the arts, including the so-called "ripple effect."

The first makes the arts appear as a failed activity compared to the "normal" economic model of a productive, money-making industry or well-supported not-for-profit activity. The second

Figure 1: Graphic Presentation of Arts "System"

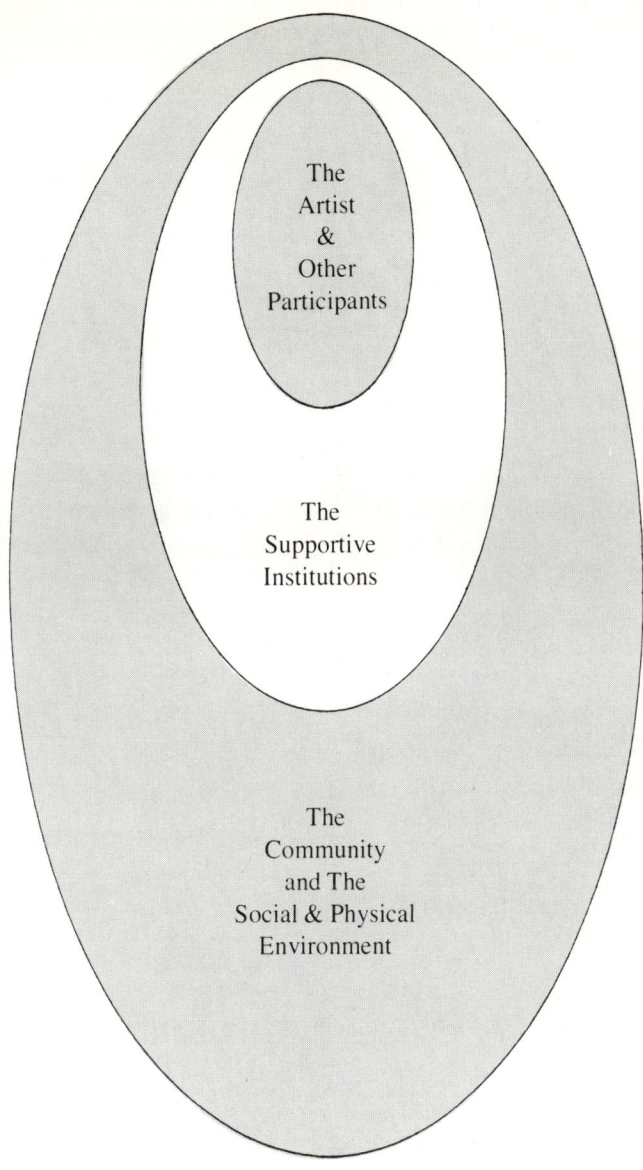

underlines what seems like economic failure and makes one feel sorry for the artists. The third simply puts the arts in the same mold as every other activity that involves various rounds of expenditures ("my expenditures create as many money ripples as your expenditures").2

A different picture emerges if one questions the role of the arts in the economic *future* of the central city. A very brief overview shows the following: Most of the large central cities all over the country—from New York and New Haven to San Francisco and Los Angeles—have serious economic problems. Economic activities are moving out of the cities to the suburbs and outlying areas beyond. Manufacturing is particularly on the move outward, since manufacturing technology frequently calls for fast horizontal movement of materials requiring large spaces for mass-production processes, and transportation is increasingly by truck. Middle-class residents are also moving to the suburbs and beyond, while poor and minority families move into the city. Wholesale and retail trade activities also leave the cities as manufacturing and middle-class families relocate. As a result, cities often face financial

Table 1: The Arts "System" in a City

("Industry," "Network," or Whatever collective term is preferred)
The various categories are not "pure" types; there are many mixtures among them

Activities	The Performing Arts	The Visual Arts	The Crafts	The Literary Arts	Architecture
The Arts	Examples: Theater, Symphony, Opera, Jazz and Other Instrumental and Vocal Music, Dance, Motion Pictures, TV and Radio, Recordings	Examples: Painting, Murals, Drawings and Prints, Other Graphic Design, Sculpture, Photography, Museum Display, Decorative Arts, Tapestries	Examples: Ceramics, Jewelry, Other Crafts, Native Arts, Interior Design, Museum Display	Example: Plays, Poetry, Other Literature, Journalism.	Examples: Design of new buildings, Designs and plans for preservation and restoration, Landscape Design, Fountains, and other environmental design features
The Artists & Other Participants	The Artists				
	The Managers, Organizers, Agents, Administrators				
	Technicians and Other Professional and Technical Support				
	Clerical and Other Assistants in Arts Activities				
	Teachers				
	Volunteers (as non-paid workers)				
The Supportive Institutions	Artistic Support Institution				
	Technical Support Institution				
	Financial Support Institution				
	Job and Income Support Institutions (Unions)				
The Community/ The Social and Physical Environment	Established Audiences				
	Potential Audiences				
	Community Support Groups				
	Governmental Support Arrangements and Agencies				
	Public Facilities				
	Private Facilities				
	Arts Settings (or Environments)				

difficulties through the diminution of the tax base and the increase in public service costs associated with the poor.

In the future, cities will have to rely on service industries for jobs, even more than they do today.[3] Already more than 70 percent of total employment in the United States is in services, and the percentage increases each decade. Some people are much disturbed by the increasing importance of service employment to the city, largely seeing this as a situation of "taking in your own washing." This is associated with the economic principle that a healthy, growing economy requires a large and growing export base; that is, industries that earn money by shipping goods outside the community, money that can then be used to buy service activities internally (such as domestic and business services). But many of the service industries in cities today (and probably even more so in the future) are of an export variety; services are sold outside the community or to people who have earned their income elsewhere and come to the city to buy these services.

This is true of many specialized services (i.e., finance and insurance services or major hospitals and universities). It is also true of many present-day arts activities and can be even more so in the future. Also, economic developments in past years suggest that we may indeed be "taking in more of each other's laundry." Just as the economy can continue to grow with a declining proportion of employment in the goods-producing activities (agriculture, mining, construction and manufacturing), so the economy seems to have been able to expand gross national product and national income while increasing the amount of "internal" service employment.

This is not to suggest that these directions are firmly established and that we can be sure the economy will flourish as goods-producing activities grow less and less important. However, until we know more about what makes a healthy national and local economy, we must assume that from the standpoint of the central city—now suffering from a declining economic base—the strengthening of service employment is good.

We also have to note that, of the services, the arts have special importance for the central city because of their potential for employing workers who might otherwise have difficulty in getting jobs, and because of the contribution the arts can make to the attractiveness of the city and therefore to its economic viability. On the first score, the arts are valuable because they can absorb talents and skills that are to be found in the various individuals and groups living in the city, particularly among minorities. Many minority youth take their first steps up the career and income ladder by playing in bands and taking part in community arts activities, in the same way that other minority youngsters start up the ladder through the world of sports. CETA, particularly, has demonstrated that many youth from poverty areas could achieve employability by a boost from public funding agencies. The contribution the arts can make to the economic viability of the city is equally important and intriguing. These days, the economic future of any area or community is tied to its attractiveness for living and working. The major impacts are not the more direct ones (those normally measured through impact analysis), but the indirect ones, the economic stimulus that results, for example, when an area is redeveloped with arts at the center (i.e., the French Quarter in New Orleans). All these questions are treated in later sections of the book. But before we proceed to the more general concepts, we need to note the special character of employment and unemployment in the arts. Here, too, we can make use of the economists' concepts and tools, particularly supply/demand concepts.

Supply

Supply in the arts emerges as that part of the labor force associated with arts activities. The labor force, though, acts differently than it does in most other economic activities. An individual may declare himself to be an unemployed actor to his labor union and to the census or Department of Labor interviewer, yet work as a real estate agent, or he may insist that he is an unemployed artist while working either part-time or full-time in a printing shop or a shoe store. Census and Department of Labor statistics give us only a small inkling of what is happening. It would take a probing search to figure out what actually occurs in the arts labor force. To provide a rounded picture from the standpoint of those who associate themselves with the arts, the following categories must have data attached to them:

Various Employment/Unemployment Categories in the Arts Industry

Employed full-time in the arts	Employed part-time in the arts	Employed part-time in the arts: part-time in another industry	Unemployed in the arts	Unemployed in the arts: employed full-time in another industry	Unemployed in the arts: employed part-time in another industry

In general, when things are slow in a particular industry, some workers will take a job elsewhere if available, and then usually declare themselves as workers in the industry that has given them employment. The attachment to the arts, however, is quite special. It is intriguing to find that performing arts unions in Los Angeles reported that over three-quarters of their registered members were unemployed at the end of 1977 when the city's unemployment rate as a whole was around 7 percent. The work of performing artists is characteristically of short duration, so that at any one time the union's "unemployment" rolls will include highly-paid actors and actresses who appear frequently—but intermittently—in theatres, movies and tv, as well as those who have not had an acting job during the past twelve months and are only marginally in the arts. Similarly, how does one calculate the employment of a well-known author who occasionally sells an article? In addition, because people in the arts are perhaps more emotionally devoted than those in most activities, the dividing line between the *volunteer* and the *worker* is very thin indeed; the volunteer is often a worker who is not being paid because the arts agency simply lacks the money. Here we see that *supply* (employed and unemployed labor force) is related to *demand* as in all economic activities, but that *supply* is both more persistent and more erratic in the arts than elsewhere.

Not surprisingly, given the background of disorganization in the arts industry, individual labor unions—mostly formed around skill groups such as actors, musicians, writers, announcers, backstage technicians, and others (in some cases organized around a medium, such as TV or movies)—have come to play a strong and very special role in supply. They have given some stability and security for at least the established members of the various arts professions. But the ties among the individual unions are tenuous and collective strength, even within a given medium, can rarely, if ever, be applied. The substantial unemployment and vast differences among various arts activities make organization across large segments of the industry extremely difficult. Yet the unions are important to the economic life of the city in influencing employment and income of people in the arts. They determine, through the rules which they set, the extent to which certain kinds of activities, such as community (neighborhood) arts activities and experimental arts efforts (as in the theatre) can be carried out with performers receiving less than the established wage. The unions face a delicate balancing act in this predominantly unorganized industry between protecting the gains already won and helping to push the arts into new areas of potential economic growth. Some contributions that the unions make, or could make, to the expansion of arts activities are discussed in Chapter 10.

Demand

The *demand* factor in the arts is equally unusual. In general, demand is simply the amount of a product or service that consumers are willing to acquire through individual purchases (out of their pocketbooks). The number of workers in an industry—supply—is then determined by the number needed to produce that particular product or service. But the arts fall within a limited category of services—medicine and education are among them—where direct payments make up only a part of the cost of producing them. These services are deemed to have a societal value which merits a special claim on the community's wealth and income. For these services, the cost of producing them is met not only through individual purchases of the service (i.e., tickets to performances and exhibits and acquisitions of works of art), but through governmental grants, foundation grants, individual philanthropy and corporate philanthropy as well. All of these add to the demand for a given service and, in turn, to the demand for workers.

Here, however, the arts depart from medicine and education. While medicine and education are substantially organized and the rationale for their public support has long been established, the rationale for consistent, substantial support of the arts by private and public wealth in the United States has not yet been developed fully or accepted widely. Art organizations, as already noted, consistently suffer from Baumol's disease. The result is a chaotic demand situation. If the "worried mayor" mentioned at the beginning wanted to calculate the arts industry's potential contribution to the city economy, he would be forced to make some wild guesses, since he would have very little firm data available about supply or demand on which to base a judgement. The situation in the United States is different from that in most European countries, where public support for the arts is firmly established.

Not only is governmental and philanthropic support for the arts less certain than in the case of medicine and education, but individual purchases do not provide as broad a base of demand, at least in the case of the more traditional art forms. Here there is an interesting split between highly commercialized art forms, such as movies, TV, radio, records, and "popular" music, and the more traditional art forms of live theatre, symphony, opera and the like. The economic view of the arts naturally raises the issue of whether audience-building methods of the former could be employed in the traditional areas, as well as new methods that might be particularly appropriate for the traditional forms. This issue is discussed in some detail in Chapter 7.

Community Arts

There are additional features that are quite special to the arts and that give a particular character to the supply and demand situation. Looming large among them is the development of what has come to be called *community or neighborhood arts*. Artists and art groups associated with particular communities and/or ethnic groups have developed innovative art forms, independent of but often related to the more traditional forms, which contribute to community cohesion. This has been part of the American rediscovery of the values of ethnic diversity, neighborhood and neighboring, and the great artistry to be found in "popular" culture and native forms. One has the sense that it may be the beginning of a significant "movement," important in quantitative as well as qualitative terms. There is now a national organization established to work with and assist such community arts groups, of which thousands are already in existence. Neighborhood arts organizations have pioneered the use of CETA (the federal government's Comprehensive Employment and Training Act) funds to employ community-based artists and organizers. They are introducing a new dimension into the most traditional of art forms, such as theater, and are using established forms, such as mural painting, in a new way. It is hard to grasp the full potential of this evolving movement but our worried mayor would be certain to be intrigued by the possibilities of this development in practical supply-and-demand terms.

Disorganization and Organization

What emerges from this overview of supply and demand in the arts is a picture of a disparate, largely unorganized set of activities that fall under the arts rubric but which are nevertheless activities that have great actual, and even greater potential, economic significance. The features which distinguish the arts industry from other industries include the following:

1. There are many part-time workers, a large proportion of whom actually prefer working only part-time (less than 35 hours per week).
2. Although only marginally related to the arts, many people declare themselves to be unemployed because of a strong attachment to arts activities. Of course, many of those claiming to be unemployed do have a substantial employment background in arts activities.
3. Strong labor unions are important in individual arts activities, but are able to influence labor conditions directly for only a small proportion of those actually involved in such activities. There are only tenuous relationships among the different arts unions.
4. There is a relatively narrow base of support through individual purchases of arts services and products in the traditional arts areas and an erratic support of the more commercial areas (essentially varying with each "output") i.e., movies, tv and popular concerts.
5. There is an equally uncertain support of arts activities through governmental and philanthropic sources, due to the absence of established quantitative or qualitative principles
6. There is minimal cooperation and coordination among different arts activities, with a limited organization of individual activities nationally and even less across-the-board local organization in most communities. Arts' organization in

general is, obviously, at a very early stage of development.

It seems clear that disorganization is at the heart of the problem of trying to understand what the arts might contribute to the economic life of the city, and that organization must be at the heart of any policy or program that looks toward greatly enlarging the contribution of the arts to local economies. What form such organization may, and should, take is a matter of concern throughout this book, probing, as it does, the economic potential of the arts in the face of the serious economic difficulties of so many of our cities. Thus, in effect, we are looking toward the change from a current model of the arts which is largely characterized by disorganization to an evolving model characterized by substantially increased organization.

This is not necessarily a costless solution. The present difficulties—i.e., unemployment—and the limited contribution to the economy could easily be traded for a much more certain situation for the arts but with more constraints on freedom and innovation. Freedom in artistic creation has long been the most precious ingredient of the arts. The challenge is to evolve organization that can strengthen the second of the the arts' dual objectives—contribution to the community—without jeopardizing the freedom that has long been a key factor in the first objective—artistic excellence.

Organization, particularly when viewed in the context of enlarging the contribution of the arts to a city's economic life, is not alone a matter of better management of arts activities—more cooperation, coordination and planning among them—or a more effective organizational "infrastructure," although it is all of these. Organization in the present context must also be seen as encompassing widely understood and firmly established sets of relationships with city and regional governments and with private enterprise (both supporters of the arts and investors in the city).

The greatest demands on organization emerge particularly when it becomes evident that arts activities should become an integral part of the physical development of the city and region. Currently, such a relationship to physical development is relatively minor, involving only the activities of preservation and restoration and the construction and maintenance of a limited number of arts facilities, public and private. The potential is another matter entirely. The arts—including architecture—can make a unique and significant contribution to the physical development of the city and region with substantial economic payoffs. They can contribute to the economic revitalization of downtown areas and older neighborhoods of the city and region; to the enlargement of tourism, the convention trade, and other attractions (and their attendant expenditures); and, in general, to the economic viability of urban communities. This is all a matter of concern in the later sections of this book, including the centrally important issues of the arts as related to city planning and zoning.

Organization, as it encompasses widely understood and firmly established sets of relationships with the city and regional governments, must also extend to the arts' role in the provision of public services. This includes the role of the arts in education, health activities, parks and recreation, transportation and other public works, public and assisted housing, law enforcement and, of course, city beautification. The arts currently have only tenuous relationships to each of these—even education, recreation, and city beautification—since they have traditionally been seen as "add-ons" in public services and facilities. When the economic potential of the arts is considered, this facet must be of central concern.

One final item about organization must be mentioned: the contribution to the economic life of the city through special events. Festivals and other special events have been associated with the arts from the beginning of recorded history. Celebrations have always naturally centered around the arts. It does not detract from the full glory of the arts as community celebration to note that such celebrations can and do have an economic component. The ability to pay for such celebrations and to have them contribute to the economic life of the total community is of no small moment.

Using the Suggested Model of the Arts

The very simple model, which has been suggested as helpful in describing the arts system by providing a logical and consistent framework for inventorying and analyzing arts activities, can also be used as a framework for discussing strategy and tactics for improvements. Thus, strategy for change might be developed for achieving general

Making a redevelopment project in the central city a work of joyous art: the Lawrence Halprin fountain in Portland, Oregon.

employment and income goals for artists and other participants; for more sharply defining the role of the supporting institutions; and for specifying the changes needed in the social and physical environment for the arts to contribute significantly to the economic life of the city. The lack of data and the present limited knowledge about the arts (as well as the limitations on funds and time of this study) prevent us from carrying such an analysis very far. Without relatively complete data on employment and unemployment in the arts, it is hard to discuss measures that might be employed to achieve a specific level of employment (aside from other difficulties in such an analysis). We are also far from the time when specific levels of public and private support of arts institutions and planned changes in the social and physical environment can be related to specific levels of employment and contribution to economic growth. However, the model does suggest potential blockages to improvements as well as the direction and scope of improvements needed to meet the goals. This has led us to look closely at necessary changes in organization and at the kinds of public policies that would substantially enhance the contribution of the arts to the economic life of the city. These subjects are at the heart of Part III of this volume.

A Focus on Los Angeles

We have tested the central features of the model of the arts by frequent references to the city and region of Los Angeles. Examples from other cities and regions have been used throughout as well, but Los Angeles has been our main testing ground. For in Los Angeles, all the features of both the commercial and nonprofit arts that deserve attention appear in vivid colors—the gaps and the tensions, the disorganization and the potential for revitalization. We have tried to use this vividness to help understand what is involved and to communicate the great potentials for the future in the arts.

Footnotes

[1] W. J. Baumol and W. G. Bowen, *Performing Arts: The Economic Dilemma* (New York: The Twentieth Century Fund, 1966).

[2] These topics are all discussed in the various papers reproduced in Mark Blaug, editor, *The Economics of the Arts* (London: Martin Robertson & Company, 1976). Some rarely discussed subjects are also touched on in these papers. This is probably the broadest treatment of the economics of the arts to date.

[3] See Harvey S. Perloff, "The Central City in the Post-Industrial Age," in Charles L. Leven, editor, *The Mature Metropolis* (New York: Lexington Books, 1978).

[4] The question of the role of export and service industries has been much debated by economists and there is far from a general consensus. For some useful discussions of the subject, see Wilbur R. Thompson, *A Preface to Urban Economics,* (Baltimore: The Johns Hopkins Press, 1965), Chapter 1, *passim,* and Hans Blumenfeld, "The Economic Base of the Metropolis," in Ralph W. Pfouts, *The Techniques of Urban Economic Analysis* (West Trenton, N.J.: Chandler-Davis, 1960), pp. 230–77.

PART II
THE ARTS IN ONE CITY: LOS ANGELES

Highlights

It would be desirable to study the arts in all of the nation's cities to determine how best to enhance their contribution to local economies. But that is too large an undertaking, particularly given the paucity of economic and other kinds of data. We have, therefore, concentrated on one city, Los Angeles (with a side glance at other cities across the country which have carried out some particularly noteworthy activities), in order to deepen our understanding of the problems and possibilities associated with enlarging the economic impact of the arts.

Part II essentially tries to characterize the arts in the city (and region) of Los Angeles to lay a foundation for the discussion of strategies and tactics of change. There are obviously many strong features of the arts, features on which to build, but there are also many weaknesses. Even our partial review permits us to see how incomplete is the arts system in Los Angeles, one of the major arts cities in the country (with the city containing some 2.8 million people and the region encompassing about 10 million). This review suggests how limited the arts system must be in other, less well endowed, cities.

Characterizing the strong and weak features of the arts in Los Angeles is a risky enterprise at best since, given the absence of accepted objective standards of quality, we must rely on personal judgment. We hope the value of such an overview justifies the risk.

The Los Angeles Art Scene: The Strong Points

The Performing Arts
The "clustering" of the movie, TV, and recording industries in Los Angeles: brings many performers and support personnel to the city and provides many jobs (some at high incomes).

A symphony of international stature.

Chamber orchestras which could evolve into world class performers.

A strong repertory theater.

Many small, experimental theaters (assisted by the ninety-nine-seat waiver plan).

A small group of commercial theaters which, if they became artistically more venturesome, could provide significant employment opportunities for stage directors and others important to the development of the theater movement in Los Angeles.

A wide variety of popular concerts.

Many high-level university and college performing arts programs.

Many clubs featuring jazz and popular music.

The Visual Arts

A major county government and privately supported museum of art and increasingly important privately supported art museums throughout the region (particularly the Norton Simon in Pasadena), including a private art museum (the Getty) with an enormous endowment whose future direction will have great impact on the region.

A strong clustering of graphic artists.

An ethnic murals movement.

Many painters and sculptors of national reputation residing in the city.

A number of high level university and college visual arts programs.

A major business center (Century City) whose plans for cultural programming may set a pattern for more direct business participation in the arts.

A major auction house which could help Los Angeles develop as a world art market.

The Crafts

Intense interest in crafts and clustering of craftsworkers.

A major crafts and folk arts museum.

A tradition of neighborhood arts and crafts fairs throughout the city and region.

The Literary Arts

A clustering of playwrights and scriptwriters.

The presence of one of the nation's best newspapers.

Architecture

The presence of four schools of architecture, each supporting exhibits.

A high development of domestic architecture (the bungalow, tract housing, pop architecture).

The Los Angeles Art Scene: The Weak Points

Governmental Agencies and Coordinating Groups

Responsibility for the arts divided among three weakly supported governmental agencies, with little coordination among them.

Lack of strong local or regional private coordinating groups.

Weakly supported neighborhood arts groups.

Little adjustment in methods of programming, ticket sales, etc., to vast size of city and region.

The Performing Arts

Lack of a resident opera company with season-long performances.

Lack of a resident major dance company with season-long performances.

Limited support of community performing arts groups.

The Visual Arts

Lack of a tradition of arts in and around buildings.

Limited outlets for displays of photographs, designs, and decorative arts.

Architecture

Lack of a tradition of wide support for distinguished buildings.

Lack of a tradition of preservation and restoration.

Lack of a tradition of extensive landscaping around buildings.

Lack of a tradition of art in public places.

2.2
Employment in the Arts in Los Angeles

A first step in any study of the contribution of the arts to a city's economic enhancement must be an inquiry into the actual employment of artists in the metropolitan area. Although the census provides only a small insight into the employment and unemployment of artists, it remains the best source for the study of employment in the arts.

Of the 2,826,565 employed workers in the Los Angeles-Long Beach Standard Metropolitan Statistical Area (SMSA) in 1970, 49,150 were classed as writers, artists, and entertainers, as detailed in Appendix Table A-1. (It should be emphasized that the occupations listed in this and subsequent tables are the *only* arts occupations presented in published census reports and are by no means complete.) While the total number of the census category "writers, artists and entertainers" increased by more than one-third between 1950 and 1970, many of the individual occupational categories showed decreases. For example, the number of actors and actresses in 1970 was only one-half the number in 1950. Other performing occupations (e.g., dancers, musicians, entertainers, etc.) similarly declined in numbers, but time series comparisons are not possible without qualifications because definitions of several of these categories are inconsistent over the years. (See discussion in technical note.) Several broadly defined categories which include technicians as well as artists (e.g., architects, designers, photographers, etc.) showed increases.

Trends over the study period are more apparent through the examination of the percentages (see Appendix Table A-1). The percentage changes between 1950 and 1960 and between 1960 and 1970 for writers, artists and entertainers as a whole are smaller than the changes for all professional and technical occupations. The percentage increase between 1950 and 1960 for this aggregate category was approximately one-third the rate of increase for professional and technical occupations (26.7 percent versus 78.3 percent) and half the rate of increase of all occupations (54.7 percent). The increase for the aggregate arts category between 1960 and 1970 (6.7 percent) was only slightly less than that for all occupations (8.0 percent) but substantially less than that for other professional and technical occupations (30.4 percent). Some occupations, especially architects and dancers/teachers, as well as writers, artists and entertainers, experienced a moderate growth of about one-third between 1950 and 1960. Artists/teachers and authors increased more substantially (over 50 percent). Designers (including technical as well as artistic designers) more than doubled in number between 1950 and 1970. Actors experienced a sizable decrease of almost one-third. The 1960–70 decade witnessed significant declines compared to the previous decade in those occupations involved directly in the arts (e.g., actors, artists/teachers, dancers/teachers), although some definitions of these categories are not comparable.

The case study of Los Angeles reveals a consistent decline in actors between 1950 and 1970. Occupations showing the largest increases—architects, designers, PR men/publicity writers—are significantly more diversified (i.e., involved in more industries) than are the performers listed. That is, census definitions include designers of machinery, tools, maps, posters, clothing, and interiors of buildings in the general category of *designer*. Thus, designers may work in non-arts fields. The same is true of PR men/publicity writers and, to a lesser extent, architects. Because of the high probability of involvement in non-arts fields, increases in these categories are undoubtedly related to the general economic growth of the Los Angeles region rather than to the arts industry. Crafts and services show extremely mixed trends during the 1950 to 1970 period. For example, in the 1950s decorators/window dressers increased by more than one-third, as did the entire crafts category; but in the next decade decorators/window dressers increased only 4.5 percent while the entire crafts occupations rose by only 0.9 percent. Jewelers and motion picture projectionists decreased fairly substantially in the 1950–1960 decade and continued to decrease in the 1960s but at a slower rate.

Projections of the number of people employed in artistic occupations in 1975 and 1980 are available from reports of the California Employment Development Department (EDD), included here in Appendix B.[1] Absolute increases are projected in all occupations listed, even those which showed decreases in census reports discussed above. Percentage changes (see Appendix Table B-1) for all writers, artists and entertainers considered together are forecasted to be slightly higher than changes for all occupations (i.e., 10.6 percent versus 8.3 percent). The performing artists are expected to experience growth at less than the rate for all occupations while the more technical fields are projected to increase more than the average of 8.3 percent. The worst aspect is the relatively small number of job opportunities projected for artistic occupations between 1975 and 1980 (see Appendix Table B-2). For example, EDD projects 161 openings per year for actors, most coming from departures from the occupation of previously employed actors. Designers' jobs are projected to increase by 514 per year.

Several general conclusions can be drawn from the discussion above. Performing occupations—actors, dancers, etc.—decreased in size in recent decades while broadly defined occupations such as designers and publicity people, which include individuals involved in technical as well as arts industries, increased. Projections suggest a possible slight increase in employment in these categories in the near future. Thus, growth is certainly not a characteristic of performing arts occupations. However, a related occupation—arts administrators—has shown growth, although it is not reflected in census reports. This growth, is reflected by the eighteen academic programs in the United States and Canada which train arts administrators, as well as numerous workshops and internships which offer short-term training. While there are no data on the number of arts administrators currently employed, this field has become increasingly important to arts organizations of all sizes.[2] Growth in this area represents a potentially important shift in emphasis within arts industries toward employment of more administrators and possibly toward stabilization of employment of performers.

Demographic and Socioeconomic Characteristics

Some characteristics of people employed in the arts can be examined with census data. These characteristics are the sexual and racial breakdown of employment, median ages and incomes.[3] The ratio of males to females varies greatly from occupation to occupation. Women account for at least one-third of all writers, artists and entertainers employed (see Appendix Table A-2). Women dominate only the dancer/teacher category throughout the study period. In some occupations, women made steady gains (see, for example, designers), but this trend is by no means typical. Women showed stronger increases (or reversal of declines) during the 1960s than in the 1950s. It is especially interesting that in some occupations (specifically acting) where men experienced declines of 36 percent throughout the study period, women increased in representation by 11 percent in the 1960s.

The data for racial composition of employment for the 1950–60 decade show that percentages were relatively the same for both sexes, with whites making up slightly over 90 percent of the total, blacks about 4-6 percent and other non-whites about 1 percent. Slight gains were registered by black male artists, authors, draftsmen, designers and musicians. Non-white males showed particularly striking increases of between one and five percentage points in occupations for which data are available. Among females the increases are less striking, especially for black females. Between 1960 and 1970 (shown in Appendix Table A-3), gains among Spanish-Americans—Mexican-Americans, Puerto Ricans and other Hispanic-Americans, by the census definition—and non-whites are particularly evident. The representation of whites in arts occupations fell from about 93–95 percent to about 87–90 percent for both sexes during the 1960s.

Data on median ages of employed "artists" are relatively scant and are available only for 1960 and 1970. Among males, persons employed in the arts have approximately the same median age (i.e., 39) as persons in all occupations in both 1960 and 1970. However, male designers and draftsmen are about seven years younger. Black and Spanish-American writers, artists and entertainers are, in the median, about four years younger than all male writers, artists and entertainers and three years younger than all male professionals. Among women, the median ages tend to be two years older than men. However, actors/dancers/entertainers had a relatively young median age of 33.7 years in 1960. All the median ages for women declined by about two years between 1960 and 1970, indicating a trend toward younger women in the arts.

Data on median income are similarly scant but are

available for 1950 to 1970 (see Table A-4 in the Appendix). With the exception of musicians/teachers in 1950 and 1960, males in arts occupations for which these data are available had median incomes of at least $300 over the median income for all occupations ($3,239 in 1950, $5,684 in 1960 and $8,542 in 1970). Females in the arts had median incomes slightly less than one-half the median incomes for males in these groups. However, compared to other employed women, women professionals and those in the arts have median incomes above the overall median ($1,891 in 1950, $2,957 in 1960 and $4,461 in 1970). Exceptions were actresses/dancers/entertainers and musicians/teachers in 1950 and 1960.

Employment Problems

While unemployment rates are not available for occupational categories, some indication of employment problems can be drawn from data on weeks worked for selected arts occupations (see Table A-4 in the Appendix). Rough estimates of numbers unemployed can be made, however, by subtracting the number employed from the number in the experienced civilian labor force, but these estimates are not comparable to nationally available rates. Furthermore, detailed estimates are possible only for 1950. Comparing these figures to the total employed, it is apparent that a fairly large proportion, i.e., 28 percent, of actors was unemployed in 1950 while only about 10 percent of musicians/teachers were unemployed.[4] (These figures are so limited in scope, and so out-of-date, that the tables are not presented in this chapter.)

Even though percent of workers employed fifty to fifty-two weeks in the previous year, or the proportion working a full year, is a fairly good indication of employment stability, it is unlikely that many people in arts occupations, because of the temporary nature of many jobs in this field, would be considered *full-time* workers by this definition. Except for male musicians, people in arts occupations fared reasonably well compared to the median weeks worked by the overall population. However, females—overall and in the performing arts—did not, in large proportion, work fifty to fifty-two weeks in the preceding year. Women in all groups averaged fewer "all year" workers than did men.

Arts Employment in Various Industries

Because occupational data presented by *industries* are probably less useful than the more detailed data discussed above, little emphasis here will be given to industrial employment data. Appendix Table A-5 illustrates the industrial breakdowns provided in U.S. Census of Population reports. From these data, nothing can be said about employment of "artists" in various industries because these occupations are aggregated with both "behind the scenes" occupations and unrelated ones.[5] The two industries in which artistic and behind the scenes employment might be expected to be the greatest, radio/television and theaters/motion pictures, showed an increase over the 1950 to 1970 period. However, this increase is relatively small when compared to the growth of all service industries.

Appendix Tables A-5 and A-6 present some demographic data on employment in arts industries. Table A-5 breaks down total employment by sex. Of the major categories, women comprise about one-half of total employment for the three study years. One exception is "professional and related services," where women represent the majority of employees. Looking again at radio/television and theaters/motion pictures, women make up only about one-third of employees throughout the study period, with some increase in female employment evident in 1970. Appendix Table A-6 (for 1960 and 1970) shows that non-white employees are underrepresented (i.e., constitute a smaller portion of the total here than their proportion of the total work force) in service industries overall and especially in arts related service industries.

More detailed breakdowns of arts industries are provided in Appendix Table A-7 (for 1972) which is taken from another source, the U.S. Census of Selected Services. Unfortunately, the only information provided by these census reports is number of establishments, number of paid employees and payroll.[6] This data source, like the industrial information from the decennial census, can provide a rough picture of total arts employment. But like the above, few breakdowns are available.

Volunteers in the Arts

A particularly important category of workers in the arts—volunteers—are not counted as arts employees by standard data sources because they are unpaid. Thus, there is little information about this group and its contributions are not considered a part of the Gross National Product. This group's importance, though, is apparent in the National Research Center of the Arts' study *The Nonprofit Art Industry in California*. Four hundred seventy one arts organizations were surveyed in fiscal year 1973–74 and reported 22,300 paid personnel and 34,100 unpaid personnel. About 75 percent of volunteers worked in administration as opposed to performing, and volunteers made up 86 percent of total administrative staff. This administrative work included fundraising, office work, ticket sales and membership drives. During the fiscal year studied, volunteers in the arts organizations surveyed worked a total of 2,928,000 hours or 86 hours per volunteer; in Los Angeles, the figures were 777,700 hours, 88 per volunteer. These hours represent a savings to arts organizations. These volunteers represent a potential demand for arts jobs or "disguised unemployment" of persons trained in the arts and working for pay at another job while keeping in touch with the arts.

Conclusions

Based on the census data, several conclusions can be drawn about employment in the arts in Los Angeles. Growth in this component of the service sector is less dramatic than for the sector as a whole. Nonetheless, growth is apparent at differing rates for different broadly defined artistic occupations. That is, technical arts fields such as designers have been increasing in size while performing occupations have diminished. Employment of women and minority males has grown in most occupations, especially the more technical ones, but white males still dominate the field. In general, persons engaged in arts occupations have the same median age as all workers. However, designers and male minority writers, artists and entertainers tend to be younger while women in most fields tend to be older than the average. Median income is fairly high, exceeding the population's median by several hundred dollars among males. While the median income for females in the arts also exceeds the overall median, the median of females in this field is less than one-half that of males. Unemployment data are particularly scanty. What is available indicates that unemployment among performers was fairly high in 1950 but percentage working fifty to fifty-two weeks—an indicator of stability of employment—was fairly high, especially in non-performing fields. Industrial data paint about the same picture.

A number of these conclusions can be disputed, based on general perceptions drawn from popular literature. Trade union estimates indicate that a large proportion of their members earn less than the poverty level from work in the arts. Thus, the median income figures from the census may be on the high side. However, census data include income from all sources. That is, an actor's income from a film made in six months would be combined with six month's income from another job, such as real estate sales. This would increase an individual's income if he designated himself an actor for census purposes. Union estimates also place the census unemployment data in doubt, commonly reporting 80 percent or more of its members unemployed *in the arts*. This last phrase is particularly important because our hypothetical actor/real estate salesman will be counted as an unemployed actor by the census only if he indicates that he is. In addition, performers usually belong to several unions to allow work in films, television and legitimate theater. Thus, an actor working in film may be unemployed in television and theater unions. Because of this multiple union membership, it is invalid to total the unemployed in each union to derive an accurate unemployment rate for performers. However, the extremely high unemployment rates calculated by unions do cast considerable doubt on the accuracy of census figures.

With these likely inaccuracies and other limitations discussed throughout this chapter, why use Census data? The Census provides the most comprehensive, consistently published data base available for small sub-national areas such as cities and counties. This data base is commonly used in all types of planning, thus allowing some comparability and possible integration of, say, economic and job development programs. The Department of Labor's Bureau of Labor Statistics (BLS) collects and disseminates labor force data on a frequent basis, but the most readily available data are usually not finely broken down in terms of detailed occupations. In addition, BLS data are collected for geographical units which are slightly different from census SMSAs (Standard Metropolitan Statistical Areas), making comparisons of different categories of data (e.g., employment, industry, housing, etc.) impossible. Labor unions will sometimes provide information on number of members, their employment status and, sometimes, demographic and socioeconomic characteristics. However, people in the arts—especially the performing arts—customarily maintain membership in several unions as previously noted. Other people working in the arts, particularly sculptors, painters, and others in the fine arts, may not belong to any union. For these reasons, reliance on union data for employment statistics leaves much to be desired. (The National Endowment for the Arts is exploring the feasibility of merging union membership files in New York City to provide an integrated source of data available on a more timely basis than the census. If this turns out to be feasible and informative, similar efforts would be logical in Los Angeles and other cities.)

Results of a Survey of Members

Probably the most comprehensive survey of union members in the performing arts has recently been conducted by the consulting firm of Ruttenberg, Friedman, Kilgallon, Gutchess & Associates, Inc., under a subcontract with the Human Resources Development Institute of the AFL-CIO and with funding from the U.S. Department of Labor.[7] This survey, administered through mail questionnaires in 1977, focused on the members of five major AFL-CIO arts unions: Actors' Equity; American Federation of Television and Radio Artists (AFTRA); Screen Actors' Guild (SAG); American Guild of Musical Artists (dancers, opera performers, concert artists, and choral members); and American Federation of Musicians (AFM). Most of the information collected relates to the year 1976. Duplications of union membership were eliminated in processing the questionnaires.

Although the survey findings must be interpreted with a knowledge that most performing artists in the United States are not union members, for the most part these results are consistent with the generalizations that tentatively emerge from census data. High proportions of unionized performing artists are underemployed in their designated professions: only about one-third of the members in all five unions worked full-time in arts jobs in 1976. On the average, they suffered longer and more frequent spells of unemployment than did other members of the total labor force, with stage performers experiencing the worst record and musicians relatively the best.

Typically, performing artists must work for several different employers during the year and especially in the case of stage actors and musicians, often must be employed away from their areas of residence at least once during that period. Many of them hold outside jobs which are likely to be unrelated to the arts; this "extra" work is concentrated in the service, sales, or clerical occupations. While their median income approximates or exceeds the national average, it remains markedly below the level attained by groups with equivalent educational attainments; performing artists tend to be well educated, experienced in their professions, and somewhat older than the average for other members of the labor force. High percentages of the artists, ranging from 40 to 60 percent depending on the union, cannot collect unemployment compensation during their periods of unemployment (in California, where qualification is based on earnings rather than duration of employment, the provisions have been more favorable for performing artists, but there are efforts underway in the legislature to reduce this protection for actors and others). Thus, many artists qualify for employment under the CETA program on the basis of low-income standards.

Despite this, performing artists demonstrate unusually high commitment to their professions, many of them continuing their education and training throughout their careers. Frequently, they must pay tuition and other costs out of their own pockets. Although many qualify, relatively few of the union members participate in CETA programs or in other governmental projects designed to assist the unemployed and underemployed. Most of them regard the arts as their principal profession, and would spend more time in the arts if work were available. It is possible, of course, that union members are more committed to artistic careers than are nonunion performers, but the data at hand suggest that performing artists as a group are professionally dedicated to an extraordinary degree.

Footnotes

[1] While these projections can be compared in a general way to the census figures discussed above, they are not entirely comparable because they are based on different sources.

[2] See National Research Center of the Arts, *The Non-Profit Arts Industry of California,* 1976.

[3] Information on other characteristics, notably educational backgrounds, is not available for detailed occupations for sub-national geographic areas. As is illustrated in this section, even the characteristics available are not finely broken down, and details are presented only for a few artistic occupations.

[4] It is difficult, because of the limitations of data, to verify these estimates with alternative sources such as union files. It does seem likely that if employment in the arts were defined more accurately by allowing specification of principal and secondary jobs, unemployment rates in the arts would be quite high. That is, the census defines employment status and occupation in terms of what respondents say they are doing in one reference week. But people in the arts frequently suffer periods of unemployment in their chosen occupation during which they must seek work in other fields. Thus, an actor temporarily working full time in real estate sales, for example, in the reference week would be classified as a real estate salesman rather than an actor. The result would be an undercount of the number of actors in an area. One possible way of counting people in the arts more accurately would be to ask respondents to specify their "principal" and "secondary" occupations. The first would indicate the individual's primary career field within which he or she may be working during the reference week and the latter a temporary job which may or may not be related to the individual's career.

[5] "Cross-tabulations" relating industry and occupation would supply much useful information about direct and indirect employment. Unfortunately, data are presented in this manner only for broadly defined occupations and industries.

[6] The latter will not be discussed here because median earnings for some specific occupations were already presented. However, a rough estimate of average wages in these industries could be obtained by dividing payroll by number of workers.

[7] See Human Resources Development Institute, AFL-CIO, *Survey of Employment, Underemployment and Unemployment in the Performing Arts,* February 1978.

2.3
The Arts Institutions: The Nonprofit Sector

A full picture of the arts in any one city would have to begin with an inventory of the arts system (as suggested in Table 1 in Part I). For such a study to be undertaken, an investigating team would have to have both time and access to institutional information. Our report faced limitations in both areas. While the primary goal is to suggest strategies for change that might have national applicability, we could not undertake the extensive research that a full inventory would require. And because we were a university team rather than a public agency, we did not have full access to the financial data of arts organizations of the city. However, despite these limitations, we do cover the significant elements of the Los Angeles arts story; it is hoped that the discussion of potential strategies in Part III will have fuller meaning because it is set against a systemic view of the arts in a major city.

We will first consider the nonprofit sector, which consists of orchestral music, theater,[1] and dance, among others. Of increasing importance is a fourth area, that of community (neighborhood) or ethnic arts. We will then turn to the mixed sector, part nonprofit, part profit: the visual arts and crafts. And finally, we will treat the area that is of unusual importance in Los Angeles, the profit sector, focusing on the motion picture and the recording industries. This discussion is intended to set the stage for a consideration of the essential question of the report: how can the arts come to play their full role in the economic revitalization of our cities?

The Performing Arts in Los Angeles: An Overview

One obvious characteristic of the greater Los Angeles region which largely distinguishes it from other urban communities of the nation is the vastness of its area and the relative decentralization of its performing arts facilities. In contrast with other cultural centers, such as New York and San Francisco, few of these facilities are located downtown; indeed, none of the major night clubs can be found there, and the Music Center complex is the *only* site for presentation of both classical and popular concerts, musicals, and plays. Tens of thousands of residents of greater Los Angeles never venture to the downtown area voluntarily, and it is probable that a high proportion of downtown visitors are attracted solely by the Music Center.

For these reasons, visits to cultural and entertainment centers virtually require private transportation; again, unlike New York and San Francisco, few of the theaters, concert hall or clubs can be reached on foot or by public transportation or taxi (except at an exorbitant cost). The Century City complex in the western area of the city does contain a major hotel (Century Plaza), a major live theater (Shubert), and movie theaters and night clubs, but this is an exception and Century City is quite distant from the downtown Music Center and other leading concert halls and from cultural facilities such as the Hollywood Bowl and the Greek Theater in Griffith Park. Two of the live theaters (Pantages, a converted movie house, and Huntington Hartford), some first-class movie theaters (notably the Chinese, a tourist mecca), and, of course, the Hollywood Bowl, all are located in Hollywood, but in recent years this has become known as a declining and generally unattractive area. In all these communities, parking is both inadequate and expensive.

On the other hand, the mild weather, coupled with an extensive freeway system, makes possible the presentation of many cultural events outdoors—at the Hollywood Bowl, where the renowned Los Angeles Philharmonic Orchestra regularly performs in the summertime; the Greek Theater, which presents jazz, classical and popular music, ballet and some opera during the summer; Burbank's Starlight Bowl; the county-owned John Anson Ford Cultural Arts Theater, which hosts the Los Angeles Shakespeare Festival and free jazz concerts (now curtailed as a result of the passage of Proposition 13); the Universal Amphitheater, run by Universal Studios, which specializes in "pop" concerts; and elsewhere.

The universities—notably the University of California, Los Angeles (UCLA), the University of Southern California (USC), Loyola-Marymount, California State University at Los Angeles, California State University at Long Beach, California State University at Northridge, and California State University at Dominguez Hills—and the dozens of private and community colleges throughout greater Los Angeles offer regular cultural and entertainment programs, sometimes in facilities such as UCLA's Royce Hall and USC's Bovard Hall, which attract thousands of nonstudents each year to events ranging from "pop rock" to classical music and dance. The performing arts departments of these schools, particularly at UCLA and USC, are major training centers for those interested in arts careers, although the music curricula appear to be much stronger in the classical fields than in the field of jazz and other contemporary music (exceptions are California State University at Northridge and Los Angeles City College). One innovative project at UCLA—Design for Sharing—provides performances and workshops on campus for pupils of the Los Angeles Unified School District and free tickets to professional performances for various groups which would normally not be able to attend: the handicapped, emotionally disturbed, and other disadvantaged persons.

In recent years, impressive cultural facilities have been developed in outlying areas, particularly the 1360-seat Ambassador Auditorium on the campus of administratively troubled Ambassador College in Pasadena; Santa Monica Civic Auditorium; and the Long Beach convention and cultural complex, with 3000-seat and 800-seat theaters. A much older facility is the 6400-seat Shrine Auditorium, the largest auditorium in Los Angeles, whose large stage makes it especially suitable for classical ballet. The Shrine, located on the edge of the USC campus, is adjacent to one of the city's redevelopment areas, and undoubtedly has lost ground to the newer Music Center with its 3200-seat Dorothy Chandler Pavilion and the smaller, more intimate, and acoustically ideal Mark Taper Forum and Ahmanson theaters. Many of the area's parks and playgrounds also have facilities which make them appropriate sites for concerts and exhibits.

Music

Greater Los Angeles has an abundance of orchestral music, with no fewer than twenty-eight orchestras within the jurisdiction of Local 47 of the American Federation of Musicians. The foremost, of course, is the Los Angeles Philharmonic, whose members are contracted for a full fifty-two-week year for performances at the Music Center in the winter, Hollywood Bowl in the summer, and national tours at various times. The Philharmonic sponsors several programs to acquaint young people with symphonic music, giving free concerts in schools, in minority communities, and even in prisons. Each year it gives a series, Symphonies for Youth, in the Music Center, plus one concert in each of the county's five supervisorial districts. In addition, the Philharmonic sponsors an orchestral training program which provides an opportunity for minority instrumental students to study orchestral techniques with members of the orchestra; nearly fifty students, with an average age of eighteen, take part in this program annually.

Other outstanding orchestras in greater Los Angeles are the Glendale and Pasadena symphonies, composed of both professional and nonprofessional players. These community orchestras receive waivers from the musicians' union, exempting them from paying full union scale to union members; the balance of the wages is paid by the Music Performance Trust Fund. (These waivers are similar to the Actors' Equity Theater Waiver Plan in Los Angeles, described later in the book). Los Angeles also supports two major chamber symphonies: The Chamber Symphony and the Los Angeles Chamber Orchestra. Both groups are made up of union members and perform a limited number of concerts per season.

One of the main attractions of Los Angeles for talented musicians is the presence of movie, television and recording studios. While a symphonist working full time and supplementing his or her income by giving lessons may earn $25,000, the income for a studio musician working fewer hours can exceed $100,000. For economic reasons, the studios often draw the best talent away from the symphonies (and, in some cases, the clubs). Most studio musicians do keep a hand in the classical repertory by playing chamber music privately and/or by taking part in the community orchestras.

Although no formal employment records are kept by the union, it is estimated that of the 16,000 Local 47 members, only about 3,000 are fully employed in musical activities. Musicians are invited to join subject to an audition and payment of the required initiation fee, and thereafter pay both quarterly and "work" dues. Before age forty, a new member receives a $1,000 life insurance policy and qualifies to join one of the union's three health insurance plans under various conditions. The union has sponsored two CETA programs for musicians. The first consisted of four ensembles, totaling forty-six musicians, which presented a series of concerts on the history of American jazz at Los Angeles junior high schools. The success of this program led to funding for six five-piece groups who performed all types of music at veterans' hospitals and social events for the elderly. (Unfortunately, administrative difficulties subsequently led to a temporary suspension of the AFM programs.)

The difficulties of earning a living in this field have forced many erstwhile classical (and jazz) musicians into other professions. Preparation for a career as a musician requires an enormous investment of time, money and effort for training, in addition to the capital expense of the instruments. By contrast, a rock musician can earn as much in one night as an orchestra member earns in a year. Despite the number of studios using musicians, the bulk of the work is performed by fewer than 400 people.

The Los Angeles area has excellent training opportunities for classical musicians, principally through the Young Musician's Foundation (YMF) and the American Youth Symphony. The YMF was organized in 1955 to recognize and foster gifted young musicians (such as Calvin Simmons, who has conducted the YMF and Los Angeles Philharmonic orchestras and is now the conductor of the Oakland Symphony). Its main component is the Debut Orchestra, composed of musicians who are age twenty-five or younger, which meets once a week to read through the standard orchestral repertoire and prepare for its five concerts each season. Union members are paid for each performance plus one prior rehearsal; other rehearsals are paid for out of the Music Performance Trust Fund. The orchestra has a music director/conductor-in-training, currently through an Exxon/NEA grant, and an assistant conductor-in-training. The orchestra also employs a manager-in-training who is paid through grant funding.

The Young Musician's Foundation also sponsors the Junior Chamber Music Ensemble, the Musical Encounters Program and a limited instrument loan program. The Junior Chamber Music Ensemble affords musicians ages eight to fifteen the opportunity to play regularly under the tutelage of a qualified coach. Under the Musical Encounters Program, four ensembles of children ages six to seventeen present two programs in fifteen local schools and answer questions about the music and their instruments. Most funds to support the YMF are raised privately and through an annual gala benefit. Grants have been received from the Municipal Arts Department and the California Arts Council.

The American Youth Symphony (AYS), under the direction of Mehli Mehta, began in 1964 with forty members, now has 100 union and non-union members between the ages of sixteen and twenty-five. Union members are paid for one rehearsal per concert plus the performance; the remainder of their wages comes from the Music Performance Trust Fund. The AYS presents free concerts to the public, four at Royce Hall and one at the Wilshire Ebell Theater. Once a year the AYS raises money from a benefit concert at the Music Center which yields about $50,000, but has never received any grant funding.

To help young musicians meet the high cost of lessons, both the YMF and AYS grant two to three scholarships annually. However, lessons cost from twenty to twenty-five dollars and a serious student often needs two lessons a week, so a $500 (YMF) or $1,000 (AYS) grant does not last very long. A number of other organizations in the Los Angeles area offer music scholarships, but these prizes are seldom greater than $150. Good teachers, both vocal and instrumental, are available in Los Angeles and many young musicians have moved to the area specifically to study with the best. Both privately and through colleges, exceptionally talented middle class students can usually get the training they require, although minority students may experience more limited musical horizons. Both the Young Musician's Foundation and the American Youth Symphony, as well as the college orchestras, give several young solo artists an opportunity to perform concertos with the orchestras in concert.

Potential conductors have an entirely different problem. For them, adequate training is simply not available in this country. While the student performer can practice his or her instrument alone, the student conductor must regularly practice with an orchestra. The Debut Orchestra is the only orchestra of young musicians with a young music director/conductor. American colleges and conservatories offer classes in conducting techniques (and USC has a small intensive program under the direction of Daniel Lewis), occasionally supplementing them with summer workshops of a few weeks' duration, although none offer the intensive experience of the major European academies.

The Young Musician's Foundation sponsors an annual composition competition, performing the winning compositions at Debut Orchestra concerts. The national headquarters of the Composers and Lyricists Guild of America is located in Hollywood, with most of its 400 members composing for movie and television studios. While entry to the field has traditionally been open to the exceptionally talented, it is often fraught with politics. In addition, the 1978 copyright law could have serious repercussions in the contemporary music world. The substantial increase in fees for royalties and performing rights, which will benefit established composers, may result in fewer new works being produced.

A major lack in Los Angeles' otherwise active musical life lies in the area of choral music. The Los Angeles Master Chorale, under the direction of Roger Wagner, is virtually the only American Guild of Musical Artists (AGMA) employer in the city. The 120-voice chorale is evenly divided between union and non-union members. Union members of the chorale are paid only for the performance and one rehearsal prior to the concert. The Chorale performs six concerts each season at the Dorothy Chandler Pavilion and others in various Southern California cities. The Chorale also has performed in films and commercials. There are probably no more than twenty-five singers in Los Angeles who are able to support themselves by their music. Los Angeles also lacks a resident opera company and local exposure to top-quality opera is limited mainly to the annual tour of the New York City Opera.

Theater

The art of theater is communally achieved. The minimum human requirements for functional theater include playwright, producer, director, designer, actor, technician, administrator and audience. If the development of theater relies heavily upon human resources, then Los Angeles should be among the most important theater centers in the world. By sheer numbers, the artists and technicians at work in the commercial performing arts—the entertainment industry—may well comprise the greatest concentration of such a work force anywhere.

For participants and spectators the actor, literally and figuratively, is the focal point of the theater, for it is the actor alone who is allowed intimacy with the audience. Acting attracts many more workers than other theater disciplines. In Los Angeles, the economic lure of film and television is a prime contributor to the supply of actors.

Acting is not ordinarily stressed as an artistic alternative for young children. It is normally assumed that a youngster with acting talent need not endure the many years of training required of a ballet dancer, an opera singer, or a symphonist. Consequently the number of acting schools and workshops for young children is scarce compared to similar training opportunities for adults. More likely, a youngster's introduction to theater and acting will be a supplemental activity of a church, ethno-cultural, or recreational group. These tend to be project- rather than training-oriented. There is little indication that elementary or junior high schools devote more than cursory attention to acting as an art.

The picture changes substantially for teenagers in high school. Hollywood, Beverly Hills, and Fairfax high schools, among others, are known to produce a large number of theater students. Thespian societies are common. More importantly, drama courses are offered as viable curriculum alternatives, although public schools tend to avoid becoming "trade schools" for any occupation. There is no such thing as a high school of performing arts in Los Angeles, as there is in New York.

Private studios and workshops for high school students and adults proliferate, charging tuition or membership fees for group training. These organizations sometimes produce plays for the public, but more commonly they train actors through scene work and exercise only. The approaches to technique by different instructors vary widely, and it is here that the distinctions between preparation for film/tv and stage become apparent; the craft must be adapted to the medium. In addition to these studios and workshops, there is at least one local organization which fits more accurately into the "academy" classification. It offers up to two-year programs in "total education for professional theater."

College and university theater is a major component in the development of the creative workforce. As previously noted, the Los Angeles area is liberally supplied with two- and four-year institutions, many offering degrees in theater arts and turning out many graduates. UCLA, California State Universities at Los Angeles and Northridge, Loyola-Marymount, and Los Angeles City College are particularly highly regarded for theater. During one week at the height of the theater season, as many as fifteen different plays may be offered in local campus theaters. Generally well attended by the public, college theaters offer an actor more audience exposure than do studios. Further, they tend to promote awareness of drama history and bibliography.

The economic environment of the professional stage actor in Los Angeles is dismal. The first hurdle is to obtain Equity membership, usually a long and difficult process requiring that the actor be cast in an Equity production. There are perhaps a dozen theaters in the area that are likely to house Equity shows, including the Shubert, Pantages, Huntington Hartford, Dorothy Chandler Pavilion, Ahmanson, John Anson Ford, and the Mark Taper Forum. Not all of these maintain ongoing production schedules. Auspiciously, the past few years have seen some additions to this group of "Equity houses."

For actors, the greatest professional level theatrical activity currently taking place is in the sixty or so ninety-nine-seat-or-less "Equity waiver" theaters (explained later in the book). Actors are rarely paid for their work in these houses. Often they contribute cash, supplies, or services in order to mount the productions. Unquestionably, there are some excellent artistic products flowing from these theaters. In one week in 1978, a theater buff could have chosen from among seventy different plays at small theaters, seventeen plays at community theaters, eleven plays at cabaret and dinner theaters, and three full-time theater tours in the city schools. There are also a number of special events during the year that use actors, e.g., the Renaissance Faire, the Garden Theater Festival, and the Children's Theater Festival.

Stage directors and designers face at least one common problem: the sources of qualified training for their specialties are extremely limited compared to those of the actor. For the director, a good theater department in a college or university will usually offer at least one course in directing, with graduate degree programs in directing sometimes offered. Outside the academic environment, there are a few workshops that provide focused director training, e.g., the Actors' and Directors' Workshop. There also is a small training program sponsored by the Association of Motion Picture and Television Producers. The most common means of directorial development is by apprenticeship. Through connections or by earnest searching, one may find an assistant director position (volunteer, of course) with a "waiver" or community stage production. For those with some directing background, the professional houses are also possibilities. Such opportunities are obviously limited. The student of directing is largely required to educate himself, and the development of directors is the weakest link in the theater system in Los Angeles. Successful film and television directors have great difficulty translating their talents to live stage production. Similarly, the path from stage direction to film is also difficult. This restricts the horizontal development of directors and inhibits the ability of stage directors to earn a living in Los Angeles.

Scenic designers often reach theater through the back door. Art and design students who have developed drawing and drafting skills are likely candidates for stage design. Because there are no private schools devoted strictly to scenic design, the two major alternatives to professional training are college or university programs and apprenticeships to working designers. Good designers often work both in film/tv and in theater, and apprenticeship with one of these professionals is a common means of entry into the field. A primary concern of a designer is to develop a portfolio of his work in order to attract more challenging jobs. Like the director, a student of stage design may have to actively seek volunteer assignments. For talented and developed designers, there are professional opportunities in both professional and academic theater. The UCLA theater arts department indicates that its MFA graduates have little difficulty finding employment locally.

Not yet discussed is the Los Angeles playwright. One local producer comments that the truly dedicated playwrights are either in New York or regularly take their work to New York. There is no dearth of playwrights in Los Angeles. However, not only are promising scripts rare, but rarer still are theater groups willing to find them, spend time developing them, and attract audiences for them. The chances for good public exposure and critical evaluation in Los Angeles are limited; the Los Angeles Actors' Theater is perhaps the best known outlet for promising new plays. Several colleges offer courses in playwriting, and the American College Theater Festival competition is an excellent avenue to exposure and critique. Nevertheless, incentives to talented playwrights to pursue the art in earnest are few.

Some Sample Employment Figures

To get some indication of employment possibilities in Los Angeles' smaller theaters, the UCLA team obtained employment figures for a theater production company operating in a 400-seat theater in Los Angeles during the 1976–1977 season. It should be emphasized in examining these figures that: (1) the data reflect the activity of only *one* theater company—they are not presented as representative of "industry averages;" (2) the company is young and struggling and showed no profit for the season, although growth is anticipated; and (3) volunteer labor was responsible for the survival of the enterprise during that season.

The two-production season comprised thirty-one weeks: ten weeks of rehearsal and twenty-one weeks of performance (147 performances) and employed eighteen Equity actors and two Equity stage managers. To those union employees the company paid a total of $56,200 or an average of $2,810 each in salaries. In addition, an average of $185 each was paid into Equity pension and welfare funds. (The average figures, however, are deceptive: all Equity personnel received scale, a minimum of $125/week; some worked as little as two weeks, while others worked as long as twenty-two weeks.)

Round-figure totals with respect to other employees during the season were as shown in Table 2.

This is the total significant *cash* compensation to the theater staff. There were other workers who were volunteers or were compensated with free

Table 2: Employment and Salaries of Staff of a Small Theater Production Company

Staff	Salaries
1 full-time technician	$ 3,600
2 designers	600
4 part-time box office workers	1,500
4 administrators	10,570
1 publicist	2,000
5 part-time miscellaneous staff	1,500

tickets or with acting lessons (an actors' workshop operates at the theater). As many as fifteen people exchanged work at the theater for anywhere from three to eighteen months of weekly acting lessons.

A Special Note on the Free Public Theater Foundation

Given the special concern of our study with the public aspects of the arts, the Free Public Theater Foundation is of particular interest. The theater's founding principle is that "the dramatic arts should be wholly accessible to the entire community and that in a democratic society a free public theater is as desirable as a free public library."

Thus, the Los Angeles Shakespeare Festival was established by the Foundation in the summer of 1973 with a presentation of *As You Like It* at the county-owned Pilgrimage Theater (since renamed the John Anson Ford County Cultural Arts Theater). Although this endeavor initially provided a "free theater" experience for those handicapped only by the price of a ticket, it did not provide the same opportunity to those for whom the theater was inaccessible. In order to reach the people who could not come to the Pilgrimage Theater, the Shakespeare Festival toured its two 1974 productions, *Macbeth* and *Comedy of Errors,* throughout Los Angeles city and county parks and charged no admission.

For the 1975 season, the managing director combined all the elements of the previous two seasons by presenting both a touring production of *Shakespeare and His People* as well as *Romeo and Juliet* at the Pilgrmage Theater. Attendance continued to build, attracting over 40,000 people, nearly double the previous season's attendance.

The 1976 season of the Shakespeare Festival provided twenty-five performances of *Othello* at the Ford Theater, fifty-two performances of *Taming of the Shrew* in parks throughout the county of Los Angeles, and twenty-eight performances of a children's theater version of *A Midsummer Night's Dream* in various parks, schools and hospitals throughout the Los Angeles area.

The organization had expanded its operations considerably during its five seasons 1973–1977. The budget grew 49 percent from FY 1975 to FY 1976, and 6 percent from 1976 to 1977, increases supported without ticket revenues. The 1977 park tour of *Comedy of Errors* played thirty-eight performances to over 20,000 people. The Ford Theater production of *Much Ado About Nothing* gave twenty-five performances to large audiences, with the last twelve reaching capacity.

An overview of the receipts and expenditures of the Free Public Theater Foundation is provided in Table 3. The size of the public contributions particularly suggests the community support of the organization. Almost 57 percent of their FY 1976 budget came from donated materials and services.

A volunteer managing director, two CETA employees, and a donated secretary/assistant are responsible for the overall administration of an organization whose ranks swell to around 120 during the height of the season. In addition, ten youths from the Summer Program for Economically Deprived Youth (SPEDY) work about twenty-five hours per week.

The Equity actors get union scale and the non-Equity actors receive honoraria. The shortness of the run and a well-defined term of tenure prevent the complete exhaustion of the company.

In the case of the Experiment in the Theater for Children (ETC) the actors are paid tiny honoraria and look on it as an opportunity to develop their skills. With thirty performances being produced for less than $4,000, it is not a great drain on the organization's resources.

The Shakespeare Festival recently received a CETA grant for two children's theater tours. One is a natural outgrowth of ETC called the Young Peoples Theater Tour. It will employ six actors, a stage manager and a production supervisor for a year, touring the elementary schools and other places where young audiences can be assembled. The total project costs will add $111,000 to the Shakespeare Festival's budget, with around 90 percent for salaries and benefits. The second tour will be in the junior and senior high schools. It will employ eight actors and one stage manager for a year and add nearly $126,000 to the budget, of which $115,000 goes for salaries and benefits.

The Shakespeare Festival has been successful at turning community resources into programming, getting a big "bang for the buck" because none of the resources are turned into negotiable reserves for the organization. When the organization tried to secure a loan to deal with cash flow problems, the banks turned it down: "No assets." But there are other kinds of assets. Bandwagons are loaned for free by the city or county, which also provide free office space. The operation is streamlined, it has no fat stored for the winter. That means the Shakespeare Festival is in a vulnerable position if it has not built up credit with the board and the community.

The Shakespeare Festival's ability to expand its programming and remain relatively stable in the face of uncertainty is largely due to its managing director, Peg Yorkin, and executive assistant, Celeste Anlauf. They put together project teams which, once organized, operate as semi-autonomous work groups. Top management provides a clear sense of mission and establishes an organizational environment conducive to good morale and high productivity.

Dance

The dance world of Los Angeles has given birth to such giants as Martha Graham and Ruth St. Denis. The Los Angeles area (including Orange County) supports over thirty companies devoted to ballet, folk, modern, or ethnic dance. The numerous teachers in the city have trained dancers who now perform in companies throughout America and Europe.

In September 1977, the first Los Angeles Dance Festival was organized, featuring most of the area's vital companies. The festival was sponsored in part by the Kinetikos Dance Foundation and UCLA's Department of Fine Arts Productions and drew record crowds. The Dance Festival and Garden

Theater Festival are the only local opportunities for Los Angeles-based companies to perform. Since there is no permanent financial support for either festival, each must yearly play the grant/foundation game, leaving little staff time for creative programming, new publicity outlets, or the like.

There are few theaters in the area that present dance advantageously. The Shrine has the biggest stage for ballet and the Music Center presents a limited amount of ballet and musical comedy. All three Music Center houses are serviceable but not designed to present dance. The smaller private houses in the city do not have adequate stage space. The Pilot is the one theater designed with dance in mind, but it is not entirely accessible to the dance community, a great loss to an art discipline so starved for space to display its work. UCLA's Royce Hall is described as a "barn" by the dance locals, with audience too distant and the rake making floor work difficult.

In March 1977, the Los Angeles Area Dance Alliance (LAADA) was formed to explore the collective problems of dance and to facilitate action to further the art form. After one year of existence, the LAADA has identified adequate space as the major need of the dance community, and it now is striving to secure adequate dance spaces in which to work and perform. Other areas in which LAADA has taken a leadership role are: the union rates and standards questions raised by the National Dance Touring Program's link to the American Guild of Musical Artists (AGMA) rate scales; a dance calendar that would coordinate and publicize upcoming dance events; and representation of Southern California's dance interests in the state legislature.

Most working dance companies in the city are supported in part by the NEA's Dance Touring Program, and all perform in local colleges and public school systems and teach classes. The activities of dance companies tend to be centered around earning money rather than creating. This generates a problem for choreographers. New works of choreography take time to create, time in which the company must rehearse rather than perform. Therefore the companies are constantly poised between the "down time" of creating and the "earning time" of performing. The support structures for the artist do not accurately relate to the choreographer's dilemma. A dance company of twelve people financially cannot take a year off to allow a choreographer full access to their talents. Hence, choreography is often hurried, forced, and geared toward selling tickets rather than artistry.

Interwoven with this choreographic problem are dance critics. The city is fortunate to have several sensitive and responsive critics who cover the dance world. However, since the companies have only one chance to be reviewed, with a concert often only running one or two nights, Los Angles does not have a system to present choreography, allow it to be revised, and then performed again. No company, with the possible exception of the Los Angeles Ballet, has a home season with multiple performances of repertory and new works.

Los Angeles supports many small schools of ballet, tap, jazz and ballroom dancing, but there are almost no public modern dance classes taught and none in choreography, composition or improvisation. Few classes of any discipline are of a professional level. The result is that the most talented dancers leave to join the schools of the major ballet companies in New York, San Francisco and Europe. On an amateur community level, there is much dance activity as it relates to recreation, fitness and weight loss.

Both the University of California and the state university system in the Los Angeles area have fine dance curricula. Several high schools also have dance programs, but these are taught as physical education rather than as an art form. Below the high school level there is almost no dance training offered in public schools. Those who choose dancing at a young age must lead a double life—a full school curriculum plus at least four hours of dancing daily. It is a rigorous and demanding routine. The only alternative for the young dancer is to enroll in a private school that will adjust its curriculum to include dance technique in the educational structure. This is often expensive and, since scholarships are almost non-existent, limits the number of children who can afford to pursue dance.

Los Angeles is a gathering place for commercial dancers, with television employing many dancers and choreographers trained in jazz. However, the commercial dancer's professional life lasts only about five years, for many are forced to dance on concrete surfaces. Recently two local disco-dance companies have been organized which provide floor shows in the area's private disco clubs. The members are all college graduates with degrees in

Table 3: Revenues and Expenses of The Free Public Theater Foundation, 1975 and 1977

	For the Year Ended October 31, 1977	For the Year Ended December 31, 1975
Revenues:		
Pledges and cash contributions:		
Foundation grants	$ 30,000	$ 27,000
City of Los Angeles	30,000	35,000
Corporate grants	37,400	10,725
County of Los Angeles	15,000	
Public contributions	41,838	26,417
	154,238	99,142
Donated material and services (Note 2)	212,128	157,057
Tuition from professional training program		8,579
Miscellaneous	30,539	2,442
Total Revenues	396,905	267,220
Expenses:		
Program services:		
Salaries and professional fees	122,070	50,394
Costumes and sets (Note 1)	14,602	3,130
Equipment rental	10,779	5,500
Employee benefits	12,680	4,695
Publicity	9,314	4,301
Payroll tax expense	5,431	3,003
Professional training program salaries		7,788
Depreciation (Note 1)		1,200
Other	3,954	1,979
Donated material and services (Note 2)	80,140	63,947
	258,970	145,964
Supporting services:		
Office and office supplies	3,130	3,686
Other	7,402	4,318
Donated material and services (Note 2)	131,988	93,083
Total Expenses	401,490	247,051
Excess (deficit) of revenues over expenses	(4,585)	20,169
Cumulative excess (deficit) of revenues over expenses, beginning of year	1,223	(17,812)
Forgiveness of debt (Note 4)		1,526)
Cumulative excess (deficit) of revenues over expenses, end of year	($3,362)	$3,883

	For the Year Ended October 31, 1977	For the Year Ended December 31, 1975
Details on Donated Materials and Services: The value of such materials and services is as follows:		
Administrative employees	$ 35,983	$ 41,132
Office space and theater rental	25,000	26,000
Utilities, janitorial, security	37,320	31,600
Administrator	24,001	15,600
Legal and accounting	19,135	14,400
Set construction	8,000	
Printing and mailing	11,000	5,803
Mobile stage	10,000	13,850
Production directors	10,675	4,803
Transportation	10,670	
Office furnishings and supplies	3,650	3,869
Other	16,695	
	$212,128	$157,057

Source: Accountants' Report on Examination of Financial Statements, dated April 22, 1977 and February 2, 1978.

dance who have found this to be one of the few ways to earn a living with their dance training.

Community (Neighborhood) Arts

A universal characteristic of urban communities in the United States is ethnic, social and economic diversity, a source of immense strength and creativity. The richness and vitality of minority cultures can, with appropriate planning and development, become the basis for broad innovation. However, with the exception of the acclaimed WPA cultural programs of the 1930s, which specifically recognized the vast but hitherto unexplored aesthetic resources of America's blacks, it was not until the civil rights movement of the 1960s that the role of minorities in the culture of this nation was widely acknowledged in public policy.

Traditionally, the bulk of public and private support for the arts in America has been directed toward the more conventional cultural forms—e.g., symphonic music, classical dance, museum art—which are predominantly European in origin.

These artistic modes have often been favored by the cultural and economic "elites" which, in large part, have been responsible for defining and applying the accepted "standards of excellence" in the arts. Thus, for many decades the phrase "good music" referred primarily to classical music composed in Europe in the eighteenth and nineteenth centuries and performed by symphony orchestras or chamber music ensembles. With few exceptions, music of African, Asian, Latin, or American origin was held in lesser esteem aesthetically and rarely was endorsed by the dominant arbiters of cultural taste.

The concept of neighborhood arts is based on a far different premise. As suggested by William H. McWhinney and James M. Woods, neighborhood arts reflect a "cultural democracy" which is at the polar extreme from traditional concepts. Arts programs and facilities have been made available to lower-income and minority communities in the past, usually based upon the assumption that the residents should be conditioned to the artistic and literary values of the dominant majority. Carnegie-

A community-produced mural adds something very special to a neighborhood: Ken's Market, Mural in Progress, East Los Angeles, 1972. Credit: Environmental Communications

funded libraries, touring art exhibits and musical performances, as well as public education, were designed to accomplish this conditioning.

A neighborhood arts program does not require the automatic rejection of majority values and standards. Nor does it necessarily imply a mindless relativism to the effect that "one type of art is just as good as any other." It merely emphasizes the multiplicity and diversity of cultural forms which deserve recognition and, in some cases, further development. McWhinney and Woods have appropriately defined what they term "cultural democracy:"

> A cultural democracy exists where the cultures of the non-dominant elements in a society are accepted along with those of the dominant. A cultural democracy provides for acceptance of one's historical, ethnic and racial identity just as a political democracy respects the individual's legal and economic rights.[2]

One important benefit from neighborhood arts, aside from the expansion of cultural resources and an enhanced quality of life, is the resultant strengthening of community pride and self-image. Communities that are invidiously depicted as culturally deprived, simply because they do not share majority values in some sense, may be reservoirs of unrecognized creative talent.

In Los Angeles, neighborhood arts have been especially identified with a number of community-based arts programs which were created after the Watts riot of 1965. Each reflected an emergent pride in the recognition and identification that had come, however violently, to a previously ignored area (some of the organizations predated the riot but their major recognition and influence came afterwards). The list is lengthy and impressive:

1. The annual Watts Summer Festival, beginning in 1966 on the first anniversary of the riot, with concerts on the Jordan High School grounds, art exhibits in a large county park, and a massive star-filled parade, all administered locally with assistance from government and business.
2. The Watts Writers' Workshop, located directly in Watts (unlike some other programs which, for public relations purposes, used "Watts" in their titles without actual location in that small community).
3. Watts Happening Coffee House, a night spot featuring talented local performers.
4. Mafundi Institute (funded initially by the Kettering Foundation), a cultural center with drama and dance classes led by tv stars and other well-known performers.
5. Studio Watts, an artistic training center for young people.
6. The Watts Media Center (located several miles from Watts), for instruction in broadcasting and other media skills.
7. Performing Arts Society of Los Angeles (PASLA), for the writing and production of plays relevant to the black experience.
8. Teen Posts, funded through the federal anti-poverty program, designed to offer teenagers in low-income communities recreational opportunities and cultural exposure.

However, a decade later, the record of these particular groups is discouraging. By mid-1976, the Writers' Workshop, Watts Happening Coffee House, Mafundi Institute, and Media Center had vanished; the Watts Summer Festival had grown progressively smaller in scope and was on the verge of extinction; most of the area Teen Posts had been closed; Studio Watts had changed its focus and had relocated its operational headquarters out of the immediate community, concentrating on the design and construction of innovative arts-oriented housing; PASLA was a small operation relocated away from the Watts area.

The experience of Mafundi is illustrative of the problems that these community arts groups faced. Located initially in an older, converted building on 103rd Street ("Charcoal Alley") in the midst of a designated urban renewal area, its programming was diverse and involved substantial numbers of young people. When Model Cities funds became available somewhat later, a new two-story building was constructed across the street, called the Watts Neighborhood Center, complete with auditorium, studios, and game rooms, and Mafundi became its only tenant. But programming and staffing declined: Kettering Foundation funds were removed, outside volunteers dwindled, and the building deteriorated and was largely unused. By mid-1974, only a grant from the National Endowment for the Arts kept Mafundi alive, and despite the efforts of the dedicated young man who was its final director and new help from some Hollywood performers and UCLA graduate students, its days were numbered. Early in 1976, the city of Los Angeles took over the building and Mafundi disappeared.

The decline of these programs does not in any way reflect a failure or weakness in the premise upon which they were based. On the contrary, the value of the contributions they made and the quality of much of the talent uncovered have never been disputed. The factors leading to their eventual weakening and dissolution apply in varying degrees to almost all programs which emerged in the aftermath of the 1965 riot.

First, the interest of funding sources in the Watts community tended to dwindle as the memory of the riot and fear of a possible recurrence faded. Much of the early programming was intended only as a pacifier, and even among those outsiders whose concern was genuine, competing interests and demands came to the fore as time passed. Some of the important programs, such as the Watts Writers' Workshop and Studio Watts, depended heavily upon the input and leadership of one or two individuals who, for both personal and professional reasons, might be drawn away to other projects.

Second, the government funding for many of the community programs dwindled during the Nixon-Ford period, and this generated another vicious circle: program administrators spent increasing amounts of time developing grant proposals or investigating alternative sources of support, which inevitably affected the quality of programming and made even more difficult the task of renewing funds.

Third, there often has been an imbalance among program elements. Political needs for high visibility have led—as in the case of Mafundi—to the construction of impressive facilities without sufficient program or staffing support. These circumstances have hardly been conducive to the innovative programming required.

Fourth, conventional funding agencies usually are reluctant to fund community-based projects and organizations without an acceptable track record. This reluctance makes genuine community control less likely and aggravates the administrative problems even of those groups which do receive funding.

A special problem affects projects which fall into artistic and cultural categories: unlike San Francisco and some other communities, Los Angeles does not have a neighborhood arts program. Thus there is no official body to assist with funding and proposal development, coordinate programs, provide technical and research support, and help clear away the typical bureaucratic obstacles to local programming. Without this resource, it is hard to build permanence into the various community arts projects, and the resulting impermanence only exacerbates the feelings of frustration and alienation experienced by so many of the ghetto and barrio youngsters.

Yet despite these problems, the community arts movement as a whole in Los Angeles remains alive and well. A range of organizations serves not only the black community, but also the city's Mexican-American and Asian-American communities. In some cases older, established, traditional arts organizations have established minority "outreach" programs. These efforts are important not only for the educational and cultural opportunities they offer, but also for the economic contributions they make to their neighborhoods and the role they play in strengthening community life in the city.

Community arts programs in greater Los Angeles fall roughly into two broad categories:

1. Those sponsored or funded by a unit of government, such as the Los Angeles County Music and Performing Arts Commission, the Municipal Arts Department of the city of Los Angeles, and the various recreation and parks departments of major cities throughout the county;
2. Those initiated by private nonprofit organizations, most of which receive some government funding. The largest and most prominent in the minority communities are the Inner City Cultural Center in predominantly black central Los Angeles (primarily for the performing arts), Plaza de la Raza in predominantly Chicano east Los Angeles (primarily for the visual arts), and East/West Players (performing arts) in the Asian-American community.

The important role community arts play in the economic and social development of minority and low-income neighborhoods is suggested by the locations of the independent community arts organizations. The city's statistical agency, the Community Analysis Bureau, using cluster analysis (which groups the city's census tracts into thirty special neighborhood clusters exhibiting similar social and economic characteristics), has identified economically distressed areas and has designated them as either Priority Areas 1 or 2. The economic characteristics of both areas are compared with those of the entire city in Table 4.

Over 75 percent of Priority Area 1 (716,000 residents in 195 census tracts) is comprised of a large contiguous area which includes east (primarily Chicano), central (Asian, black, Hispanic), and south central (primarily black) Los Angeles. By the major economic indicators in Table 4, Priority Area 1 exhibits the lowest economic levels of prosperity compared to the city as a whole. Mean family income is 46 percent below that of the city, while the percentage of families in poverty is 122 percent higher. Unemployment is 74 percent above the city mean. The percentage of families on welfare is 124 percent higher than for the entire city.

More than 90 percent of Priority Area 2 (135 cen-

Table 4: Economic Characteristics of Los Angeles's Poorer Areas, 1974

	Median Family Income	% of Families in Poverty	% Unemployment	% Families on Welfare
Priority Area 1	$ 6,090	22.5%	12.7%	23.5%
Priority Area 2	9,859	17.5	7.3	10.1
City Average	$11,200 (Median)	10.5	7.3	10.5

Source: Los Angeles Community Analysis Bureau, *The State of the City: Priority of Needs, 1974*.

sus tracts, 545,400 residents) is immediately adjacent to Priority Area 1, bordering east, central, and south central Los Angeles. Median family income is 12 percent below that of the city as a whole. The percentage of families in poverty is 67 percent higher. The unemployment levels approximate those of the city, as does the percentage of families receiving welfare.

Priority Area 2 does not exhibit severe economic problems to the extent of those experienced by the primary area, as evidenced by the data. Although Priority Area 2 is not as heavily minority as Priority Area 1 in its population composition (50 percent compared to 85 percent), it is considered a transitional area undergoing rapid demographic change, and is largely blue collar in terms of its labor force. According to the Community Analysis Bureau, the entire area is beginning to exhibit signs of deterioration. Against this background, it is instructive to note the location of the city's major community arts organizations, as shown in Table 5.

As shown in Table 5, five community arts organizations are located in Priority Area 2, while six are in Priority Area 1. Only one (the Bilingual Foundation for the Arts) is not located in either area. Furthermore, every arts organization, with the exception of two (BFA and Nosotros), is situated in a census tract where minority groups comprise a majority or near-majority of the population.

Table 5: The Location of Neighborhood Arts Organizations

Community Arts Organization	Economically Distressed Area	Minority Population in Census Tracts**
Bilingual Foundation for the Arts*		
Brockman Art Gallery	Priority Area 2	83%(B)
East/West Players	2	35%(C)19%(B)5%(A)
Centro de Arte Publico	2	50%(C)
Goez Art Studio	1	92%(C)
Inner City Cultural Center	1	70%(C)15%(A)
Mechicano Art Center	2	47%(C)
Nosotros	2	30%(C)
Plaza de la Raza	1	73%(C)
R'Wanda Lewis Afro-American Dance Company	1	90%(B)
Self-Help Graphics	1	91%(C)
Watts Community Symphony	1	89%(B)

* Even though BFA is located in the San Fernando Valley, it primarily serves the East Los Angeles area which is designated as a part of Priority Area 1

** A-Asian American   B-Black   C-Chicano/Latino

It is evident that independent organizations involved with community arts serve economically distressed areas having large minority populations. By the very fact that community arts organizations are located in areas with limited resources, they demonstrate their commitment to the community, and in doing so, provide some employment opportunities and a degree of stability in low-income areas.

Along with this distinct economic role, community arts organizations also serve to give coherence and meaning to minority communities. Many function as multifaceted community centers. Certain groups, such as the Inner City Cultural Center, have worked for constructive community change and have acted as centers of social interchange for children and adults. The organizations have attempted to bring together various elements of the community—schools, gangs, churches, businesses, labor—to work with artists in generating new cultural forces. The result of all this is the development of community cohesion and pride and the enrichment of the neighborhood as a basic and important unit of urban life.

Community arts groups are innovative. For example, the R'Wanda Lewis Dance Company has provided handicapped students with a form of new therapy through dance and movement. Self Help Graphics' Barrio Mobile Art Service is literally an art studio on wheels providing services to inner city schools which have drastically reduced arts curricula because of cutbacks. East-West Players provides workshops for students in the Asian-American community. Goez Art Studio, along with other arts groups, has helped to bring national attention to the mural movement in east Los Angeles, and Brockman Gallery serves a similar function in behalf of black artists and sculptors.

Community arts programs fill a void where established arts institutions have failed to adequately address the creative needs of minorities. They also provide an avenue for artists to be recognized in the established art world by providing encouragement within a supportive framework. Surprisingly, many Los Angeles community arts organizations have continued to function despite extremely limited budgets. The Municipal Arts Department provides small grants to some arts organizations, but only a few are directed to minority communities. The California Arts Council has provided nonmatching grants to community arts organizations and the Expansion Arts Program of the National Endowment for the Arts also funds neighborhood arts programs. While such grants form a small proportion of the funds needed by community arts organizations, these sums represent a beginning that hopefully will grow in the future to more significant dimensions.

The greater Los Angeles area has vast resources in the nonprofit arts sector, encompassing virtually all aspects of the performing, graphic, and fine arts. Environmental and economic attractions have brought large numbers of talented artists to the area, but unemployment remains high and there is little coordination among the many programs and organizations in this broad field.

Community (neighborhood) arts clearly play an important role in the cultural and economic life of Los Angeles, both enriching the life of the whole city and working to strengthen group identity and cohesion. Their location in several low-income areas of the city gives them an economic importance—and potential—that is unique among arts organizations. We consider the strengthening of neighborhood arts as being fundamental to the enhancement of the economic and social role of the arts in the city.

Footnotes

[1] Theater is actually "mixed" nonprofit and profit, but is included in this sector because we emphasize the former.

[2] "Arts in the Neighborhood," Research Paper No. 19, Management in the Arts Research Program, UCLA, September 1973, p. 14.

2.4
The Arts Institutions: The "Mixed" and For-Profit Sectors

Visual Arts and Crafts

Los Angeles is not known as a particularly thriving center for the visual arts. The presentation of visual art in the greater Los Angeles area is provided primarily by traditional institutions such as museums and galleries, but is augmented by the recent emergence of alternative spaces. The Los Angeles County Museum of Art (LACMA) is the major museum in the area, but it has limited resources for fostering art in the community. The contemporary art department has a limited budget and primarily restricts itself to exhibiting local artists, ensuring that some local artists enjoy the legitimacy of a major museum. The curators of contemporary art thus wield considerable power on the local scene.

In terms of community outreach, LACMA provides a continuing series of classes, films and lectures, but these are not widely publicized except to members. However, large numbers of students are introduced to the museum through its tours for all local school systems.

The J. Paul Getty Museum in Malibu and the Norton Simon Museum of Art in Pasadena are privately-endowed museums which contain impressive collections of art, each reflecting the tastes and preferences of its founder. The Henry Huntington Gallery in San Marino specializes in English sixteenth through nineteenth century painting and draws the public to its beautiful botanical gardens and extensive library as well as to its art. In Exposition Park, adjacent to the Coliseum and the USC campus, the county administers several museums with historical, scientific, artistic and photographic collections and some facilities for the performing arts. This is the only major publicly-owned cultural complex located adjacent to a predominantly minority (black) area.

Galleries

The gallery network in Los Angeles appears to be undergoing expansion and diversification. While La Cienega Boulevard may still reign supreme as the established commercial art center, pockets of activity are developing in other parts of the city as well. The relocation to Venice of some prominent galleries attests to this recent surge of art exhibitions in previously dormant places. Whether these moves have been precipitated by escalating rents on La Cienega or by the desire to distinguish themselves from the "decorator-oriented" galleries which seem to prevail there is uncertain. In any case, the geographic spread enhances the accessibility of galleries to a broader public.

La Cienega's Tuesday evening art-walk is also aimed at attracting a fresh crowd of gallery-goers. Reports indicate the attendance is sporadic, however, despite oft-repeated newspaper announcements. One surmises that public outreach is not an objective for those galleries strung out along Santa Monica Boulevard or in Venice. Off the beaten track and poorly announced from the street, they clearly do not invite casual foot traffic, but rather cater to a more knowledgeable art crowd. Relying mainly on newspaper and periodical reviews and private mailing lists, these galleries appeal to a deliberately select group of viewers.

It seems that a growing geographic base is not sufficient to render the gallery network a pillar of support for local visual artists: profit-making concerns in a fairly conservative art market induce a certain reluctance on the part of many galleries to show contemporary works which may not prove saleable. While New York galleries are often in the vanguard with respect to emerging artists, most Los Angeles galleries seem to hang back, looking toward the museum establishment for its seal of approval. Even those galleries more independent in spirit have a limited impact on the plight of local artists. Only so many can be successfully shown, and at the common 50-50 consignment rate, the artist cannot expect substantial or steady pecuniary support. (One fairly well-known local artist has an excellent rapport with her dealer and considers herself fortunate to have earned $7,000 in one year through the sale of her work.)

Alternative Spaces

A nationwide phenomenon known as the alternative space has emerged within the past few years to lessen the difficulties artists face in merely getting shown. Emerging alongside the movement toward less saleable art work, the alternative space is designed to act as a non-commercial, nonprofit gallery which caters to art forms which have no other outlet. A few such spaces have appeared in Los Angeles, the most prominent being the Los Angeles Institute of Contemporary Art (LAICA). In addition to providing exhibit space for experimental art forms such as performance and video, LAICA provides such services as an artists' registry, public lectures on the legislative and financial concerns of artists and a quarterly journal. Recent foundation grants and CETA awards have permitted LAICA to broaden its public outreach by sponsoring outside exhibits which may prove vital to the Los Angeles community as a whole. Other visual arts organizations have cropped up with similar intentions. For example, the Foundation for Art Resources, organized by three commercial gallery owners who recognize the weaknesses in Los Angeles' support system, is essentially an umbrella organization with no space of its own, aiming to facilitate various art activities throughout the city. Although not officially alternative spaces, college art galleries correspond more closely to this particular category than to any other, especially with regard to exhibiting artists who are emerging from educational institutions. However, these galleries often have an academic, art historical focus which links them more with museums.

Artists Studios

While the notion of making art conjures up images of the solitary artist, isolated in his or her studio pursuing a unique, compelling vision, artists can also be one another's prime resources. In a realm where no official alliances exist, casual comradeship can help to disseminate valuable information. At times more formal workshop or rap sessions have arisen to meet immediate needs. But in any situation where demand (for exhibition opportunity) exceeds supply, group spirit only carries so far; local artists have been known to withhold pertinent information from one another to further their own careers. One of the few collective graphic workshop/studio spaces recently was forced to close its doors because members were continuing to use the facilities without paying their share of the costs.

While certain museum curators and gallery dealers make a habit of frequenting artists studios to survey local talent, the artist most often must actively engage in self-promotion before gaining even a modicum of recognition. Nonetheless, the studio network would seem to provide a direct link for communication and the exchange of new ideas. Exhibition in the private sector is probably on an upswing, with corporate collections being displayed in various office buildings throughout the city, especially in the downtown area. Especially noteworthy is the ARCO-sponsored space in its downtown Los Angeles Plaza, which functions as an alternative space and has changing exhibits.

Direct corporate patronage is also apparent in commissions such as the Jim Dine collection in the newly renovated Biltmore Hotel. Other outlets include the Cedars-Sinai Hospital, which displays art on its walls for sale, or the tours of collections in private residences sponsored by various organizations.

Art Training

A student's first training in visual art is likely to come from the educational system. This may be due to encouragement in school or at home; nevertheless, the amount of training available at lower school levels is limited. New directions in programming are developing, however.

The California Arts Council sponsors two of these. Artists in Schools and Communities provides a system whereby resident artists contribute services and teach classes in local schools and communities. Alternatives in Education is a three-year pilot program designed to demonstrate the usefulness of art in teaching traditional academic subjects.

More extensive training has traditionally been expected to come from the college and university level. Some of the more well-known campuses producing visual artists include UCLA, Art Center College of Design, Otis Art Institute, California Institute of the Arts, Scripps College, University of California at Irvine (Orange County), and California State University at Long Beach. Programs at these schools range from specialities in conceptual art to graphic design and illustration. A beginning art student generally will find it hard to locate an institution which caters to varied interests. California State University at Long Beach, probably the closest to offering a truly comprehensive visual art program, can only offer admission to a small percentage of the would-be art students clamoring at its gates.

Apprenticeships also provide an important form of training. However in Los Angeles, apprenticeships between established artists and those who are "up-and-coming" seem sporadic and based almost entirely upon connections or being in the right place at the right time. This is another function of the loose communication network in Los Angeles and its lack of overhead guidance. A hopeful direction has been provided by the California Arts Council in encouraging this most precious of artistic relationships, its Maestro-Apprentice Program. This program is not only for visual artists, but masters of all art forms. Each year, the arts council will select a limited number of "maestros" from around the state and award them stipends for their work with chosen apprentices.

In addition to the art training in the public school, the Municipal Arts Department has developed an extensive training program at the Barnsdall Park Junior Art Center. Classes are provided free of charge to youths between the ages of four and seventeen, integrated with viewing experiences in the Municipal Gallery. The aim is to expose young people to both the product and process of art in a meaningful, participatory fashion.

This same goal provides much of the energetic impetus behind the operation of the Municipal Gallery. Previously a somewhat weak component of the Los Angeles art scene, the gallery has recently experienced a regeneration, primarily due to the dynamic directorship of Josine Ianco-Starrels. Viewed by many local artists as a vital resource, Ms. Starrels is known to review artists' portfolios with a real desire to understand their work. She devotes at least one show per year to emerging Southern California artists and is widely lauded for mounting educational but non-didactic exhibitions.

Other municipal endeavors focus on a grass roots approach as well. The city-administered Watts Towers Art Center, Citywide Mural Project and a proposed Art Park all promote the expansion of the arts into non-traditional places. The heightened public awareness for which these projects strive can be expected to play a key role in the future state of the visual arts in Los Angeles.

On a statewide level, the California Arts Council has a number of programs available which support visual artists in addition to those previously mentioned. Artists in Social Institutions funds artists' projects in such places as hospitals, prisons, and mental health centers. Visual Arts Assistance aids artists in obtaining supplies for projects earmarked for display in public places.

The physical scope of artistic activity in the Los Angeles area is limited, focused mostly in the Hollywood and Westside communities. There has been an attempt on the part of the Los Angeles Municipal Arts Department to increase outreach in the east Los Angeles (Chicano) area, but progress is slow. Activity is also limited in the San Fernando Valley, although new projects like the proposed Art Park may remedy this situation. One of the major stumbling blocks is the sprawling nature of Los Angeles itself, inhibiting communication among the various groups and cultures existent here.

In addition to the immediate Los Angeles area, there are a number of activities in peripheral areas. The Long Beach Museum makes a practice of showing contemporary art although it does not have a permanent collection. Orange County also has its share of activities, including the Newport Harbor Art Museum and the string of galleries and festivals in Laguna Beach.

In general, it is the geographic nature of Los Angeles that makes it difficult to isolate problems, and, once isolated, to solve them. The large physical area not only spreads out artistic activity for spectators, but separates artists and divides them into many small clusters of activity.

Crafts

Craft, folk and ethnic arts cannot readily be placed into a category separate from the visual and fine arts. We tend to use the word *craft* when the function of an art object precedes its aesthetic form. In *folk* art there need be no conscious acknowledgement that aesthetics transcend function. The additional distinction of *ethnic* art is only in terms of its religio-cultural focus.

If we reconstruct basic assumptions from the behavior of craft artists in Los Angeles, it seems they believe that given enough time to develop a market for their works, the craft artist can be self-sufficient. Beyond the continuing demand for studio space, the primary demand of the craft community is for exposure through exhibitions and publications. These functions are performed by the Craft

A mural by a fine arts group (of Los Angeles after it has slid into the ocean) has become a landmark for tourists and natives: Isle of California *Mural, South of Santa Monica Boulevard, Los Angeles, 1970–72. Credit: Environmental Communications.*

and Folk Art Museum. To extend exposure, the museum maintains a slide registry and a museum shop as an important channel of distribution for contemporary crafts. While it originally functioned on a consignment basis, it now makes outright purchases from the artists. This has helped the ever-present cash flow problem of the artists and has increased the museum shop's return on gross assets from 6 percent in 1976 to 15 percent in 1977.

Craft fairs in many neighborhoods of the city and region are the predominant channel of distribution. These fairs are well-attended and provide a very frequent sales outlet. The annual sales of student work at UCLA and at Otis Art Institute also provide a valuable outlet and market test.

While channels of distribution are increasing and awareness of the vitality of the craft artist is growing, the lack of communication between the entire arts community and the general populace is still the greatest problem for the artist trying to make a living. At this stage, members of the general public need to be better convinced of the validity of crafts as an art form and need to gain confidence and experience in exercising their own aesthetic tastes.

The For-Profit Sector: Motion Pictures

The year 1977 was the most successful in motion picture history, at least in terms of gross box office revenues. In current dollars, revenues amounted to approximately $2.325 billion, about 10 percent above the previous record year of 1975 and 17 percent above 1976. Even after an adjustment for inflation, the 1977 figure was still about 2 percent above 1975 and 13 percent above 1976. Amazingly, the income from just one picture—*Star Wars*—represented about 10 percent of all revenues for 1977.[1]

Total admissions in 1977 also climbed to a new high. The 1977 figure of 1.047 billion exceeded the previous record of 1.033 billion in 1975. This extends an upward trend in movie admissions since 1974, when the total was about 1.012 billion, for the approximately 15,000 theaters in the United States. Movie box office revenues in 1973 constituted about 45 percent of total U.S. spectator amusement expenditures, obviously a significant percentage but down considerably from the 53 percent ten years earlier and the 82 percent figure for 1946—the first peacetime year after World War II. Consumer expenditures on movies represented about 2.5 percent of total U.S. recreation expenditures in 1973, compared to about 21 percent in 1935 and a high of almost 26 percent in 1943. Total payroll for the industry (including theaters) was $1.424 billion in 1973, with average employment at 203,000 nationally.

According to Department of Commerce estimates, capital investment in the industry amounted in 1965 to approximately $2.9 billion, of which 94 percent was invested in theaters. It is estimated that about $500 million is invested annually in the motion picture industry, with an added $250 million invested in television. About 700 circuits operate slightly over half of all the movie houses in the nation, with about 70 percent of film rental gross on an average A-picture coming from about 1,000 "key run" bookings. A particularly intriguing trend in the industry in recent years has been the proliferation of multi-auditorium theaters in suburban shopping centers and malls. This enables the industry to attract audiences with a variety of tastes and preferences in movie entertainment into already well-attended commercial centers.

The audience for movies remains predominantly young: in 1975, 46 percent of total admissions were in the below-age-21 group, and another 28 percent of attendees were in the age 21-to-29 bracket. By contrast, only 6 percent of admissions came from the age-50-and-older group, although this category accounted for 32 percent of the U.S. population.

Metropolitan Los Angeles is the largest film production center in the United States—perhaps in the world. It is here that the large film studios are located—Universal, Columbia, Twentieth Century Fox, United Artists and others. In addition, most network tv programming is now produced in Los Angeles. As a result, there are more film technicians and creative personnel in Los Angeles than in any other place.

The organizations that serve these people are also located in Los Angeles: the guilds and unions, the laboratories, the large distributors and film booking offices, lawyers specializing in entertainment, management firms, agents, representatives of the massive exhibition networks. The trade publications which relate to the film industry are also based in Los Angeles. *Daily Variety* and the *Hollywood Reporter* are as evident as the large-circulation daily newspapers at Hollywood, Beverly Hills and Burbank newsstands.

Employment in Hollywood reached its peak just following World War II, and the trend has generally been downward since that time, although there has been some recovery since the low point in 1971–1972. One recent favorable trend has been the return of most film production to the United States. During the 1950s and 1960s, foreign production sharply reduced the number of jobs in southern California, but rising costs and the effects of two devaluations of the dollar finally reversed this trend. Between 1968 and 1973 the proportion of pictures being filmed in this country rose from 47 percent to 71 percent. On the other hand, the foreign market for both feature and television films remains strong: in 1975, the American film industry received $530 million in rental fees from other countries, representing approximately half of the cost of producing U.S. films.

The Commerce Department's *U.S. Industrial Outlook, 1977* projects continued growth in movie production from 1976 to 1985:

> Production of feature films is expected to be maintained at a high level in the next several years and the supply of films should be sufficient to meet the demand of the exhibitors. Multi-auditoriums, offering a wide choice of movies that appeal to diverse ages and movie tastes, will probably con-

tinue to increase indoor movie attendance. The growing population of young moviegoers and top box office attractions will boost box office receipts during the next decade.

The decrease in the annual rate of growth for motion picture box office receipts in 1976 is not expected to extend into the future. The trend should reverse and box office receipts should increase to about $5.7 billion by 1985, reflecting an average annual rate of increase of about 10 percent from 1976 to 1985.

In recent years, total employment in motion picture production and distribution in California (which includes both feature films and tv series) has risen substantially, largely as the result of profits from blockbuster films such as Paramount's *The Godfather,* Universal's *Jaws,* and, above all, Twentieth Century Fox's *Star Wars*. Employment in the peak production month of August rose from 54,200 in 1972 to 65,200 in 1977.[2] However, the major studios have found it necessary—and, in most cases, highly profitable—to diversify their operations and investments beyond motion picture production: for example, MGM operates the Grand Hotel in Las Vegas; Universal runs an entertainment center and a popular tourist attraction in addition to other enterprises; both Warner Brothers and Paramount are parts of massive conglomerates; and Twentieth Century Fox, now buoyed by the astounding revenues from *Star Wars,* has acquired two television stations and the Coca-Cola Midwest Bottling Company and proposes to take over the Aspen Skiing Company.[3]

Two additional trends in the industry have recently diminished the proportionate role of major studios in Hollywood employment: (1) the rise of the independent producer and (2) the movement of some production to areas outside Los Angeles. According to the Security Pacific Bank's "Monthly Summary of Business Conditions in Southern California," dated February 28, 1977:

> Independent film producers have been playing a major role in the nation's motion picture production—to the detriment of the major film studios. In 1975, for example, independent film producers made 45 percent of the nation's motion pictures, compared with only 29 percent in 1960. This tendency has resulted in a diversification of film production to areas outside of Los Angeles County. Although Hollywood is still recognized as the nation's center of motion picture and television production, 32 percent of total motion picture production is done outside the Los Angeles area. In addition, the amount of filming on studio backlots has declined in favor of filming on location.

Conversely, the continuing expansion of studio production for television, encompassing both dramatic and comedy series and feature films made especially for tv, and the expected growth in number of moviegoers—from 109 million in 1975 to an anticipated 120 million by 1985—provide substantial basis for optimism about overall employment prospects.

Educational Opportunities

Two of the top film schools in the country are located in Los Angeles—UCLA and USC. In addition, the American Film Institute (AFI) is the only professionally oriented conservatory of film in the United States. The Sherman Oaks Experimental College provides classes in film and tv writing and music scoring. Management and legal skills are taught at UCLA, USC and Loyola. All of these schools sponsor seminars in legal and business problems of specific interest to filmmakers. The UCLA extension program provides extensive course offerings in the technical, creative and business aspects of film and of recording. The various guilds and unions have a few apprenticeship programs and almost every producer trains young assistants in the skills necessary for the creation and execution of motion pictures.

Los Angeles provides endless opportunities for exposure to films of all periods, from all countries. FILMEX annually gathers together the best examples of the filmmaking art from around the world and exhibits them in an ever-growing festival. The 1978 festival lasted four weeks. Screening rooms at AFI, UCLA and USC show experimental and classic films while a new facility, the Los Angeles Film Center, is scheduled to screen noncommercial films daily as soon as it is inaugurated. One of the world's best film and videotape archives is located at UCLA and excellent libraries can be found there and at the AFI; thus, opportunities for research abound.

Entry into the industry is restrictive: the supply of willing and interested candidates far outstrips the demand for them. Because of the tendency toward large-budget productions, the major motion picture studios are unwilling to allow untried and untested producers and directors to practice their art. Unless the young filmmaker is willing to suffer the rigors of a career as an independent, he must turn to the few companies, such as American International Pictures and New World Pictures, which produce the contemporary equivalent of the "B" picture. The lack of a "B" product, traditionally the testing ground for new talent, is a result of legal decisions (such as the Paramount Decree) which forced studios to abandon their exhibition outlets, resulting in diminished Hollywood production. Currently, the best entries into the business are provided by talent agencies and law firms.

Minority Employment in Motion Pictures, Radio and Television

The concentration of mass entertainment industries—notably, motion pictures and television—in Los Angeles County should in principle offer a readily accessible source of employment for artistically talented members of minority groups. However, the available figures fail to indicate the degree of progress in minority employment which might reasonably be anticipated.

The apparent lack of progress is especially striking in motion picture production, where a superficially strong affirmative-action program was put into effect in 1970. Adopted "voluntarily," but in the context of considerable and mounting pressure from civil rights organizations and the federal government, the plan was aimed at allocating about one-fifth of job openings to minorities, identifying goals for particular crafts and even specifying the names of minority individuals who were to be given jobs previously denied to them.

The settlement applied to behind-the-camera crafts, and to clerical and administrative occupations, where the major charges of discrimination had been focused. Not only was there to be a quota for minority employment, but the agreement specifically forbade hiring or union membership on the basis of "family or personal relationship with someone employed in the industry." In certain of the trades, it had been virtually impossible to secure regular work unless the aspirant had a family or close personal tie with an already employed union member. Under the new agreement, no pre-employment tests were to be applied unless they had been professionally validated.

Perhaps of greatest importance, a minority labor pool was set up to encompass minority persons physically and mentally able to work in the industry. The agreement specified, by identified union locals, how minorities were to be referred to jobs from that pool, and at the end of a maximum two-year period the minority and general referral rosters were to be merged. All referrals were to be on a completely nondiscriminatory basis, and during this period the industry was required to make regular progress reports to the federal government. On-the-job training programs were to be initiated on a broad scale, to enable minorities to qualify for skilled jobs.

The plan was accepted in the industry only with reluctance, as a largely self-enforcing alternative to a stronger enforceable court decree. Furthermore, Hollywood was suffering a massive recession at the time, and unemployment averaged over 50 percent in the crafts. When, for all practical purposes, governmental monitoring ended in or around 1974, much of the industry seemed to return to previous practices.

So-called "EEO-1" report summaries are now available for the total industry, under the Freedom of Information Act, and minority employment figures for the broad occupational groups (professional, managerial, craft, technical, service, etc.), covering the period 1970–75, show little progress. Indeed, among firms with one hundred or more employees which reported to the Equal Employment Opportunity Commission during that period, the percentage of black employment in motion picture production actually dropped from 9.3 percent in 1970 to 6.6 percent in 1975, while the percentages of Chicano, Asian and Indian employment rose only slightly. In occupations which in theory should have been most affected by the agreement—technical and craft—there were as many indications of retrogression as of progress.

There has been some improvement in motion picture employment of performers, which perhaps reflects the expansion of films directed to ethnic audiences. This progress, however, has not yet been accompanied by a similar advance in employment of minority producers, directors, writers, and technicians; Indeed, in 1975 only a third of the so-called "black-oriented" pictures were either written, produced or directed by blacks.

Minority employment in radio and television reflects some progress between 1970 and 1976, but the most significant growth occurred in 1972 and 1973 and has decreased considerably since then. Minorities are represented in much higher proportion among part-time than among full-time employees; similarly, their percentages in the lower five job categories (office and clerical, craftsmen, operatives, laborers, and service workers) are more than double their proportions in the upper four categories (officials and managers, professionals, technicians, and sales workers).

In the field of noncommercial television, the proportion of total minority employment rose substantially between 1971 and 1976, but again, the major growth occurred in the first years of that period and was much slower in 1975 and 1976. The underrepresentation of both minorities and women continues in the upper occupational categories.

The absence of minorities from certain key roles in radio and television is especially noticeable in the managerial and entrepreneurial fields. Even those radio stations which appeal particularly to black listeners are usually owned and operated by whites; in 1975, there were only forty black-owned commercial radio stations in the entire country. The *first* black-owned television station began broadcasting in Detroit in mid-1975.

A favorable trend over the last decade has been the increasing appearance of minorities, especially blacks, in television commercials. This has the dual effect of diminishing the "lily-white" image formerly projected by this medium and of expanding employment opportunities for minority performers in a field which provides much of the income for members of the Screen Actors Guild.

Progress in minority employment, most notably in the profit-making sectors of the arts, is directly linked with a vigorous implementation of affirmative action. But statements of good intention are far from enough: not even the superficially strong "voluntary" agreement in the Hollywood crafts was sufficient to overcome resistance based on long-standing practices of tight labor supply control, pervasive unemployment, favoritism and nepotism in hiring and promotion, and outright racial discrimination. Experience shows that such settlements mean little in the long run unless monitoring and enforcement are continuous and pressure from outside the industry—from governmental and organizational sources alike—is maintained.[4]

To the degree that the affirmative action goals are achieved, the need for trained minority and female performers, technicians, writers, producers, and craftsmen will intensify. Community arts organizations and programs can be expected to play a vital role in meeting this need.

The Recording Industry

In at least some crucial respects, the recording industry is the largest and most popular of the artistic industries. Of the total seventy-four million households, approximately seventy-three million have record players. In 1977, records became a $3 billion industry, an all-time high. Record sales continue to exceed motion picture box office revenues, even though movie income in 1977 also broke all previous records. Such increases, of course, reflect the impact of inflation, and in the case of records, the figures are based on manufacturers' suggested list prices although substantial numbers of records are sold at a retail discount; on the other hand, the statistics for the recording industry exclude foreign sales, which constitute about half of all sales made each year.

Profits largely depend on extraordinary volumes of sales for a relatively few records and tapes, just as the revenues from motion picture production are associated with the popularity of a few blockbusters among total studio output. Pop albums, featuring either rock performers appealing primarily to whites or soul artists appealing mainly to blacks, are the major source of profit, with sales of seven million or more for especially popular offerings. So-called "crossover" artists, such as Stevie Wonder, have large followings among both blacks and whites and, in many cases, appeal strongly to adult as well as to teenage audiences. Blacks constitute a rising proportion of the market for records: according to one estimate, about 40 percent of the dollar volume in the industry is generated by black music.[5]

As the average age of the American population rises, adults become a more significant proportion of the record market. Research performed by CBS Records shows that persons age eighteen or older now make up 77 percent of all record buyers and account for 82 percent of aggregate record purchases. It appears that large numbers of those who typically were frequent record purchasers in their teens continue to buy records as they grow older.

Sales of tapes and cassettes also are booming, providing much of the profit for the recording industry. Tapes now account for about 35 percent of all sales, with strong demand generated through the popularity of home and car stereo systems. It is probable that within a few years tape and cassette players in automobiles will be nearly as pervasive as record players in homes.

Innovative or improved merchandising, marketing and advertising methods undoubtedly have contributed to growing sales volume. Discount chains have multiplied in recent years: The Wherehouse, one of the large chains, has opened almost one hundred outlets in California since the fall of 1970. Record "supermarkets" are opening in urban and suburban areas throughout the country and the membership of the Columbia Record and Tape Club grew from 2 million in 1972 to more than 3.2 million in late 1977. Some executives foresee a further boom if tapes and cassettes can be sold in as many diverse locations as are paperbacks, e.g., markets, liquor stores, transportation terminals.

Tempering this optimistic picture is the fact that a minority of albums produced and sold are responsible for profits. A Cambridge Research Study in 1975 reported that the break-even point for pop albums averaged approximately 61,000 copies, and that almost 80 percent of pop releases fail to attain that volume of sale. In addition, relatively few corporations control much of the total record output in the United States: the two biggest companies, Warner Communications (Warners, Atlantic, Elektra/Asylum, and asociated labels) and CBS (Columbia, Epic, Portrait, and associated labels), hold 40 percent of the U.S. record business, six other companies are responsible for between 30 and 35 percent, and another four or five account for about 5 or 10 percent more. The remaining 15 or 20 percent of sales is divided among hundreds of smaller companies that experience heavy turnover.

The rising sales of 8-track cartridges and of cassettes contribute significantly to the profit record, as noted before, but sales trends for reel-to-reel and quadraphonic sets—once regarded as having good market prospects—have been in the opposite direction. Indeed, sales of reel-to-reel units have dropped to such a degree that they are no longer reported by the industry. This experience demonstrates the unpredictability and capriciousness of the market, which continues to perplex record company executives. While they know which artists are popular, they confess that the reasons why some records sell well and others of apparently equal merit fail evade them to this day.

Los Angeles is now responsible for the recording of more popular music (rock, pop, jazz, rhythm and blues, disco) than any other city in the country. Since the sixties, when the market emphasis shifted away from show tunes and classical music to pop and rock, Los Angeles has been the commercial center of the business. Connections to the film and tv industries, as opposed to Broadway theaters, have made southern California ever more attractive.

Most of the major record companies and music publishers are now headquartered in Los Angeles. Associated businesses—trade press, agencies, and booking, promotion, management and design firms—are very much in evidence. Independent producers and studios outnumber those which are affiliated to specific companies, and more and more records attain gold (500,000 records sold) and platinum (1,000,000 records sold) status.

Ties to the motion picture and tv businesses have pushed record sales to previously inconceivable heights (witness the success of *Saturday Night Fever*) and the emergence of disco music has opened up new marketing avenues. Los Angeles is becoming increasingly attractive to musicians. A walk down Sunset Strip, with its billboards, reveals the importance of popular music in the economy of the city.

Professional exposure can be had at many different levels, from small clubs to large auditoriums. All types of music can be heard in Los Angeles. Facilities ranging from the Dorothy Chandler Pavilion, the Santa Monica Civic Auditorium and UCLA's Royce Hall to night clubs such as the Roxy and Concerts by the Sea present artists who represent the best of classical, jazz and popular music. The 13,000-seat Inglewood Forum and Los Angeles Sports Arena facilities, as well as UCLA's spacious basketball arena, the Pauley Pavilion, are also the scene of jam-packed rock concerts. Many studio musicians are employed by record companies, recording studios and touring bands or appear as regulars in the orchestras of popular tv shows such as Johnny Carson's. Visual artists may work creating promotional items and advertising as well as record jackets.

Footnotes

[1] *Variety,* January 11, 1978, p. 1.

[2] *SPNB California Databank,* Research Department, Security Pacific Bank, Los Angeles.

[3] See, e.g., "Robust Fox on Prowl for New Acquisitions," *Los Angeles Times,* Outlook Section, p. 1, January 8, 1978.

[4] Some recent studies of motion pictures and television, conducted and published by the U.S. Commission on Civil Rights, confirm the inadequacy of progress in minority and female employment and continuing deficiencies in their portrayal on movie and tv screens. See *Equal Employment Opportunity in the Motion Picture Industry,* September 1978, A Report of the California Advisory Committee to the United States Commission on Civil Rights, and *Window Dressing on the Set: An Update,* January 1979, A Report of the United States Commission on Civil Rights.

[5] Barbara Isenberg, "The Record Biz Rocks 'n' Rolls to New Heights," *Los Angeles Times,* Calendar Section, December 4, 1977, pp. 1, 76–77, 80.

2.5
The Role of Festivals and Special Events

A unique opportunity to broaden the scope of arts activities beyond the reach of existing cultural institutions lies in the realm of festivals and special events, taking art and transforming it into celebration. Arts festivals have distinguishing qualities which can make an important impact on the city's social and economic life:

1 **Mobility:** Festivals often move art and arts activities out of their usual buildings and into the community, utilizing public spaces and attracting visitors to new locales. This aspect of festivals has a direct economic impact on the community, for it demands additional employment to prepare and staff the site and expands the business of restaurants and shops in the area.
2 **Intensity:** Festivals bring many arts activities together in a short period of time, a convenience that encourages audiences to attend more performances or exhibits. People may spend an entire day or more in the area of the festival and, as noted, this encourages the business of restaurants and shops in the area.
3 **Community/Anti-Elitist Orientation:** By taking arts activities out of their traditional settings, festivals encourage more people to attend. This is a way of "bringing art to the people" and can lead to increased future patronage of the arts. Of course, festivals do not always take place at a location outside of the art institution itself. But when they are held on the grounds of a traditional institution, they often have an open house quality and thus attract people to a gallery or recital hall who might not otherwise have visited.
4 **Scope/Size:** Festivals bring many artists and visitors together in one locale at one time (or in a number of locales over a short period of time). This enhances a sense of community and involvement as well as generating increased exposure to the arts.

These qualities can enable arts festivals to play an important role in community cohesion and development and can provide unique opportunities to bring together artists and patrons for a common purpose. Some examples of ongoing arts festivals in Los Angeles will help to illustrate.

All City Outdoor Art Festival

The Municipal Arts Department of the city of Los Angeles has sponsored an annual outdoor art festival for twenty-five years. Usually held in late June, it provides an opportunity for artists of Los Angeles (geographically defined as those within a thirty-mile radius of City Hall) to show their works and to offer them for sale. Each artist may submit only one work. In 1977 there were 1,500 works submitted, of which more than 100 were shown.

In addition to the art exhibit, the festival includes various related activities: a bazaar; entertainment (big bands, classical music, jazz, and folk dance) coordinated through the Bureau of Music of the city; and craftspeople demonstrating their works. The festival is now held at Barnsdall Park, the site of the Municipal Art Gallery and other community art facilities.

When it first began, the Outdoor Art Festival lasted seven to nine days and averaged 50,000–60,000 visitors during that period. Due to financial and other problems the festival was cut back to three days (Friday to Sunday) six years ago. During those three days it is open from 11:00 A.M. to 7:00 P.M. and averages about 35,000–40,000 visitors.

The impact of such a festival goes far beyond the socio-cultural realm. Over a thousand artists and craftspeople have an opportunity to exhibit and sell their work and the economy of the city is bolstered. The festival contributes to the following:

City revenue: The city receives revenue from the collection of sales tax by the craftspeople and from the licensing of food concessions at the festival by the Department of Parks and Recreation.

Employment: Part of the responsibility of three full-time employees of the Municipal Arts Department is the Outdoor Art Festival. In addition, the following part-time jobs are created: twelve to fourteen people to receive and set up works (about two

*An annual festival that brings thousands of visitors: Renaissance Pleasure Faire.
Credit: Art Blum Agency.*

days of nine hours each); twelve to fourteen people working five to six days to install exhibits; fifteen people to work in actual festival operations; ten people to tear down the exhibits; five to six people on a clean up crew; and five to ten people to work at the concessions. In addition, a contracting firm is hired to set up fences and display areas prior to the show. This job usually requires about fifteen workers budgeted at about $15,000. About seventy part-time jobs (without the contractor) are created by the Outdoor Art Festival for which about $5,500 is budgeted. The total budget for the festival is about $25,000.

Los Angeles Dance Festival

The first Los Angeles Dance Festival was held in September 1977. Ten dance companies participated in seven different performances held at UCLA and the Music Center downtown. The budget for the festival was approximately $27,000, of which about 15 to 20 percent was used for administrative expenses. The only employee of the festival was its organizer, so that most of the budget went to the ten dance companies that performed in the festival. Funding came from a variety of sources, including the National Endowment for the Arts, the California Arts Council, the city of Los Angeles, various individual and corporate contributors, and box office receipts. Ticket prices varied from $3.50 to $5.50.

The 1977 Los Angeles Dance Festival played to mostly sold-out houses and more than 6,000 people attended. Due to the success of the first festival, the 1978 budget was projected at $50,000, with twelve concerts planned. Six were held at UCLA, the remainder at other locations in the Los Angeles area. In addition to these concerts, there was a twenty-four-hour program of dance films.

The first two Los Angles Dance Festivals clearly increased interest in dance in the Los Angeles area. An innovative feature of the festivals was that most of the concerts presented shared programs. By pairing different types of dance companies together in one concert, the festival offered its audience exposure to dance forms they might not otherwise have chosen. These types of marketing methods create new audiences, expanding interest and participation in the arts and increasing their economic impact on a community.

The Garden Theater Festival

The Garden Theater Festival is probably *the* major celebration of the arts in the Los Angeles area. Its rapid development over the past six years shows an ever-increasing impact on the Los Angeles community.

The mission of the Garden Theater Festival is to provide a wide variety of cultural events and entertainment to the public at no charge and to bring attention to the arts in Los Angeles. Primarily a festival of performing arts, it began in 1973 as a three-day, sixty-hour weekend of mime, theater, dance, poetry, comedy and music. All events (including performances, exhibits and food) were free to the public and support came from local artists and businesses.

An overwhelmingly favorable response to the festival led to its subsequent development and expansion, with funding contributed by city government. Over the past five years it has also received increasing support from local individuals, organizations and businesses, including a number of major local foundations, corporations and universities. The Garden Theater Festival has also received financial support from the National Endowment for the Arts and the California Arts Council. Most of the funds received by the festival are used to pay artists' honoraria, both union and non-union. No staff member is paid a salary. Much of the work necessary for the actual staging of the festival is done by city employees; thus, the festival has little impact on employment of those other than artists.

The Garden Theater Festival activities in 1977 included a major celebration of the arts—the Fifth Annual Los Angeles Performing Art and Folklife Festival at Barnsdall Park—a three-day festival at UCLA, an Independence Day Celebration and fundraising benefit at the late Will Geer's Theatricum Botanicum in Topanga Canyon, and a Thanksgiving Day arts festival for the inmates of the Lompoc Prison.

The Barnsdall event was the highlight of the season and drew an audience of more than 100,000 people during a three-week period. Approximately 2,000 performing artists contributed to more than 500 hours of programming, representing the wide spectrum of cultural and ethnic resources in Los Angeles. In addition to the many performing events, the 1977 event also added a folklife program, a series of symposia, a film festival, an exhibit of contemporary art in the Municipal Art Gallery (located at the park), and a number of exhibits and special events (such as an opening reception). Another significant addition was a Fringe Festival held in twenty-two theaters within a five-mile radius of the park, allowing these theaters a chance to offer programs as part of the Garden Theater Festival.

Plans for the 1978 Garden Theater Festival were not realized because of the public funding cutbacks that came with the passage of Proposition 13. Thus, one has to look to earlier years to appreciate the potentialities of this type of endeavor.

The expansion of the Garden Theater Festival's staff through 1977 suggests the direct impact that the growth of an arts festival can have on local employment. In addition, the festival has contributed to an extended use of public facilities and spaces and has had a major impact on bringing together cultural and ethnic resources of the Los Angeles community and making them accessible to the overall population. Since its beginning, the Garden Theater Festival has presented free to the public more than twenty performing arts events held throughout the greater Los Angeles area, utilizing both indoor and outdoor facilities. More than 2,000 artists from approximately 1,000 arts groups have participated in the festival, representing all of the cultural and ethnic resources of the area. A total of 2,225 hours or 3,137 performances has been presented under the auspices of the Garden Theater Festival. But most importantly, the combined total attendance for all of the festival events numbers close to one-half million people.

The three festivals described above represent successful ongoing attempts to expand interest and participation in the arts in the Los Angeles area. On a smaller scale, but also worthy of mention, is the Annual Festival in Black, sponsored by the city for three days in sprawling MacArthur Park.

Los Angeles festivals could be extended statewide; the Garden Theater Festival has proposed a California State Arts Festival to take place in 1981. The current proposal outlines four stages. Phase one includes plans for an extension of the Los Angeles festival as outlined above. Phase two outlines the First Annual San Francisco Performing Arts Festival. The third phase plans for an extension of the festival into six other cities throughout California. The final stage foresees a First California State Performing Arts Festival to take place in 1981 in Monterey as a four-day event over the Labor Day weekend. It would bring together representative artists from each of the eight participating communities in a cross-cultural celebration of the arts. Such an event could further be expanded past 1981 to encompass events throughout the state of California.

Festivals such as these are established periodic events, often taking place on an annual basis. Related activities exhibiting many of the same characteristics as festivals fall into the category of "special events." These are one-time celebrations of a particular event, anniversary or phenomenon which may occur within the art world itself or totally outside the realm of the arts. For example, a special event within the context of the arts would be a series of concerts in commemoration of the anniversary of a composer's birth. Such an event is natural to the arts. However, its overall impact on the community-at-large usually is minimal.

Perhaps the greatest impact on a community comes from arts festivals which celebrate special events outside the realm of the arts. They afford a unique opportunity to widen the access to and scope of artistic activities and to increase community involvement. Arts activities connected with a special event lose most, if not all, of their elitist air simply by being part of a community-wide celebration (so long as they are not priced too high). The arts have a unique opportunity to increase their audiences and at the same time involve more members of the community in the celebration, enhancing the celebration activities. As an effective way to express the history—past, present and future—of a community, the arts naturally belong in a celebration of many kinds of events. The arts clearly have a role in commemorating a bicentennial or world's fair, as well as in celebrating the Olympic Games. Some specific examples of upcoming special events in Los Angeles that could easily involve arts activities include the Los Angeles Bicentennial in 1981 and the 1984 Olympics in Los Angeles. Both are massive special events with almost unlimited possibilities for arts activities. Furthermore, the time sequence offers the possibility for a continuing festival, beginning with the bicentennial celebration and building up to the Olympics.

These two events can be viewed as somewhat different from each other in scope. The bicentennial represents an ideal time for bringing the various sectors of the community together under one common goal and purpose. Los Angeles is a truly international city in its mix of ethnic, racial and cultural elements. All of these groups have arts activities within their individual communities. Through the use of neighborhood centers, mobile units, community organizations (such as schools and churches) and public facilities and agencies (such as parks and libraries), these many diverse elements of Los Angeles' community can be brought together in celebration of the bicentennial.

The bicentennial is a time to advance not only the social elements of Los Angeles, but also its economic life. Much of Los Angeles' business is arts-oriented and there is every reason to include the booming tv, movie, recording, fashion and design industries in this celebration. Los Angeles is a distinct center of the arts, and it must be recognized as such. The bicentennial affords an opportunity to provide people with a better understanding of what lies behind the glamour. Architecture represents another excellent medium for depicting the history and development of the community. Los Angeles has rich environmental settings, an important part of any celebration. Much can be learned about the diverse elements of a culture from its architecture. There are many architectural art forms prevalent in Los Angeles, such as murals, billboards, interiors and landscapes, and, of course, parks and beaches provide marvelous natural settings for arts activities.

The bicentennial is a time to invite outsiders to celebrate the anniversary of the city. The potential for tourism for such a celebration is great, and by simply using the community's resources, the economic impact could be significant.

The 1984 Olympics, to be held in Los Angeles, will be a natural outgrowth of these celebrations and will provide an excellent opportunity to display the arts of Los Angeles and the nation. Although it is not widely known, the rules for the Olympic Games state that arts activities should be held in conjunction with the games. In the ancient games there was an inseparable nexis between sport and art. Athletes were the models for most ancient Greek art and the artist played an important role in the celebration of the games and, in fact, the entire Greek way of life. Because of this important relationship, the founder of the modern games, Baron Pierre de Coubertin, stressed the concept of a melding of mind and muscle and pushed for the inclusion of arts in sporting events.

The first modern Olympic Games actually to include the arts took place in Stockholm in 1912 (the Fifth Olympiad). From then through the 1948 games, competitions were held in the arts along with the sporting events; exhibitions were held and medals were awarded to the winners. Various problems ensued and from 1952 on, arts exhibitions have been held in lieu of competitions. The scope and success of these activities have depended upon the hosting nations. Since 1956 the exhibitions have usually focused on the arts of the hosting nation with the exception of the 1968 Games in Mexico, which featured a full year of international arts activities in celebration of the Olympiad.

During the 1984 Olympics there will be a very large increase in the number of visitors to Los Angeles. With limited availability of tickets to sporting events, it will be necessary to stage other events within the city for visitors to attend, something which an arts festival could provide. Sales of tickets to arts events in conjunction with tickets to sporting events could substantially increase revenue for the arts. By having tickets sold in advance for activities at decentralized locations, congestion could be alleviated. This Olympic arts festival could be spread over a much longer period of time than the actual two-week staging of the games themselves, possibly even as long as a year, thereby encouraging tourism over a longer period of time and increasing the economic impact of the Olympics.

An arts festival could also generate income by the selling television and film rights to cover arts events along with the rights to broadcast the actual games. This would increase interest in the arts by making them more accessible to the public through the media. The long-range economic effects of such a festival must also be taken into account. It might expand the future market for the arts in Los Angeles, thereby creating additional employment, and it could contribute to the development of Los Angeles as a west coast cultural center and increase the city's future attractiveness to tourists. It might also provide for additional growth to segments of the already rapidly growing Los Angeles media industry.

There are many socio-cultural benefits of an Olympic arts festival which would contribute to upgrading the city's quality of life. Besides existing facilities, there will be a need to develop other sites for the festival. To ease the concentration of people, these will have to be developed in outlying communities as well as within the city. Such new centers will benefit the community for many years after the games. The arts festival would also aid in the development and recognition of various arts within the community (including traditional, non-traditional and ethnic arts), bringing together diverse elements of the community for a common purpose.

These examples of ongoing and proposed events in Los Angeles make it clear that the potential impact of arts festivals and special events on a community is significant. The socio-cultural implications of such events are implicit: by enhancing aesthetic opportunity they help to build a sense of community and make the city a more desirable place in which to live and conduct business. The economic effects of such arts activities are also vital to the health and development of a community. They can contribute substantially to enhancing employment and may bring new business to the community by stimulating tourism. Furthermore, festivals and special events contribute to the overall development of interest and participation in the arts, and this generates a positive economic and socio-cultural impact on the community.

2.6
Government Support for the Arts

Los Angeles City Government

In considering the arts in any one city, it is important to look at the support given to the arts by agencies of municipal government. Three perspectives are useful here: an examination of the city budget for the arts as a whole; an inquiry into the specific support given to the arts by the different agencies; and finally a look at the budgets of certain significant programs to determine the proportion of their funding by city government.

When we turn to the Los Angeles city budget as a whole in 1976–1977 directly related arts activities consumed about $1 million in funds, while indirectly related arts activities consumed over $20 million in local funds for public facilities. In addition, $215,900 was allocated to private organizations as contracts for providing public services.

"Directly related" arts activities can be defined as those events and programs predominantly of a cultural nature, including music, theater and dance performances, art museums and art exhibits, and art, dance and music instruction. These types of activities are part of the annual programs of the Bureau of Music, the Municipal Art Gallery, the Junior Arts Center, the Watts Tower Art Center and historic preservation efforts. About 65 percent of the $956,715 budgeted for these activities is absorbed by administrative and salary costs, with only 21 percent paid directly to artists. The remaining 14 percent is allocated for program (or operation) expenditures.

"Indirectly related" arts activities are those events and programs which are only partially arts-related. These include zoos, marine and maritime museums, industry and commerce museums, natural history museums, botanical gardens and libraries. Also included are programs involving architectural approval processes—the Street Mural Program and Arts and Crafts Centers, and the Griffith Park Observatory. As was the case in directly related arts expenditures, in 1976–1977 indirectly related expenditures consisted largely of administrative salary funds. These constituted 80 percent of the $20,480,384 budget item. Artists' salary funds constituted less than 1 percent of that budget item, with the remaining 19 percent allocated to program expenses.

When we turn to the specific agencies of the city involved in the arts, we must look at the Municipal Arts Department, the Recreation and Parks Department, and the Board of Public Works.

Municipal Arts Department

Of the three agencies, the Municipal Arts Department is most heavily involved with the arts. The department is concerned with the delivery of cultural services. Major functions include encouraging citizen appreciation and participation in cultural activities and the development of young people's arts skills. The Municipal Arts Department operates the Municipal Arts Gallery and Gallery Theater; Hollyhock House, Frank Lloyd Wright's first Los Angeles-designed residence, which is now open for tours; and the Junior Arts Center and the Watts Tower Arts Center, both offering free arts instruction. Other responsibilities include the world-renowned Towers of Simon Rodia in Watts and the musical Triforium, a sixty-foot-high concrete and glass tower adjacent to City Hall which converts music into color by computer. The department's Bureau of Music arranges over 500 free musical programs annually throughout the city. The other major component, the Cultural Heritage Board, designates historical-cultural monuments and, in addition, supports the Cultural Heritage Foundation which maintains Heritage Square, a preservation site for Victorian-era buildings. The Municipal Arts Commission acts as an advisory body to the department and is responsible for approving the design of all buildings on city property.

The Municipal Arts Department's budget can be divided into two elements: cultural appreciation and support of cultural opportunities by other organizations.

Cultural appreciation consists of six activities, listed below along with their respective 1977–1978 budget allocations:

1 Architectural Approval .... $ 38,806
2 Music Activities $257,329

3 Art Activities $182,442
4 Cultural Heritage . . . . $ 31,500
5 Junior Arts Center $259,664
6 Watts Tower Arts Center . . . . . . $ 77,995

Architectural Approval involves less than 3 percent of the agency's budget. This activity includes review and approval of the design and placement of buildings, bridges, marquees, and art objects on city property. There has been a 7 percent increase in plans reviewed since 1975.

About 20 percent of the agency's budget is used for Music Activities. This encompasses sponsoring youth and adult choruses, community sings, band concerts, special programs for holidays, song festivals and musical concerts. The presentation of music programs has increased by 2 percent since 1975.

Art Activities take about 17 percent of the agency's budget to conduct and sponsor art exhibitions and community art events in City Hall and at the Municipal Art Gallery in Barnsdall Park. Art programs have not increased since 1975 and attendance has dropped by 18 percent.

Only a tiny fraction (2.5 percent) of the agency's budget goes to Cultural Heritage to locate and designate cultural and historical monuments worthy of preservation. Since no public monies are allocated for restoration purposes (except for public buildings), increases in this activity are not measurable.

The Junior Arts Center uses about 20 percent of the agency's budget for art classes for ages five through seventeen in painting, ceramics, photography, weaving and drawing. Class attendance has increased by 50 percent, causing a corollary increase in courses offered by 37 percent since 1975. Similar to the Junior Arts Center (except it is for all age groups) is the Watts Tower Arts Center, which accounts for 6 percent of the agency's budget.

The other chief service provided by this department is support of cultural opportunities by other organizations. Seventeen percent of its budget, or $227,000, is allocated to thirty-seven separate organizations (see Appendix: City Support of Other Cultural Organizations).

The largest amounts of city support in 1977-78 went to the Hollywood Bowl-Los Angeles Philharmonic ($50,000), the citywide Garden Theater Festival ($30,000), the Free Public Theater ($30,000), the San Fernando Valley Arts Council ($20,000), and the Los Angeles Ballet ($10,000). (See Table 6.) Altogether, two-thirds of the Municipal Arts Department's "Special" budget, directed to eligible nonprofit organizations, goes to these five groups. Only the San Fernando Valley Arts Council might reasonably be described as a "neighborhood" organization. (It should be noted that this area is predominantly white and middle- to upper-class in composition). Although there has not been any significant increase in the amounts awarded to each organization, the number of organizations receiving funds has increased by 42 percent since 1975, constituting an 8 percent increase in funds.

The administrative costs for this agency constitute 17 percent of the agency's budget, and have not been factored out of the previous calculations of the percentage of each activity's allocation of the annual budget.

Department of Recreation and Parks

This city department administers cultural programs through its Cultural Affairs Section. There are eight subsections that operate at one or more of seven facilities. For the past three years the budget allocation has barely fluctuated, decreasing 3 percent since 1975 to $525,094. Approximately 9 percent of the budget is generated internally from operating revenues. Most of the expenditures are for staff salaries, constituting 93 percent of the budget.

The eight subsections are as follows:
1 Performances
2 Volunteer
3 Adaptive Recreation
4 Photography
5 Dance and Drama
6 Arts and Crafts
7 Costume Workshop
8 Barnsdall Art and Craft

The Performances Section coordinates activities between artists and their potential audiences. It publishes a calendar of cultural offerings, distributes tickets, and coordinates tours for performing groups.

The Volunteer Section recruits and trains volunteers specializing in cultural activities. Among its purposes is to register interested individuals, distribute training information and provide individualized training upon request.

Table 6: Budget and Expenditures of the Los Angeles Municipal Arts Department, 1975–78

Category	Budget FY 1977–78	Est. Expenditures FY 1976–77	Expenditures FY 1975–76
Total			
Salaries	$ 883,040	$ 851,621	$ 706,121
Expenses	190,162	169,050	185,785
Equipment	3,046	4,238	8,477
Special*			
Hollywood Bowl-LA Philharmonic	50,000	50,000	65,000
Brentwood-Westwood Symphony	2,500	2,500	2,500
Committee on the Arts (Symphony)	2,500	4,000	1,875
Hollywood-Wilshire Symphony	2,500	3,000	2,500
Japanese Symphony	2,500	3,200	2,500
Metropolitan Symphony	—	—	1,875
Northeast Symphony	2,500	2,500	2,500
San Fernando Valley Symphony	2,500	2,500	2,500
Southeast Symphony	2,500	2,500	2,500
Watts Symphony	2,500	2,500	—
Chamber Symphony	5,000	5,000	1,250
Westchester Symphony	2,500	2,500	—
So. California Choral	—	—	5,000
Chamber Music Ensemble	—	—	2,500
So. California Chamber Music	2,000	2,000	—
Free Public Theater	30,000	30,000	35,000
East/West Players	2,000	2,000	—
LA Junior Police Band	—	—	7,000
LA City Youth Band	5,000	5,000	5,000
LA Ballet	10,000	10,000	—
Garden Theater Festival	30,000	30,000	35,000
City of Angels Opera	—	—	25,000
R'Wanda Lewis Dance	2,000	2,000	—
Young Musicians Foundation	3,000	3,000	2,000
San Fernando Valley Arts Council	20,000	—	2,873
West Coast Theater	2,000	4,000	5,000
LA Solo Repertory	2,000	2,000	—
Rose Parade	6,000	6,000	—
Filmex	—	40,000	—
Bilingual Foundation for the Arts	2,000	—	—
LA Actors Theater	2,000	—	—
Aman Folk Ensemble	2,000	—	—
Self-Help Graphics	5,000	—	—
Educational Opera	5,000	—	—
Total, Special	207,500	216,200	209,373
Total, Municipal Arts Department	$1,283,748	$1,241,109	$1,109,726

*"Special" programs are those carried on by private non-profit arts organizations in Los Angeles which receive financial support from the Municipal Arts Department. All other programs supported by the department are city-operated—e.g., the Municipal Art Gallery, the Junior Arts Center, and the Watts Tower Arts Center.

Note: For Fy 1977–1978, the budget for city-operated programs is $847,738, for "Special" programs $207,500, and for general administration $220,492.

The Adaptive Recreation Section is designed to enhance recreational opportunities for the handicapped. This program encompasses the educational and recreational needs of the handicapped and is placed within Cultural Affairs for administrative reasons.

The Photography Center serves both the general public and departmental training needs. It provides classes, instruction and equipment for all aspects of photography. Perhaps its most obscure function is the administration and maintenance of the artifacts and memorabilia of the Hollywood Museum, yet to be established.

The Dance and Drama Section assists department personnel in the areas of drama, dance, preschool activities and women's rhythmic exercises. This section works with the Performing Arts Committee, consisting of representative staff directors from each area, and assists in the planning of the Garden Theater Festival.

The Arts and Crafts Section provides training and material for the general public and in-service training for staff directors and volunteers. This section plans and develops classes, helps with special exhibits, hobby shows, and workshops.

The Costume Workshop Section is actually under the Dance and Drama Supervisor, who is charged with the maintenance of over 17,000 costumes. In addition to designing and manufacturing the costumes, this section provides assistance in the design and construction of sets and the recommendation of the appropriate costume for a specific script.

The Barnsdall Art and Craft Center is a high quality training center, not to be confused with the Junior Arts Center located within the same park. For a nominal fee, the center provides individualized training for the general public as well as advising other departments on craft programs, exhibits and demonstrations.

Although established in 1935, the Griffith Park Planetarium could not be considered a performing arts facility until now. Still predominantly a museum of science and an observatory, the domed theater is now attracting most of its visitors for its Laserium light concerts, which set beams of laser light to classical and rock music. This is not a city program, but instead is produced by Laser Images, Inc., to which the city leases its facilities.

The Cultural Affairs Division of the Recreation and Parks Department administers the Theater Arts Players of Los Angeles (TAPLA), a CETA-funded seventy-one-member troupe composed of five companies that perform free of charge at nonprofit community agencies throughout the city. In addition, the Cultural Affairs Division administers the Los Angeles Citywide Murals Project, also a recipient of CETA funding.

Board of Public Works

The Motion Picture Coordination Section of the Board of Public Works functions as a one-stop permit center for motion picture and television producers and commercial photographers wanting to "shoot" on city or private property. The section determines the city agencies having jurisdiction over that property and coordinates their approval prior to issuing a film permit. The board has also designated certain areas of the city as special filming areas to encourage motion picture production.

Many other city agencies are also involved in some way with the city's cultural life. They include departments that are responsible for city property that may be used for performances or exhibitions; provide special services for the cultural community; administer funds for, sponsor or coordinate special culturally related programs; and regulate through permits, inspection or zoning, various cultural activities or facilities.

Los Angeles County Government

County Parks and Recreation Department

Within the city boundaries the county has a very limited program for arts and cultural facilities, as it emphasizes activities for county areas which are usually outside the city proper. An exception to this is the programs conducted at Hancock Park, the site of the County Museum of Art.

One such program is the Festival of Arts, a four-month summer weekend event combining the talents of craftspeople and performing artists. The county provides booths, advertising and staff for an average of twenty artists and craftspeople each weekend. They are charged a nominal twenty-five dollars per weekend for each booth, which covers about half of the total cost of the show ($15,636). In addition, the county provides the stage, seating and equipment for performing artists who entertain these crowds. The performing artists are minimally compensated for their work by the Music Performance Trust Fund. About half of the monies budgeted for this program are allocated to county recreation staff.

The county also conducts arts and crafts programs similar to the city's programs at recreation centers located within county "islands" and oriented to the demographics of the community. For example, Plummer Park, located in West Hollywood, sponsors theatrical productions within a small theater.

County Museum of Art

The county's greatest contribution to the city's cultural assets is the Los Angeles County Museum of Art located in Hancock Park within the Wilshire District of Los Angeles. Although the county provided the land, the construction was paid for by private donations.

The museum is a complex of three buildings around a central sculpture plaza. The permanent collection is housed in the Ahmanson Gallery, along with the Museum Shop (books and souvenirs whose revenues go toward the museum foundation). The center building, the Hammer Wing, houses the touring exhibitions, and also a small contemporary art exhibit. The third building, the Leo S. Bing wing, houses a 500-seat theater, a cafe and various administrative and educational activities.

The combined funds provided by the county government and Museum Associates Funds, a nonprofit corporation, increased steadily from 1969 until the passage of Proposition 13 in 1978. The increased funds were used chiefly to offset cost-of-living increases in staff salaries. The complex has enjoyed a broad base of support and has the highest membership volume of any arts facility in the county. A statement of financial condition covering 1972–1975 provides an overview of the income and outlays of this important operation. Among other things, it establishes the relative importance of the county's contribution. It is noteworthy that more than half the annual budget comes from the Los Angeles County appropriation.

State Government

The California Arts Council (CAC), the state's arts agency, has experienced some recent growth, increasing from a budget of $318,000 in 1975–1976 to $3.4 million for 1977–1978. National Endowment for the Arts (NEA) support of the CAC budget has averaged 20 percent of the total budget during the three-year period.

The increased funding has been helpful to California artists and arts organizations. For 1977–1978, over $1.5 million was granted to 275 artists and arts organizations throughout the state. Some $800,000 went to 160 arts groups; $630,000 to support a program for artists in schools and communities; and nearly $100,000 for arts programs in social institutions, including hospitals, mental health centers and prisons. As for Los Angeles-based recipients, forty-nine groups received $290,000.

Despite its apparent success in filling a void of state support for the arts, the CAC budget hardly compares to that of its New York counterpart. The New York State Council on the Arts's budget for 1977–1978 was $30 million.

The California Arts Council, whose predecessor was the twelve-year-old California Arts Commission, has experienced some growing pains that accompanied its rapid expansion. In 1975, the governor appointed a new nine-member council to oversee the CAC. However, unlike previous appointees, all of the new members were artists, with the exception of one, as were the two top administrators. In this unprecedented move, the governor expressed the philosophy that artists should dictate the policies of the state arts agency. The move, while applauded by artists, has resulted in some disillusionment.

According to the *Los Angeles Times* (January 7, 1978), many of the governor's appointees admitted that artists are not necessarily good administrators. Artists willing to work in that capacity must be willing to forego their artistic activities to meet the time demands required of such a position. Since the majority of artists are not experienced public servants, they find it somewhat difficult to work in an environment where they must evaluate the work of other artists and arts organizations. At the same time, artists must become accustomed to

Table 7: COUNTY MUSEUM OF ART Statement of Financial Condition: 1972–75

Combined County of Los Angeles and Museum Associates Funds	FY 1972–73	FY 1973–74	FY 1974–75
Source of Funds:			
Investment Income	$ 104,690	$ 126,579	$ 132,689
Los Angeles County Appropriation	2,446,327	2,317,685	2,598,963
Admission Fees[1]	91,817	99,475	23,813
Other Revenue[1]	66,649	151,597	39,687
Annual Memberships	734,022	809,478	763,674
Bookshop Sales, Net	134,901	154,849	107,844
Theater Income	64,141	77,212	86,108
Auxiliary Operations	39,657	153,890	82,916
Council Activities	100,583	108,014	99,202
Gifts (Cash)	416,257	340,777	303,868
Total	$4,199,044	$4,339,556	$4,238,764
Transfer from Reserve	—	—	39,121
Total	$4,199,044	$4,339,556	$4,277,885
Expenditures:			
Educational, Curatorial, Exhibitions and Publications	$1,310,554[2]	$1,741,428[2]	$1,803,080
Maintenance, Operations, and Administration	2,352,944[2]	1,909,806[2]	2,148,778
Bookshop and Auxiliary Activities	90,200	99,724	105,055
Council Activities	63,107	83,757	89,647
Additions to Collections—Purchases	120,734	86,529	131,325
Total	$3,937,539	$3,921,244	$4,277,885
Transfer to Reserve	261,505	418,312	—
Total	$4,199,044	$4,339,556	$4,277,885
Acquisitions Fund Balance:			
Acquisitions Fund			
Balance (Beginning of Fiscal Year)	$ 567,161	$ 681,842	$ 890,624
Receipts	836,078	2,623,250	1,679,726
Subtotal	$1,403,239	$3,305,092	$2,570,350
Purchases and Miscellaneous Expenditure	721,397	2,414,468	1,688,920
Balance (End of Fiscal Year)	$ 681,842	$ 890,624	$ 881,430

[1]This revenue is returned to the County of Los Angeles to offset a portion of the county's total appropriation for the operation of the museum. Admission fees in 1974–75 are reduced from prior years due to the fact that the admission fees were charged to the museum's tenth anniversary exhibition and the Islamic Art exhibition.

[2]Changes in the relative amount of these expenditure figures between fiscal years 1972–73 and 1973–74 are the result of more accurate cost distribution methods.

functioning under the political pressure which is routine for decision-making positions in any state agency. Despite the problems encountered by some CAC members, several have adjusted to the new environment and have used the experience to develop their skills. Other members have chosen to resign in order to return to their creative work. The experience, however, has not been wholly negative, since the CAC has provided a forum where concerned artists have learned how to work within the political arena to advance state support for the arts. Artists should not be excluded altogether from holding such posts. What is needed is a combination of artists and non-artists who are sensitive to the unique needs of the arts and possess sufficient background to deal with the difficulties of decision making within a state agency. In this way, an environment could be created for the training of those artists with the desire and capacity to gain expertise as political spokespersons for the arts.

It is to be hoped that with the reorganization of the arts council, the state will begin to invest more in arts activities. Given the relative size and wealth of California, the state might well be expected to support the arts not far from the level established by New York state.

CETA Programs in California

Since passage of the Comprehensive Employment and Training Act of 1973, states, cities and counties designated as "prime sponsors" under the act have been funded by the federal government for the purpose of developing and implementing employment, training and related programs, directed primarily to unemployed, underemployed and/or low-income persons residing within the various jurisdictions. Title I of CETA is "decategorized," in the sense that the prime sponsor is authorized to apply the funds to any combination of programs and activities—classroom training, on-the-job training, work experience, job referral and placement, counseling or special services—which, in its view, best meets the needs of the area served. Titles II and VI remain "categorized," since they authorize funding only for public service employment. Title II, a part of the original legislation, theoretically is directed predominantly to the longer-term, chronically unemployed, while Title VI (which was added somewhat later) is intended to serve the cyclically unemployed; but there is evidence that these legislative distinctions have not been closely observed in many cases. Title III of CETA provides mainly for special programs directed to disadvantaged groups such as migratory workers, the young and the elderly, women, handicapped and so on, and proposals usually are funded by the Department of Labor on a competitive basis. Summertime programs for disadvantaged youth also are funded under Title III. The bulk of congressional appropriations under CETA have been directed to Titles I and VI.[1]

In many respects, the recent CETA arts programs are similar in concept and implementation to the widely acclaimed WPA cultural programs of the 1930s, which used federal funds to bring innovative art, theater, music and literature to thousands of communities and millions of Americans throughout the United States. Although it existed only for a brief period (1935–1939), the WPA's Federal Theater Project permanently influenced the course of the arts by developing free or low-cost productions which could be seen by the many people who rarely or never had access to the commercial theater, by recognizing and giving expression to the creative talents of minorities, and by granting artistic opportunity and employment to dramatic innovators. Like CETA, the WPA was primarily a job-creating program, and thus it was required to serve employment as well as aesthetic goals. Probably the chief difference between the WPA and CETA approaches is that the latter is decentralized in planning and administration, with cities, counties and other local units making the key decisions affecting the employment of artists. This decentralization means that artists and arts organizations must deal and negotiate with prime sponsors in securing funding, but the basic legislation and federal regulations and interpretations also have an impact on the decision-making process.

In California, the CETA program in San Francisco remains the most innovative among the various prime sponsors. As of late September 1977, there were 146 CETA artists and art technicians in its Neighborhood Arts Program, including fifty-one just hired from a list of about 700 active applicants. Most of the newly hired people have been assigned to work in connection with the nine decentralized community cultural centers which are now operating or are soon to open, covering programs in ceramics, graphics, photography, dance, theater and music. Through CETA funding, master and trainee technicians, an architect, draftsmen, arts therapists, new personnel for the SCRAP (Scroungers Center for Reusable Art Parts) program which collects materials from business and industry for use in schools and community programs, two printer-designers for the printing department, artist consultants, a grants-writer, a coordinator of a new theatrical costume bank and many others have been hired. In addition, state CETA funds have made possible the employment of two full-time assistant building managers at the South of Market and Bayview-Hunter's Point cultural centers. The Neighborhood Arts Program now sponsors fourteen community workshops taught by CETA artists, and thirty-nine other workshops taught by non-CETA staff. CETA artists also teach in the public schools and several have received California Arts Council grants. Annual expenditures for the Neighborhood Arts Program (exclusive of CETA funding) have risen from $72,800 in 1967–1968 to $321,500 in 1976–1977.

Arts funding under CETA has expanded in Los Angeles since the Theater Arts Program of Los Angeles (TAPLA) was first authorized and funded in 1976. One-third of Title VI funding is reserved for community-based organizations and arts organizations are increasingly numbered among the recipients. As of late October 1977, 113 Title VI job slots had been provided to eleven nonprofit arts groups throughout the city. The California Confederation of the Arts also served as an "umbrella" agency for more than a dozen smaller organizations designated as "worksites" under the CETA program (See Table 8). This latter arrangement gives administrative and technical support to small arts groups which otherwise might lack the capacity to meet CETA standards. In addition, another 109 Title VI jobs had been authorized for the Municipal Arts Department and other city agencies (see Table 9).

As a result of a recent amendment to CETA that requires the provision of services under Title VI which communities otherwise could not afford to offer, many of the newer programs are in the creative arts. As of early August 1977, about 4 percent of all the special public service projects in the country were in the arts field.

Proposals for CETA funds are evaluated by city CETA staff and the Personnel Department. Appeals are heard by the Proposal Review Committee of the Advisory Board, and final decisions are made by the City Council. Except in special instances, usually where there are key political considerations in one or more council districts, recommendations of staff usually are ratified by the other groups involved in the process.

Arts projects, like other CETA-funded projects, are those which have some public service aspect, e.g., presentations of arts events free or at low cost in public places such as parks and playgrounds. Provisions for administrative and equipment costs are very limited, since 85 percent of the funding usually has been reserved for the wages, salaries and fringe benefits of eligible employees. Each community ("prime sponsor") decides how much of total CETA funding is to be allocated to the arts.

A review of all proposals submitted for funding under CETA Title VI for FY 1978–1979 shows that the "arts/cultural" category was second only to "education" in number of projects proposed and number of participants covered (among the total of nineteen categories). Of the fifty-one arts organizations submitting proposals, twenty-eight were already funded under CETA. It is significant that almost two-thirds of the projects submitted were located in the three labor market planning areas (1, 2 and 3) which contain the highest percentages of low-income households and unemployed persons. This information demonstrates that significant numbers of artists are CETA-eligible and that CETA-aided arts organizations are important sources of employment in low-income areas (See Table 10).

Public Funds Received by Community Organizations

One way to assess the role that government plays in the arts is to look at several important community arts organizations to determine what proportion of their budgets is derived from the city and from other public sources. Such an inquiry can also tell much about funding for the arts more generally in Los Angeles.

Table 8: Comprehensive Employment and Training Act, Title VI (Public Service) Los Angeles Worksite Agencies Under California Confederation of The Arts September 1977

Coordinating Agency	Grant Amount	Number of Positions
California Confederation of the Arts	$ 1,016,615 Worksite Funding $ 48,461 Administrative Funding	89

Agency	Grant Amount	Number of Positions
Aman Folk Ensemble, Inc.	21,510	2
American Dance Theatre	68,280	8
Artists for Economic Action	130,088	10
Brockman Gallery Productions	89,532	11
California Confederation of the Arts	47,403	4
Free Public Theatre Foundation (Changed to Subgrantee Status)	217,256	17
Los Angeles Institute of Contemporary Art	37,218	3
Los Angeles Solo Repertory Orchestra Association, Inc.	23,817	2
Los Angeles Theatre Alliance	83,862	7
Performing Tree, Inc.	11,553	1
Plaza De La Raza, Inc.	25,479	2
R'Wanda Lewis Afro/American Dance Company	59,243	6
San Fernando Valley Arts Council	89,341	7
Scorpio Rising Theatre Foundation	96,207	8
Social and Public Art Resource Center	15,826	1
Total	$ 1,065,076	89
Grand Total (All CETA VI Programs)	$12,675,519	1200

Plaza de la Raza

Plaza de la Raza is perhaps the most diversified and stable community arts organization serving the Los Angeles Chicano community. Its operating budget was approximately $259,000 for fiscal year 1978. Nearly half (45 percent) of the total comes from a $114,000 basic administrative grant by the Los Angeles Office of Urban Development (OUD) and is used for salaries (for a staff of five) and supplies. This funding began under the Model Cities Program in 1971, but since 1975, it has come from Housing and Community Development (HCD) "block grants." Other significant sources of support are the California Arts Council ($8,000); U.S. Office of Education—Ethnic Heritage Studies ($50,000); and CETA Title VI ($35,000). Private sector grants total approximately $53,000, with the largest gifts from the Irvine Foundation and the Sears Corporation. Thus, 80 percent of Plaza's support is derived from the public sector and 20 percent from the private sector in the form of corporate and foundation support.

Plaza de la Raza has also embarked upon an effort to obtain operating funds directly from the federal government through the Community Services Administration (CSA). CSA puts primary emphasis on community services in economically distressed areas, a criterion that is compatible with the goals of Plaza.

Plaza has applied for a five-year planning grant from CSA for $225,000 per year. Management is fairly confident of obtaining the grant, at least for the first year, which would double its budget and

Table 9: CETA Employment—Los Angeles, October 1977

The city of Los Angeles has made direct grants to eleven arts groups to undertake public service programs in neighborhoods throughout the metropolitan area. A total of 113 Title VI jobs has been provided to these private, nonprofit organizations, with another 109 Title VI jobs assigned to the Municipal Arts Department and other agencies of the city government.

Recipient organizations include:

The Aman Folk Ensemble, an ethnic dance group touring children's and other community facilities (8);

The American Dance Theatre, a training company that tours among special audiences (14);

Brockman Gallery Productions, a collective of visual artists executing works in public places (10);

The Center Theatre Group, a dramatic touring company to do follow-up training after performances in schools (13);

Los Angeles Actors' Theatre, a troupe conducting free community performances (13);

Music Center Presentations, a group of strolling musicians who celebrate the Mexican-American Hertiage (9); and a liaison group to coordinate private sponsors of cultural presentations with available performing artists (2);

R'Wanda Lewis Afro-American Dance Company, a touring company in the schools (7);

Social and Public Art Resources Center (SPARC), a visual arts project to create works in public places, and to involve the community with the design and development of this art (9);

Songwriters Resources and Services, service group to assist new songwriters through festivals, evaluations, and promotions of their works (2);

Theatre in Progress (Garden Theater Festival), a group conducting free community festivals of performing arts in different areas of the city (16);

Twelfth Night Repertory Company, a group sending small teams of actors to work with children in raising cultural and social awareness through theater (5).

Source: "A Bulletin on Federal Economic Programs and the Arts," National Endowment for the Arts, October 28, 1977, p. 14.

would in effect alter the private/public composition of its funding from 20 percent/80 percent to 10 percent/90 percent, thereby increasing its reliance on the public sector.

The long-term strategy, however, is to secure a new stable and independent source of funding. In all likelihood, housing and community development grants will be phased out for service-type organizations within the near future. Increases in funding afforded by CSA will provide Plaza the opportunity to hire and train its own resident teachers for the many classes and workshops offered in the performing and visual arts and other related educational programs. At the present time, most of the organization's programs are supported by grants, while teachers are provided by the school district and local colleges.

Plaza has a unique twenty-five-year leasing arrangement (with a renewable option) with the Los Angeles Recreation and Parks Department whereby it plays one dollar a year for the use of its site in east Los Angeles' Lincoln Park. The building complex is owned and administered by Plaza's corporate board, which also heads the organization's fundraising efforts for a $2.5 million building program.

R'Wanda Lewis Afro-American Dance Company

Compared to most other Los Angeles community arts organization, R'Wanda Lewis Afro-American Dance Company is relatively self-sufficient economically. R'Wanda Lewis's 1977

Table 10: Funds Received by San Francisco Neighborhood Arts Program During 1975–77

Foundations:

Zellerbach Family Fund	
Supplies and truck maintenance	$ 8,000
Make-a-circus	5,000
Private Donations for Bicentennial Gardens for (8 gardens)	5,000
San Francisco Foundation	
Talespinners	5,400
Make-a-circus	11,000
Coordinating Council of Literary Magazines poetry publications	2,000
Strybing Arboretum Society (for 2 gardens)	750
Commission on the Aging Talespinners	450

City Funds:

Publicity and Advertising Funds Pickle Family Circus	2,000

State Funds:

California Arts Council	
Pickle Family Circus	7,500
Pickle Family Circus	3,500
Poetry Anthology	1,500

Federal Funds:

Office of Community Development
(Projects sponsored by community organizations or Housing Authority Tenants

1975

Housing Authority Gardens	3,000
Housing Authority Murals	11,000
Community and school gardens	6,000
Community and school murals	9,800

1976

Community, school and Housing Authority Gardens	10,000
National Endowment for the Arts	
Pickle Family Circus	10,000
Small Press Grant (3 poets—anthologies)	16,000
Golden Gate National Recreation Area	
Mural Project at Pier 2	8,000
Pickle Family Circus	4,000
Neighborhood Bicentennial Awards—City Planning: 5 gardens and 2 murals	49,000
S.C.R.A.P. 1976–1977	
San Francisco Foundation	5,000
C.A.C.	6,850

Information provided by San Francisco Neighborhood Arts Program annual operating budget of $125,000 was used to maintain a staff of twenty (of which ten were on a part-time basis), including performers, technical and administrative support services. Needless to say, salaries were low. Approximately 60 percent ($75,000) of the budget was derived from earned income through touring and local group performances. The remaining 40 percent ($50,000) came from public sector support, of which $20,000 was from the National Endowment for the Arts. Other public sector support, as a percentage of total support, included the California Arts Council (5%); the Los Angeles County Performing Arts Commission (5%); and local city government—the Municipal Arts Department, Recreation and Parks Department, revenue sharing and CETA Title I (10%).

In 1978, R'Wanda Lewis was awarded a CETA Title VI grant for $256,000, more than double the previous year's operating budget and providing an additional thirty-one positions (some part-time) for performers and technical support. As a result of the increase afforded by the CETA funds, the organization's operating budget for 1978 is approximately $380,000. Moreover, it has drastically altered the overall funding composition, which had remained constant the past few years. Instead of the 60/40 private-public support ratio, it is now 20/80. Because the organization is now more dependent upon the public sector for support, its fiscal vulnerability is increased in the event that there are CETA cutbacks.

Self Help Graphics

Self Help Graphics is administered by a nun who is a visual artist. Even though the organization is not formally affiliated with any religious organization, the Order of Franciscan Sisters and Fathers has provided funds, particularly in times of severe cash flow problems. Were it not for this support during past crises, it is doubtful whether Self Help Graphics would still be in existence. Self Help's budget for FY 1978 is approximately $67,000, an increase of $15,000 over FY 1977. A staff of three coordinates the organization's program. Public sector support amounts to 92 percent of the total budget, while private support comprises the remaining 8 percent. Approximately 60 percent ($40,000) of the total budget is provided through revenue sharing funds administered by the Los Angeles County Parks and Recreation Department. Two organizational grants from the California Arts Council account for 26 percent ($17,000) of the budget, while 7 percent ($5,000) is provided by local city government through the Municipal Arts Department. The remaining 8 percent ($5,500) is provided by the Franciscan Order.

There is also cooperation with other programs in which Self Help Graphics provides the use of its facilities but does not directly receive funds for these purposes and therefore does not include them as part of the budget. Self Help hosts a visual artist who is paid $7,600 directly by the California Arts Council through its Artists in Schools and Communities program. Self Help furnishes the space, supplies and materials to enable the artist to work with local schools and community groups. City government employs young people on a part-time basis and provides supervision of neighborhood youngsters at Self Help, contributing $4,000.

Over the past few years, revenue sharing funds have proven to be Self Help's most stable funding source and are regarded as the cornerstone of the organization's economic health. To a lesser extent, the California Arts Council has also provided constant funding.

In order to decrease such a heavy reliance on the public sector, Self Help will soon begin to operate a small silkscreen studio to help support its overall efforts. Although Self Help works closely with the schools, it has chosen not to contract services with the district in order not to lose its organizational autonomy.

Analysis

What we see is a heavy reliance upon government grants for economic support of the community arts organizations surveyed. Moreover, the bulk of public support is derived from nonarts funding agencies. One of the few exceptions is the Garden Theater Festival, where the city of Los Angeles provides more than 25 percent of its support. This may be explained by the organization's citywide involvement. Support on a more limited scale is provided for community arts organizations by the private sector, mainly foundations. From our knowledge, the picture which emerges here, in relation to public/private financial support, is characteristic of Los Angeles community arts organizations.

The existing community arts organization may aptly be described as the survivors of the Los Angeles community arts movement that attained its full momentum in the late 1960s and early 1970s. To a degree, the continued existence of these organizations has been made possible by the diversification of their funding sources, which has helped to maintain fiscal flexibility, a key element for survival. This diversification is generated in large part by an awareness among community arts organizations of the need to develop alternative sources of income within the scope of their available services. Some organizations have become extremely vulnerable as a result of a heavy reliance upon grants. Those organizations capable of generating earned income find that it provides a financial cushion in the event of funding cutbacks by allowing at least a marginal source of income as an interim safeguard while strategies can be developed to attract new support.

Perhaps one of the greatest problems faced by community arts organizations is that of developing credibility. Without a previous track record, funding is extremely difficult, particularly in the formative stages of development. The scenario is familiar: without credibility there is little possibility of program development, and in turn, there is little likelihood of obtaining the track record which is absolutely necessary for success in the grantsmanship process. The task has proven a difficult one and has led to the demise of many new community arts organizations. However, once credibility is established, it continues as a self-reinforcing process with the expansion of services and clientele paving the way for the development of new funding sources. This is almost a prerequisite for funding diversification.

Management skills represent another important element in economic survival. This area is perhaps one of the weakest among emerging community arts organizations. Good budgeting and accounting techniques are essential for maintaining adequate financial records and cash flows to meet anticipated operating expenses. Again, the community arts survivors have succeeded in developing management capabilities, sometimes with difficulty and very little assistance from outside sources. This is an impressive accomplishment in itself, considering the limited resources at their disposal, especially during early growth periods. Systematic technical assistance to neighborhood arts groups through a community agency established for that purpose would substantially improve the survival chances for many of them.

Footnotes

[1] In late 1978, a CETA reauthorization bill was passed which substantially changes the thrust of the legislation, although it retains most of the "decentralization" features. The emphasis has been shifted to the training and employment of the long-term unemployed and lowest-skill groups, with restrictions upon the capacity of prime sponsors to hire in the higher-salary jobs and limitations on the tenure of public service employees, a focus on the "transitioning" of CETA workers to unsubsidized private employment, and addition of a new title providing for special programs in the private sector. Severe cuts in allocations for public service employment are possible.

PART III
STRATEGIES FOR CHANGE

Highlights

Economic Role of the Arts: The arts are not likely to provide a panacea for the economic problems of central cities. But they do have a significant role to play. Many of the arts are central-city-oriented because of economies of scale (they have to draw audiences from the entire metropolitan area). Others are "footloose;" they can follow consumers to the suburbs or congregate in the central city, so this may be an ideal sector in which to intervene. Government and private-sector incentives designed to create jobs in the central city may be particularly attractive to the arts. Thus the arts, while not the most rapidly growing part of the service sector, may be one of the most strategic and pivotal contributors to the economic life of the central city. The arts meet some of the special employment and income needs of the poorer population now clustered in central cities. This population has talents and skills that can be tapped by the arts. The arts also contribute to community cohesion, a critical feature in the ability of communities to provide for their own needs. The future viability of the central city is closely tied to whether or not it is a good place in which to live and work, since today many locational decisions by business depend on this factor. The arts can and do contribute importantly to the drawing power of the central city.

Framework: In terms of the tripartite framework which has been established in this book to describe and analyze the arts system, attention here is concentrated on the supportive institutions and the community, together with the social and physical environment. The core element of the analytical framework—the artists and other participants—is kept very much in mind but not discussed directly (except for a limited discussion of training needs). The central problem is not seen as a lack of artistic excellence or an inadequate labor force for the arts. Rather, it is seen as being in the realm of organization and public/private support.

Marketing: A logical starting point for expanding the economic scope of the arts is to concentrate on methods for increasing the size of audiences. Sound marketing requires, first, effective dissemination of information. There are advanced media and other techniques to be learned as well as personal methods. Ties to tourism are important, as are the use of special events. Arts organizations spend 5 to 8 percent of their operating expenditures for promotion, where a figure of 10 to 15 percent is thought to be needed. Subscription sales are critically important. Cooperative or umbrella marketing agencies offer significant possibilities for the future.

Stimulating desire for the arts by education is of key importance. Awareness and appreciation of the arts must begin early in life to ensure future consumption. How to prevent public school funds for arts instruction from being cut (they are usually the first to be cut) should become a matter of concern for all arts organizations. Ancillary institutions for arts learning have been established and should be expanded.

Voucher ticket sales (through which the consumer purchases a block of tickets to a variety of events) may be general or limited to special audiences. Outlets for the sale of unsold theater tickets at a reduced rate (pioneered in New York) is an innovation with great potential.

Financing: If the arts are to play their proper role in the economy and culture of our cities, access to the arts must be broadly available to the public. This requires a fundamental rethinking about economic support of the arts and the responsibility that government bears toward artistic enterprise. The key is to rationalize the market exchanges of four interrelated sectors: (1) government, (2) for-profit enterprises, (3) the nonprofit sector, and (4) the individual, as organization member and as consumer.

The present rules of the game prevent all of these sectors from being as supportive of the arts as they might be. Scarcity as an explanation of price setting is based on a model of man which asserts that he receives economic value not only from the consumption of goods and services, but also by excluding others from doing the same. Scarcity in reality then becomes a brute force mechanism for establishing prices which insures that the wealthy get served first. However, the principle of scarcity runs counter to the principle of broad access to the arts. When the demand curve (as a graphic presentation of a complex reality) is looked at as representative of individual behavior, it can show that different people and institutions are willing to pay different amounts for the consumption of the same good. If the arts are able to develop other ways to get consumers to express their full economic valuation of artistic goods and services, scarcity can be discarded as the sole mechanism and access to the arts can be more fully realized.

For the nonprofit sector, public service budgets can permit a more appropriate kind of accounting than the present concentration on the bottom line of an organization's financial statement. Residual exclusivity would be reduced.

Government subsidy provides for the delivery of arts goods or services which could not otherwise be afforded by the public. It represents the fee-for-public-service cost which must go with any claim by government that it is assuring access to the arts. Beyond that, to foster or preserve the arts for future generations, government must provide additional resources.

Part of the cost is appropriately covered by wealthy individuals in the community, as well as the private and semi-private collectivities, the corporations and foundations. This is the area in which these individuals and collectivities can exhibit their sense of social responsibility—the desire to increase the quality of life of their community—as well as the judgment that the value associated with support of the arts is greater than the cost incurred.

Along the same principles, this analysis calls for local governments to return to the arts a reasonable share of a hotel tax (or similar levy) equal to the contribution of the arts in attracting visitors and their capital to the city.

Federal Government Support: The national government supports the arts in a variety of forms. Except for the highly important support provided by the National Endowment for the Arts, federal financial assistance is related to other non-art purposes, such as employment, training, education, and transportation. This turns out to be a two-edged knife. It significantly broadens the total government assistance provided to the arts but, at the same time, puts the arts in a Procrustean-bed situation where they are stretched or cut to fit some preordained general purpose. In each of the federal programs, there are not-unreasonable adjustments to existing rules of the game that can be enormously helpful to the arts without subverting the overall purposes of federal grants and programs. CETA is used as an example of how this might be done. Similar principles would apply to other federal programs.

The proposal for the creation of an office of cultural affairs in the executive office of the president, to increase the visibility of the arts and to provide a continuing overview of federal programs touching on the arts, deserves support.

Unions: Unions can play a significant role in enhancing the strength of the arts within the economy. Currently, unions help to stabilize the arts industry and serve to control the labor market. In collective bargaining, unions have to act as an adversary against employers and managers. With the expansion of financing by government and other collectivities, future collective bargaining might logically be between management and unions on one side confronting the sources of funding on the other.

With the shifting of fundraising to collectivities, the union leader should be encouraged to play a larger role in obtaining funds, increasing audience support, and perhaps even making financial contributions to the arts organization—in the interest of enhancing arts employment.

The encouragement of additional employment opportunities for actors and related professionals by the Actors Equity ninety-nine-seat waiver plan (a waiving of its work rules in theaters of ninety-nine seats or less) in Los Angeles and San Francisco, in effect since 1972, has had enough success to suggest that other arts unions might well follow Equity's example.

Another strategy for increasing employment in the arts is the establishment of a performing arts trust fund, a concept pioneered by the American Federation of Musicians. The fund provides a self-circulating financial mechanism which not only benefits the community, but also helps to maintain the livelihood of many artists. There are numerous avenues for financing a trust fund: an agreed-upon proportion of royalties, programs sold at arts performances, parking fees, and various forms of residuals.

A united arts fund drive could be an effective means of generating support for all arts organizations in a community.

Beautifying, Restoring and Revitalizing the City: The arts can serve in many ways to vitalize the city. In a truly foundational sense, architects and architecture can help create an environment which is not only well-organized, but poetic and symbolic as well. Buildings and clusters of buildings—like other major works of art—help to attract people to city areas, at times providing welcome additions to sections lacking the pedestrian traffic necessary for increased business activity.

Preserving and adapting historic buildings are in many instances economically more feasible than new construction and can provide a significant job market (because of their labor-intensive nature) for craftspeople and architects.

Existing support for architecture and building from the corporate sector (in one case encompassing programs to encourage minority builders, to help displaced tenants, and to provide funds for city improvement and restoration) might well be emulated. But it is the broadening of public support upon which the future contribution of architecture to the economic and cultural life of the city will depend. This should cover (1) the reservation of land for future community use, (2) expansion of support for public facilities and housing, (3) tax incentives for town-scale projects, (4) revisions of property tax systems and of zoning and building codes to encourage city development, (5) establishment of trust funds for community redevelopment, (6) creation of a national development corporation (already proposed by President Carter), (7) special zoning and codes for cultural facilities and historic restoration, and (8) provision of design services for construction in government grants. Also, critically important is the establishment of "1 percent funding" to support art work associated with new building and to provide art in public places.

Many of the large older cities (including Los Angeles, which is about to celebrate its 200th anniversary) are obsolete in large sections because they are the product of the previous industrial age and have not adapted to the post-industrial period. They are presently not the ideal sites for either manufacturing or the new service industries, nor for middle- and upper-income families. The population is responding to this obsolescence by settling in outlying areas. The central cities can stop the (net) out-migration of people by becoming good places in which to live and work. This requires that the amenities unique to the older areas become the basis for effectively competing with the younger outlying employment centers. These amenities include the centralized location of downtown and the assets and charms of the older buildings and spaces—and the arts.

The redevelopment process and the state laws regulating it are receptive to financing cultural facilities in the city. However, to be eligible for tax-increment financing (which is key to financing redevelopment), cultural-facility investments must demonstrate an ability to contribute to the economic viability of the city and not just the quality of life. Under such terms of reference, measuring the economic benefit of cultural facilities requires consideration of other factors than projected gross revenues from ticket sales. It requires inclusion of a broadly defined economic "multiplier" effect. Experiences in various cities suggest that arts facilities and activities, when imaginatively developed to attract a maximum of local and tourist visitors, can be a major economic asset to the local economy. The multiplier measurement should be able to capture that. There are significant possibilities, as demonstrated in various cities across the country, in mixed-use facilities, the use of public spaces for cultural activities, historic restoration, and the use of special opportunities to revitalize the city (the projected people mover project in Los Angeles is discussed as a case in point).

Public regulations dealing with land use and structures can be changed in certain instances to have a favorable impact on the expansion of the arts. Examples are changes in the current zoning laws to accommodate artists in parts of the city where the mixing of studios and living accommodations are now prohibited. Such changes can encourage the development of "artist colonies" which might well become an important symbol of the post-industrial city. A comprehensive proposal for zoning, designed to enable artists to practice their professions in a variety of urban settings, is set down in Chapter 14.

Community Arts: Neighborhood arts must play a key role in the revitalization of our central cities. This is particularly important because they are associated with minority cultures that represent a majority or near-majority of the population in most large cities. By stimulating a more general interest in and appreciation of the arts in a variety of forms, a decentralized arts program could have a long-run impact upon patronage of the arts in both the nonprofit and profit making sectors.

A public organization that can speak for all neighborhood arts in a city is needed. Private, nonprofit arts organizations can retain their individual and independent identities, but receive financial and technical assistance from such an agency.

For the neighborhood arts programs to develop in the long run, there must be educational programs to build future community involvement with the arts. Creative skills may be related to a range of career occupations, including many which are outside the arts field, and educational research might well focus on new instructional and counseling techniques for identification and development of this relationship.

Universities in urban areas have the potential capacity to serve artistic needs in minority communities but, with few exceptions, this potential remains undeveloped.

Neighborhood recreation and cultural centers need to be developed and/or expanded for local residents as a locus for arts events and education.

Parks and playgrounds, child day-care facilities, shopping malls, work places, post offices and other public buildings, housing projects and other such facilities can serve as conduits for both the performing and visual arts. Musical instruments, art supplies and other equipment should be available for use by residents, especially young people, in classes and workshops. Construction, staffing and programming of such neighborhood facilities should be a specific element in urban redevelopment planning and in the general plan for the total community.

The problem of security might be diminished through the proper planning of programs and facilities to minimize risks of crime; for example, shopping malls and other centers which are well-lit and well-policed, with adequate and secure parking areas, are ideal locations for artistic events. Consideration should also be given to the establishment of "cultural parks," akin to industrial parks, (indeed, in some areas cultural and industrial parks might occupy the same space and facilities) which can encompass these security measures as an element in their planning and construction.

All of these elements should be the responsibility of a neighborhood arts program, which might well be along the lines of the San Francisco model.

Department of Cultural Affairs: Large cities need a public agency that can not only provide specific cultural services and programs, but can coordinate the city's arts activities, foster its overall cultural development, and create a comprehensive policy for the city.

A new department of cultural affairs would combine the major existing departments providing arts services and programs. It should take leadership in developing and articulating a comprehensive cultural policy for the city and have the power to implement it. It would stimulate the development of the arts by: (1) supervising city aid to cultural institutions, (2) helping to determine funding allocations, (3) administering free programs to the public, (4) providing technical services to cultural organizations, groups, and individual artists, and (5) coordinating the efforts of the other city agencies that affect cultural activities, and cooperating with the county. The agency should also be allowed to play an active role in the development of historical districts and redevelopment projects. Also, the department should work closely with such agencies as the city planning department and the community redevelopment agency in overall planning efforts to encourage the arts component in development strategies.

The department should have a division to foster the development of community arts organizations. Guidance and assistance should run from securing permits for community arts festivals to obtaining major funding for innovative programs. It should explore opportunities for cooperative partnerships in projects of mutual benefit among the city and community art groups.

The department should take an active interest in nurturing the development of for-profit arts activities. There are helpful public regulations that can be sponsored to meet needs of these industries (such as the "one-stop" permit arrangement for using public streets and facilities in film-making in Los Angeles). Also, the city can help provide useful information on available training facilities to youthful unemployed workers and press for-profit arts employers on "affirmative action" hiring.

Arts in Economic Development Efforts: The post-industrial city must depend on service activities, rather than manufacturing and trade, as the mainstay of its economy. But service activities have different requirements than traditional manufacturing or trade activities, and this should be reflected in economic development (promotion) efforts by city agencies. Just as public-private task forces are organized to try to hold on to a garment industry or jewelry exchange, task forces need to be organized to increase employment in the arts and to help magnify the economic impact of the arts. City efforts in this regard would be greatly enhanced if the federal government's grants for economic development (through HUD and EDA) made specific provision for the arts in relation to their economic development grants.

Corporations contributing to the arts and interested in the economic viability of the central city might well consider the economic dimensions of the arts in making decisions on grants and sponsored art shows and performances. Their knowledge about economic stimuli should be sought by city agencies in evolving programs to attract tourists and private investment to the city.

Cultural Planning: Planning is required if the arts are to achieve the objectives which have been set for them, including a major contribution to the local economy. This can be done by introducing a cultural element in the general plan (prepared in almost every city in the country) which can serve as a framework for specific governmental decisions.

A cultural element should do the following: (1) provide basic information about the arts activities in a city and the people involved in them (a constantly maintained inventory of the arts); (2) make plans for broader and more flexible use of public (and, to some extent, private) facilities for arts activities, experimental arts groups and arts education efforts; (3) probe for ways in which the arts might be tied into various private activities and public services in order to enlarge the scope of arts employment and income; and (4) make plans for the fuller use of the arts in urban development and redevelopment.

3.7
Increasing Paying Audiences
Marketing Factors to Encourage Expansion of of the Arts

For the arts to play a greater role in the revitalization of our cities, support must come from a variety of sources. Perhaps the most obvious and elementary source is the paying audience. What follows is a marketing approach to increase the size of the audience for the arts. Marketing is a series of techniques used by business to bring to the attention of consumers the goods or services it has developed for their use. Such techniques can substantially enlarge the audiences for the arts.

Information Dissemination

Before a consumer can decide to purchase a product, that person must be made aware of its existence. There are many ways to communicate this information to the public. When one turns to standard advertising, there are a number of options from which to choose, each effective for attracting a different sector of the population. In marketing terms, media mix describes the combination of media sources designed for different elements of the audience. Sales representatives can help an arts organization to determine the potential reach (audience make-up) of its particular forms of media. Examples of the media available are metropolitan newspapers, community newspapers, weekly and semi-weekly shopping newspapers, and commercial radio and television stations, as well as direct mail and posters. Radio and television make public service announcement time available to nonprofit organizations, giving arts organizations an excellent opportunity for broad exposure. In addition, there are transit advertising and billboards. No matter what method is used, the more complete and excellent the presentation, the more effective it will be. Seeking advice from media experts can aid in determining the best media source for a particular need.

Yet many parts of the population to be reached will not respond to this kind of information. Mass mailing of printed material is relatively low in cost in proportion to size of audience reached. Door-to-door campaigns, perhaps with the distribution of novelty items such as buttons, flyers or bumper stickers, increase familiarity with a product and can stimulate valuable word-of-mouth and peer influence support. The specific communication device used by an organization should be geared to the type of audience desired, the event being communicated, and the kind of organization presenting it. A community arts organization might rely less on a newspaper than on flyers or a mailing campaign if its population is not prone to reading metropolitan newspapers. An arts organization attempting to diversify its audience ethnically might consider publishing in languages other than English. Thus, a personal, individual approach works best.

In some cases, the product can be advertised in an indirect manner. The fundraising campaign of the San Francisco Ballet exemplifies this technique. When the company came close to extinction a few years ago, the dancers took to the streets, ballet shoes in hand, to solicit funds. By this the company gained notice for its product and stimulated a new, interested audience.

Another example of indirect advertising is "star endorsement." The star, an individual who has achieved a degree of fame, can be someone in the community, such as a politician or a community leader, or someone from the arts who bears a message about the product in question. The arts organization or product may achieve fame by its link with a star that is part of the product, or the star may serve only as an initial attention-getter necessary to stimulate a future audience.

Tourism provides another means of publicizing the arts. Every city has a chamber of commerce; many have tourist councils. These organizations charge nominal fees for membership which allow for inexpensive advertising in their publications. Publication in hotel activity magazines, advertisements or inserts in tour brochures, and connections to major tourist attractions can stimulate audience development. In addition, tourism can increase the availability of the product for the hometown audience.

Special events can be used to inform the public of

the existence of the artistic products. Conventions and the convention bureau or an exposition can inform new audiences, a significant proportion of which may be local residents not yet familiar with hometown artistic resources. Displays or demonstrations of the artistic product at conventions motivate and guide newcomers. Additional information aids such as a culture map, including directions to events and possibly containing promotional ties with restaurants, will attract people who may have never participated in such events.

All the above suggestions require two important sets of resources—funding and staffing. Organizations spend between 5 percent and 8 percent of their total operating expenditures for promotion. Marketing consultants and media representatives suggest an expense figure in the 10 to 15 percent range for proper promotion of a product. An increase in promotion expenditures can not only increase direct and immediate audience support in the form of ticket revenues, but it can lead to long-term advocacy and increase public funding for the arts.

Adequate promotion requires qualified writers, designers, graphic artists, public relations staff and, possibly, filmmakers. If budget constraints do not permit employment of such personnel, it may be possible to have their services donated or to obtain specific grants for their work. If the board of directors of an arts organization is well selected, it should include people with a variety of talents and contacts valuable for promotional purposes. Newspaper, television and radio sales personnel can assist with ad editing and layout. Ad agencies may be willing to donate trained personnel. Billboard companies may have unused space and available design staff. Recently, the advertising agency which sells Southern California Rapid Transit District (RTD) bus advertisement space to outside vendors donated materials and installation costs to a Los Angeles mural association and the RTD allocated space. Many corporations have in-house promotion staff who may be able to donate time and advice as a community service. The National Advertising Council sponsors certain ad campaigns and can be approached about initiating such programs. Printing materials are expensive, but equipment can be used cooperatively to reduce cost. The Neighborhood Arts Program in San Francisco operates a graphics duplication service for its member groups, suggesting a possible approach for groups in other areas.

Another alternative is a cooperative, or umbrella, marketing agency. This organization would work closely with member groups to monitor their information dissemination, such as press releases and public service spots. It would consult with member groups regarding their media mix and the content and placement of information. If it also provided design service, such an organization could play a major role in improving communication about available artistic products, thus bringing about the desired goal of increased consumption. Perhaps funding sources would be willing to subsidize such an organization, for it would allow the arts associations to concentrate on the production of their artistry.

One of the keys to a successful advertising campaign is the level of knowledge the arts organization has about itself. If the organization has not clearly defined the audience most suited to its product, and has not identified the needs and perceptions of that desired (and existing) audience, it may fail in its attempts to inform the public about itself. The tone of an advertising and information program depends on such organizational self-knowledge.

An arts organization can acquire such self-knowledge through market research which analyzes what the present audience thinks of the product an organization offers. Many organizations may need market research techniques just to learn who their present audience actually is before branching out to deduce the make-up of a future audience. Although the use of market research techniques may be too sophisticated or expensive for many arts organizations, this can be offset through shared or donated resources, or the use of marketing students at local universities. A cooperative marketing agency could include a broad-scale market research facility, perhaps staffed by volunteer investigators supervised by trained professionals. Arts organizations could hire the unemployed for their market research efforts as well as for personal selling and literature distribution, with monies available for various employment projects.

An innovative attempt at market research and self-knowledge is being carried out by the Los Angeles Center Theater Group of the Mark Taper

Forum. An anthropologist on staff studies the communities and populations that live near the theater and measures their opinions and preferences regarding the performing arts.

The UCLA Department of Fine Arts Productions recently conducted an audience survey by placing a questionnaire in audience programs at a variety of events. Ushers reminded participants to complete the survey and collected the questionnaires after each intermission. Not only will the information be used to redirect their advertising campaign, but better information about the perception of quality of the productions will be gleaned from this effort.

Stimulating Desire by Education[1]

Once an organization has effectively informed an audience of the existence of a product and has geared its information to the needs and make-up of that audience, it may discover that the audience needs further stimulation to purchase the product. Using the information gleaned from market research efforts, the arts organization can proceed to educate the informed audience about the nature of the artistic product. This is the most difficult task facing an arts organization or governmental cultural organization.

It is preferable to expand public awareness and appreciation of the arts early in individual's lives to insure further consumption. Thus, children become the ideal focal point for arts education. Unfortunately, public school funds for arts instruction are the first funds to be cut. To offset diminishing public arts education, ancillary institutions for learning have been established. In Los Angeles there are the Improvisational Theater Project sponsored by the Mark Taper Forum, Young Audiences, Design for Sharing (UCLA's Community Service Project for the Performing Arts), the Performing Tree and the Junior Arts Center.

The Performing Tree began initially as a Junior League-sponsored project "created to convince educators of the value of the arts in education" by bringing the performing arts to schools.[2] This organization began with seventy-two elementary schools. It contracted a diverse and highly skilled group of performers who liked working with children and who wished to involve them in their art. The teachers in the pilot schools were also taught the numerous possibilities for adding performing arts to the classroom.

The Performing Tree has grown into a nonprofit organization with forty-two of the original schools paying their own way. In addition, 180 other schools pay the Performing Tree to come into their schools. So much interest has been generated in this organization and its concept that new project ideas are being considered, such as artists-in-residence programs and workshops designed for individual schools. In 1979, the Performing Tree received a grant of $47,500 from the California Arts Council to be used for artists-in-schools and other programs.

The Junior Arts Center (JAC) stresses the importance of the visual arts for children ages five to seventeen. It is sponsored by the Municipal Arts Department, Los Angeles' cultural agency, to teach each year 5,000 children various forms of visual expression. It operates on a city budget of some $260,000, offering seventy-five different classes, gallery exhibitions, special events and community programs.

Yet the audience development and educational efforts of the JAC are stymied to some degree. For instance, most of the children enrolled are young, leaving gaps in the high school age range. For those students who do "grow up at the Junior Arts Center," no opportunity for future artistic education is offered. The ideal in audience development is continuity throughout one's life. The JAC has suggested that it send graduate pupils back into their communities, letting their successes speak to new students and their parents with the hope of gaining new audiences and support. This "missionary" approach, if properly funded, would provide jobs for young people in the arts, be reflected in communities often less directly served by other outreach programs, and slowly begin a broadened education process.

These programs serve both to broaden the horizons of the participants and educate them about the relationship of art to their lives, and to stimulate others whom the participants encounter. Any satisfied customer, whether student, parent, or teacher, can positively influence another's response. A marketing "multiplier effect" will occur, one which will cause greater growth of the audience for artistic products.

Innovations in Education for Adults

Programs for adults are important not only to increase their interest in the arts, but also to support the educative efforts of those programs aimed at their children. Few formal examples of education for adults exist other than the conventional, self-initiated programs at junior colleges and universities.

The Los Angeles Center Theater Group has an innovative program that buses a group of University of California at Santa Barbara (UCSB) alumni and students to Los Angeles to view the Mark Taper Forum's productions. The group regularly fills the entire theater for a preview of each play performed. One of UCSB's professors leads the group and provides a seminar before each play, using members of the group to demonstrate points of discussion. Following the performance, members of the cast or technical staff discuss the play with the group.

Informal adult education takes place in the shopping malls of southern California. Shopping center developers and management are becoming increasingly enlightened about the use of their space for arts events. They see the malls as the town squares of the latter twentieth century and in some cases are consciously constructing the space to play this role. Malls house temporary exhibitions of artists' work and many are the sites of performances. Although the mall areas are often less than perfect acoustically, they provide a place for people to view artistic products in an unintimidating atmosphere. Mime is effective in this type of setting, as are small musical ensembles. Puppetry captures the attention of children and adults. Other suitable locations where many adults gather are factories and large companies. Noon concerts are becoming increasingly popular in many metropolitan areas. Trade unions have traditionally supported the arts and may want to expand educational and recreational art programs for their members.

People integrate art into their daily lives and can acquire a natural acceptance of it through artist-in-residence programs and community arts organizations. A successful program of the New York State Council on the Arts had visual artists take up residence in vacant space in small towns in upstate New York. The artists were paid a salary, given materials and encouraged to assimilate into the towns. The program allowed for as much contact and dialogue as the artists wished to undertake in order to enhance understanding of the art forms produced by the artists and of art in general, and to strengthen the recognition of artists as active members of society.

The Inner City Cultural Center, a Los Angeles community arts organization, serves as a community center, cafe, art resource and historical library, performing arts space, and artistic educator within its community. It owns its own building and manages rental property in adjacent space, and it has plans to spruce up the facades of this income property as well as to convert a nearby alley to a mall-walkway-performing area. The organization intends to strengthen its role as a community focal point as well as an artistic center, and the physical renovation helps economic development in the area by revitalizing an inner-city environment.

The California Department of Transportation (CALTRANS) recently initiated an Art on Highways program. Over $100,000 has been earmarked for the Los Angeles district office to contract with an east Los Angeles mural organization to design and produce ten murals on or near the city's highways. The goal of the program is more than decorative: it hopes to place artistic products in areas accessible to a great number of people, using art forms that are representative of a cultural element of the Los Angeles community and suited to a variety of locations.

The Purchase Process and Price

Once informed of the availability of the product, educated to the value of it, and stimulated to purchase it, the consumer must go through a purchase process to acquire it. If either the purchase process appears difficult or the cost of the product prohibitive, the consumer may be inclined to do without the product. By contrast, both price and purchase process can represent attention-getting marketing devices which aid the sale of the product and may even be the initial stimulus for getting the consumer interested.

The Theatre Development Fund set up a ticket booth (TKTS) in New York's theater district and later in lower Manhattan. Theater producers send their unsold tickets to the booth for sale on the day of the performance at half price. This innovative approach met with much opposition at first, but since has been credited with contributing significantly to the growth of Broadway audiences.[3] TKTS has the special benefit of catering to a wide variety of audiences, both tourist and local, who wish to see a live performance but not necessarily a hit show. In addition, TKTS has returned $17 million to New York theater producers which conceivably would have been lost otherwise.

The Ford Foundation financed the New York TKTS in its early stages. In Los Angeles (as in other cities), funding could be obtained either through foundation support or perhaps in combination with the state arts council or NEA grants. Operating expenses could be offset with a ticket surcharge of fifty cents to one dollar as in New York.

Perhaps one of the most difficult aspects of the project in Los Angeles (and other automobile-oriented cities) would be the development of a locational strategy for the ticket booth(s). Because of the enormous spread of the city, more than one location having heavy foot traffic (a rarity in Los Angeles) would in all likelihood be necessary to generate enough demand to adequately serve the concentration of performing arts activities in the downtown, Hollywood and Westwood/Century City areas. A computerized network tying all of the sites and the arts institutions may be needed. Perhaps the selection of a pilot site would be useful before operating other TKTS booths in Los Angeles to provide information helpful in planning further development.

Tickets to performing arts events are increasingly sold at retail stores. A food chain in Minneapolis sells tickets for the Guthrie Theatre. A grocery store is an excellent outlet for the attraction of a new and diverse audience who may have intended only to purchase groceries. With proper advertising and promotion at the store, this type of consumer could be stimulated to purchase an artistic product of which he or she was not aware. The store benefits from the informed arts product purchaser who had to enter the store to purchase tickets. A computerized ticket sales company handles the major portion of San Francisco's ticket sales. Known as BASS, the Bay Area Seating Service, this organization operates from retail record stores. Once again, record stores reap ancillary benefits from housing the ticket seller. BASS gets publicity as the primary ticket seller for a variety of arts and other events.

Some organizations are investigating the possibility of voucher ticket sales in which the consumer purchases a block of tickets to a variety of events presented by many different arts organization. The consumer can thereby sample a potpourri of events without standing in a multitude of box office lines, and receives a price discount on the voucher packet. New York has a voucher system initiated by the Theatre Development Fund, the same organization that sponsors TKTS, as does San Francisco through the Performing Arts Services (PAS), a nonprofit service organization which sells vouchers to selected groups. PAS screens the people who are eligible for vouchers: the audience it is trying to reach includes senior citizens or retired persons, physically disabled persons (non-senior citizens), vocational or high school students, elementary, secondary or vocational school teachers, professional artists, union members, non-union clerical workers, and community service program employees or participants. Each voucher ticket costs a dollar and up to ten tickets can be purchased in a six-month period. The purchaser is sent a calendar of events with information about transportation, seating information and redemption for specific performances of the 150 participating performing arts organizations.

The voucher application form also serves as a market research tool. It queries the applicant about age, sex, education level and the type of artistic events the consumer has attended in the past three months. The sponsor uses this computer-oriented data to get to know its collective audience better and to inform its member performing groups of the makeup of their audiences.

PAS is intended to be a marketing tool for member peforming groups. These arts organizations receive mailing lists of voucher holders, free publicity through the calendar of events and the directory of member groups which each voucher holder receives. Much word-of-mouth publicity as well as written communication about the groups will be generated by and for voucher holders. According to The Ticket Voucher Program description generated by the Performing Arts Services, voucher systems have stimulated such marketing tools as "group advertising" and " 'arts lines' that give phone messages about voucher program events throughout the Bay Area." Thus, PAS is an organization which has put into effect many of the suggestions outlined above to encourage people to try a new artistic product.

Convenience of Product

The fourth and final step in the process of enlarging the audience for artistic products involves making the product accessible to that audience. Buildings need to have clearly lighted, properly placed signs to get attention. Access roads need to be marked and maps provided to indicate the physical location of an arts organization or product. As simplistic as this idea may seem, it is extremely helpful and important. In addition, arts organizations should consider providing transportation to arts events, possibly including it as part of the total artistic event. The Hollywood Bowl series of the Los Angeles Philharmonic was faced by a difficult parking situation. The arts organization worked with city authorities and the Southern California Rapid Transit District (RTD) to facilitate access to the events. A large fleet of city buses was chartered to run from a number of locations around the Los Angeles area, charging a reasonable fee of fifty cents a ride to take patrons to the Hollywood Bowl. Bus tickets were sold along with event tickets. Riding the bus became part of the enjoyment of the evening. By using a difficult situation to its fullest advantage, a problem was resolved effectively. Recently the San Diego Opera Guild sponsored a successful fundraising association event which chartered a train from Los Angeles to San Diego for an opera starring Beverly Sills. Just as the RTD receives ancillary benefits for carrying Hollywood Bowl patrons safely and comfortably, the train company similarly has an opportunity to build its clientele.

The event can be taken to the audience as well as the audience to the event. The Los Angeles Philharmonic Minority Youth Orchestra presents concerts in the neighborhoods of its young members. The youth program, which provides private training with the members of the philharmonic, is designed to broaden the horizons of all involved: students, orchestra members, parents and community members.

Conclusion

There are many marketing options from which art producers can choose to increase their audiences. The potential consumer needs to be informed of the products available by a variety of media, educated to desire the product, given a choice of purchase locations and price options, and made to feel that the product is accessible. If arts organizations can present their artistic products effectively to the public, a larger audience will emerge and will contribute to the economic as well as cultural revitalization of our cities.

Footnotes

[1] For an excellent, in-depth treatment of the interplay of the arts and education, see David Rockefeller, Jr., *Coming to Our Senses*, (New York: McGraw-Hill, 1977).

[2] Dan Sullivan, "A Tree Grows in Los Angeles," *Los Angeles Times*, September 25, 1977, p. 46.

[3] Walter Kerr, "TKTS: Giving Broadway a Future," *New York Times*, October 1977.

3.8
Organizing the Finances of the Arts: An Overview

If the arts are to play their hoped-for role in the economy and culture of our cities, access to the arts must be broadly available to the public. This requires a fundamental rethinking about economic support of the arts and the responsibility that government and business bear toward artistic enterprise. While many of the traditional terms of economic analysis are usefully applied to arts organizations, others need revision. Some new insights on the financing of artistic endeavors can be provided by employing a supply/demand approach that is appropriate to the arts and, in addition, by applying the concept of public service budgeting. The result allows a new way of viewing and understanding the role that government and private groups should take as partners in financing the arts.

The Multi-Market Structure of the Arts

Arts organizations typically offer three interrelated classes of products and services. First, multiple products are associated with a single performance. The Founders Circle patron has a different experience than does the customer in the last row of the third balcony. The price scaling of the house is a simple manifestation of this multiplicity. Correspondingly in the visual arts, a corporate evening at the Treasures of Tutankhamun is a different experience than that of a viewer who stands in line for hours waiting for a chance to get inside. Second, many arts organizations provide a variety of merchandise which is somehow related to its image of mission. Museums are often more developed in this domain than are the performing arts. All products showing the affiliation of the patron to the arts event or organization are in this class, from T-shirts and tote bags to expensive recreations of ancient Egyptian jewelry. The demand for these products is highly dependent upon the market for the artistic output of the organization. Price for these products is more understandable in terms of the character of the arts organization than in terms of the price of somewhat comparable items distributed through other channels. The third class of products and services deals with the "market" of grants and contributions. For all not-for-profit, tax-exempt [501 (c) (3)] arts organizations, this represents a legislatively-created market wherein the government provides indirect encouragement for individual and corporate consumers to "exchange" with the arts for what economists sometimes call the "psychic" value of the arts.

Arts organizations are created for aesthetic purposes. The accomplishment of their artistic mission is the primary reason the government grants them not-for-profit status. To continue pursuing an artistic mission, the organization must maintain financial solvency. The financial reality an arts organization faces is simply that in the long run, the total revenue it receives from delivering the three classes of products and services must exceed its total expenses.

In order for the management of an arts organization to deal adequately with the problem of long-term financial stability, the degree of interdependence of the markets for the three classes of products and services must be recognized. For example, consider the issues involved in establishing a price for a performing arts organization's most expensive seats. The Founders Circle of almost every major performing arts group is fully subscribed. If considered independently of all other exchanges, the point of revenue maximization would be found by increasing prices until the increase in revenue per subscription was balanced by the drop in revenue due to a decreasing number of subscriptions. Considering the broader class of performance-related exchanges, an arts organization may wish to fully subscribe the Founders Circle, even at a price less than that indicated by the revenue maximization procedure, in order to minimize unauthorized migration from less expensive seats to the Founders Circle.[1] Considering other interdependent classes of products and services, the organization might investigate such questions as: "How do increases in the price of the most expensive seats impact the contributions in excess of ticket price from that group of subscribers?" An arts manager need not make these complex pricing decisions on the basis of conjecture. In most arts organizations some relevant data are available or could be gathered. The point is that revenue decisions concerning products in one market have implications for revenues in other markets.

Interrelated Sectors

The multiple exchanges between an arts organization and its publics are complex and interdependent. The complexity at the micro level of an individual arts organization is mirrored at the macro level by the exchanges among sectors of the economy.

In considering the arts within the mixed economic system that we have in the United States, we need to be concerned with the market for exchanges among four sectors: (1) government, (2) for-profit enterprises, (3) the not-for-profit sector, and (4) the consumer. *Government* gets its wealth through taxation of all sources of revenue—land, capital assets and wages. It has a most elaborate, guaranteed and enforced cash flow system. *For-profit enterprises* encompass those enterprises which organize to respond to the rules of the economic market. Enterprises which profit tend to survive, while others do not. The *not-for-profit sector* is used here in the narrow sense to include just those organizations granted tax-exempt status by the federal government. This is the government's licensing mechanism which admits qualifying organizations to full competition in a market of exchanges involving grants and contributions. The *consumers* in this market are individuals, foundations, corporations and governments at all levels—when they allocate their resources to the arts or other not-for-profit organizations.

An expanded set of rules, compared with those of the economic market, apply to the exchanges with not-for-profit organizations. In many ways these rules are closer to the ideal of free enterprise than are the rules governing the for-profit sector. As a consumer one may decide how much to allocate to the not-for-profit market, although government has imposed some rarely reached ceilings. One may decide with whom to exchange in the classes of general charitable, scientific, educational, public service, and arts and cultural organizations. These are the broadest of latitudes. Gone are the restrictive requirements of resource allocation in the profit sector. In the profit sector the guiding rule, though often ignored, is to seek to maximize profits. This is the generic mission and guiding direction of for-profit enterprises. The tastes and values of people and corporations are much broader than that which can be rationalized in terms of the unidimensional criterion of dollar profits.

Here it is good to note that the classic "rational economic man" really thinks in one dimension. "Psychologic man" (if one may counterpose another facet of man) thinks and feels in many dimensions and "exchanges" with the environment across all of those dimensions. A genuine free enterprise system would certainly enfranchise as many exchanges in as many ways as possible. The very broadest class of exchanges would certainly include the "psychologic man's" many dimensions of exchanges as well as the "economic man's" one dimension of exchange. To assert that the free enterprise system is synonymous only with the organization of the profit sector is to narrow the concept of free enterprise. The market exchanges are limited. Government first knocks out what it calls "illegal" exchanges. Among the legal exchanges which remain are transactions which in some degree run counter to the rules of the economic market. Government then says, here is a set of organizations whose not-for-profit mission should be the primary determiner of their direction. They are free to proceed, *if* they can acquire sufficient resources from the exchanges they make.

Most visual and performing arts have a consumable product of some sort and consequently compete for resources with the profit sector. The profit sector may respond that *its* rules should govern. That simply is not true in law or in fact.

The facts are borne out by a careful look at the economists' demand curve. In many cases, government is hampering the ability of the arts to exchange for all of the resources implied by the demand curve. We need to go back to the simple demand curve to see the nature of the resource problem of the arts.

A New View of the Demand Curve

Figure 2 presents a traditional economic display. *Price per unit* is the ordinate and *quantity demanded* is the abscissa. The chart gives an approximate representation of how demand changes with price per unit. When the price is low, as indicated by p_1, the quantity demanded is high, as indicated by q_1. As the quantity available decreases to q_2, the price consumers are willing to pay increases to p_2. Economists traditionally explain the rise in price that consumers are willing to pay by alluding to the scarcity of the good or service. The scarcity explanation is based on a model of man which asserts that he receives economic value not only from the consumption of goods and services, but also by excluding others from doing the same.[2]

However, the principle of scarcity runs counter to the principle of access to the arts. It is thus incumbent on the arts to consider richer explanations of this phenomenon. When the demand curve is looked at as representative of individual behavior, it suggests that different people are willing to pay different amounts for the consumption of the same good. If the arts are able to develop other ways to get consumers to express their full economic valuation of artistic goods and services, access to the arts can be more fully realized. To a certain extent all arts organizations are currently attempting to do this, but a more systematic investigation of the demand curve and its implications can clarify and assist these efforts.

The quantity of services an arts organization should deliver cannot be determined from the demand curve in the same way that it is for products in the profit sector.[3] Over a period of years, an arts organization experiments with the delivery of different quantities of services and experiences the resulting revenues and costs. The mission of the organization, the constraints of shared facilities and touring, the labor-management agreement, the diverse requirements for creative vitality of the artists, the responsiveness of local, regional and national communities, and a number of complex economic dependencies all enter into the deliberations concerning what quantity of services should be delivered. For convenience, and without loss of generality, we can let the quantity which results from the deliberations be denoted as q_1. From the demand curve we can tell that if the arts organization prices its services at p_1, all of that quantity will be consumed with resulting ticket revenues of $p_1 \times q_1 = r_1$. This revenue is represented by the sum of areas 3 and 5. A *public service budget* could be developed to determine what it should cost to deliver q_1 artistic services or goods when the organization is living up to its obligations and potentials and exchanging fairly with its members. The total costs could be such that the organization would have to charge price p_2 for all q_1 goods or services to recover all costs (i.e., $p_2 \times q_1$ = total cost).

It is necessary here to clarify the concept of *public service budget*. When the government grants an arts organization 501 (c) (3), not-for-profit, tax-exempt status, the standard formulas which produce equilibrium prices for goods in the marketplace do not apply in the same way. The cost is separated more completely from the revenue. Since a single marketplace does not account for all the revenues an arts organization may be able to garner, the marketplace does not provide cost guidelines for not-for-profit organizations to the same extent as it does for for-profit enterprises.

Public Service Budgets

Interesting and appropriate cost guidelines for not-for-profit organizations are presented in *The Public Service Budget of Arts and Cultural Organizations: A Better Measure of Full Financial Disclosure*. The concept of public service budgets is introduced in the belief that:

> "The real measure of a nonprofit organization's effectiveness is not the bottom line of its financial statement, but the services it offers in relation to their costs. The books can always be balanced by reducing the quantity and quality of these services."[4]

A public service budget tries to assign costs to the services the organization should be providing, "not in the best of all possible worlds, but as (the organization) ought to be in this world, if it were functioning at its normal and natural rate and living up to its obligations and opportunities."[5] Many arts organizations devour the resources they need to provide services. In order to meet budget demands, they postpone repairs and the physical plant deteriorates. Museums are forced to curtail their viewing hours. The American Ballet Theatre felt compelled to sell its Chagall sets. As stated in *The Public Service Budget:*

> . . . the factor of invisible erosion can be costed out . . . in specific cases dollar figures can be put on activities which a reasonable and balanced scale of operation could require, but which at present are not being

Figure 2: Division of Cost Responsibilities

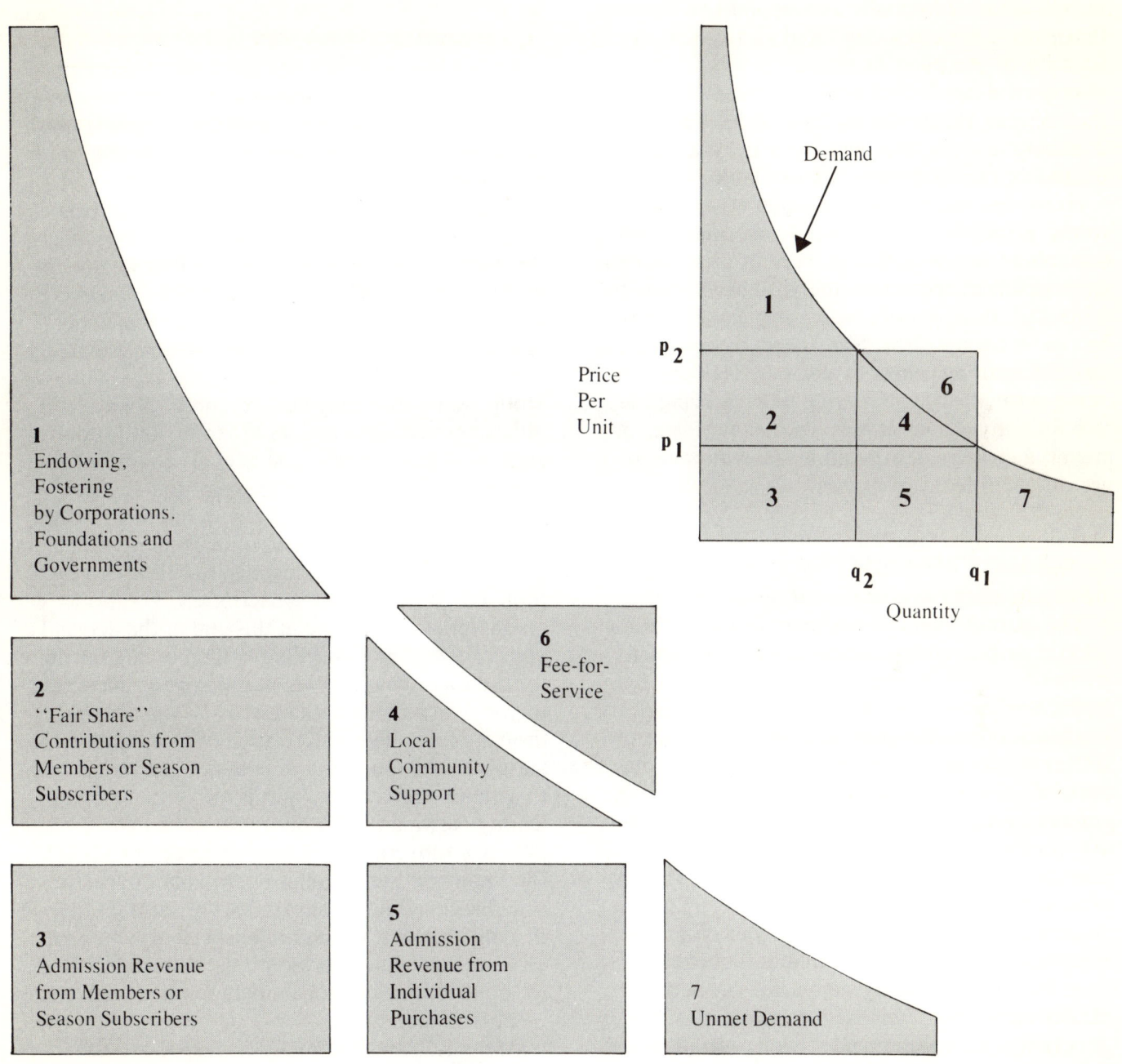

set in motion because of immediate budget limitations.[6]

While accepted financial records should be kept for reporting, public service budgets are much better suited for planning. They help an organization to see more clearly what is being and/or should be done and what that is and/or should be costing.

The public service budget determines the cost required to deliver q_1. There are then seven areas of cost responsibility, represented diagramatically in Figure 2. Area 7 represents unmet demand. Even at price p_1, arts organizations will exclude some people who would attend if there was more quantity available and at a lower price. The extent to which even this level of exclusivity is tolerable in a democratic society is not known. However, when the quantity of goods or services delivered by an arts organization is determined in line with the parameters of a public service budget rather than through the price-scarcity relation, residual exclusivity is greatly reduced.

At price p_2 and quantity q_2, services would be delivered according to the demand curve. The effect of pricing at p_1 is the delivery of $q_1 - q_2$ additional services. The cost of these additional services is shared between area 4 and area 6. Area 4 is discussed below. Area 6 is the government subsidy associated with the delivery of arts goods or services which could not otherwise be afforded by the public. It represents the *fee-for-public-service* cost, which must go with any claim by government that it is assuring access to the arts.[7] This does not represent endowing, fostering or preserving the arts for future generations. To endow, foster or preserve, government at all levels will have to provide additional resources.

Fees-for-Public-Service

Persuading government at all levels first to recognize and then to implement its fee-for-public-service responsibility is extremely important to an arts organization. An example of effective municipal responsibility is the Los Angeles Shakespeare Festival, which has survived largely because of fee-for-public-service monies. It produces a play in each of fifteen city parks, one park in each city council district. The fifteen city park productions are matched with fifteen county park productions. For these public services (and the Ford Theatre production) the festival received (in 1976) $30,000 in cash from the city, $13,500 in cash from the county, and $208,000 in "in-kind" contributions from the city and county combined. The necessity of gaining fee-for-public-service revenue is obvious to organizations with no admission revenue, but is just as necessary for other arts organizations. Without such revenue, arts organizations are placed at a competitive disadvantage in gaining revenue from other sources of income discussed below. Governments must also realize that unless they respond to the legitimate fee-for-public-service requests of arts organizations which do charge admission, more and more arts organizations might appropriately conclude that they should drop their admission charges in order to get such revenues.

Good management sense shows us the danger of relying too heavily on a single source of revenue.

Community Support

Area 4 is the domain of community level support. At price p_1 there are people in the community who would be willing to pay more for the goods and services they receive from an arts organization. In Los Angeles, Shakespeare's Angels is the organization the Shakespeare Festival established to raise these funds from the community. As long as the costs of area 6 are picked up by the government, such organizations can compete effectively with all other pulls on the community members' resources. Arts support groups can compete freely and effectively for community resources with groups supporting medical research, private and public universities, and all other 501 (c) (3) organizations as long as reasonable goals can be established to determine their share of the costs.

The two areas associated with admission revenues are 3 and 5. For arts organizations which produce a season, it is reasonable to tie area 3 to the revenues from season subscription. The primary characteristic of people at this end of the demand curve is that they are often willing to pay far more for their association with an arts organization than the price of a block of tickets. This is an accurate, though incomplete, description of most season subscribers. The multitude of benefits associated with this major source of support is well articulated by Danny Newman in his book, *Subscribe Now!*[8] Not only are subscriptions a major source of cash for financing the ongoing operations of an arts organization, but the subscribers are also the source of contributions which are associated with area 2. This area could represent the "fair share" goal for contributions of subscribers to the overall costs of operations.

Areas 1, 2, and 3 formally correspond to people who would be willing to pay prices greater than, or equal to, p_2 for the goods and services of an arts organization. While this certainly includes wealthy individuals in the community, it is worthwhile to recognize that great wealth has shifted to include the collectivities (i.e. corporations, foundations and governments). Arts organizations need to retrieve revenues from these collectivities in order to achieve a financially stable revenue balance. Since area 2 is already associated with

84

individuals, it is somewhat arbitrary but useful to associate area 1 with the collectivities. This is the area in which governments express their desires to endow, foster or preserve the arts above and beyond their fee-for-public-service obligations. This is the area in which corporations and foundations can exhibit their sense of social responsibility—their desire to build the quality of life in their communities—as well as the judgment that the value associated with support of the arts is greater than the costs incurred. This is where local governments should return to the arts a share of hotel taxes equal to the role of the arts in attracting visitors and their capital to the city.

Area 5 represents the revenue from individual ticket sales. The individual ticket purchasers are the pool from which the vast majority of future season subscribers are drawn. An unsold ticket represents a loss to the public and to the arts organization.

An Illustrative Budget

If we ignore the impact of merchandising revenues, we can illustrate how this division of cost responsibility can be used by an arts organization in setting financial goals.[9] Take, for example, the case of a major resident theater producing five plays a year. Let us say it has a 555-seat house which is around 90 percent full for forty-eight performances of each play. Let us assume the average ticket price is ten dollars and at that price the theater covers 50 percent of its costs from admission revenues. If we know that 70 percent of the attendance at each performance comes from season subscribers and 30 percent comes from individual sales, we can set approximate goals for each area in Table 11.

We can consider area 3 to be season sales. Subscription costs for five plays are fifty dollars and at 90 percent capacity there are 350 subscribers at

Table 11: Using the Model to Set Goals—A Theater Example

Area	Source of Revenue	Reason		Goal at 90% (000's)		Goal at 99% (000's)
1	Foundations Corporations Governments	Fostering, endowing and preserving the arts	min	$180	min	$162
2	Season subscribers and wealthy individuals	Fair share contributions		840		756
3	Season subscribers	Subscription to five plays		840		924
4	Individual ticket purchasers	Fair share contributions	max	180	max	162
5	Individual ticket purchasers	Admission		360		396
6	City, county, state and federal governments	Fee-for-public-service	min	180	min	162
7	Unmet demand			0		0
	Approximate gross revenue			$2,580		$2,562
	Surplus (deficit) of revenue over total operating expenses			180		162
	Surplus (deficit) as a proportion of total operating expenses			.075		.068

each of the forty-eight performances. These 16,800 subscribers produce $840,000 in attendance revenues. Because we assumed that 50 percent of costs were covered by admission revenues, area 2 is equal to area 3. The theatre should try to raise another $840,000 from season subscribers and other wealthy individuals in the community.

On the average, 150 individual admissions are purchased for each performance. Over the forty-eight performances of five plays this amounts to 36,000 individuals. This number would undoubtedly contain some repeats. But while this group is in the minority at any single performance, in total it is much larger than the season subscription group—in fact, almost twice as large. A theater cannot expect this group to contribute as heavily as the season subscribers, but less than a five dollar contribution per attendance will meet the maximum goal of $180,000 for area 4.

Because the demand curve is negatively sloping, area 6 is somewhat larger than area 4. This theater should seek a minimum of $180,000 from government at all levels as the fee-for-public-service which allows for wider public access. The contributions of individual ticket purchasers and the government's fee-for-public-service total $360,000—matching the revenues from individual sales.

The standard economic rationale holds that for an arts organization to be economically worthy of either public or private support, area 1 must be larger than area 6. Although this model does not rely fundamentally on this rationale, for strategic purposes we can set area 1 to be at least as large as area 6. However, there is every reason to guess that area 1 is actually considerably larger than area 6. This indicates the theater in this example should seek a bare minimum of $180,000 from corporations, foundations and governments to endow, foster and preserve the arts.

While this completes the example for a 90 percent full house, we can ask how the picture changes if the theater increases its audience to 99 percent capacity. This kind of expansion has a minimum cost associated with it since there is no increase in the number of performances. Ignoring the minor costs associated with the production of more printed programs and possibly slightly greater maintenance services, we can see how cost responsibilities are now divided among the areas.

If there is uniform expansion of season and individual sales, the number of subscribers increases to 385 per performance. This results in $924,000 in subscription revenue. Individual sales are up to 165 per performance, leading to $396,000 in revenues. This means attendance revenues total $1,320,000 or 55 percent of total operating costs ($2,400,000). The total cost rectangle allocates 70 percent of the operating deficit to season subscribers ($756,000), which reduces the goal for their contribution by $86,000. A maximum of 15 percent of the deficit is the goal set for contributions of individual ticket purchasers. This indicates their fair share contribution is reduced to $162,000 at a maximum, or just over four dollars per attendance. The fee-for-public-service is a minimum of $162,000, with an equal minimum contribution from corporations, foundations and governments. These latter categories should be urged to go beyond minimum contributions, since at the minimum the theater will experience an $18,000 reduction in gross revenue. All of these goals and comparisons are summarized in Table 11.

As clear as the cost responsibilities appear to be in this portrayal, there still exists fundamental confusion. The federal and state governments created, through legislation, all the markets of exchange except ticket revenues. This rationale has two foci. For the possessors of wealth, it gives them a greater degree of control over the allocation of their resources. Instead of giving some revenues to the government, they can direct those revenues to efforts they wish to support. On the government's side, the legislation provides an excuse. Governments usually can claim that they are providing tax incentives for private sources of wealth to fund these activities. Such a claim can be offered only to the extent that private wealth accomplishes public goals. But private wealth rarely provides access to the arts. Governments can provide such access by living up to their fee-for-public-service responsibility. The tax laws provide no excuse for governments to ignore this responsibility.

There is one fascinating possibility which arises when all parties involved in providing resources for the arts live up to their respective responsibilities. If the revenues associated with areas 1 through 6 are returned to the arts organization, they might possibly make a profit. Being a not-for-profit organization means that no person can pocket this surplus. It will be turned into resources the arts organization can use for increasing access and for improving quality, proving there is no incompatibility between democracy and high artistic standards.

Policy Implications

Much of the product of nonprofit arts organizations represents a public service, the cost of which may or may not be covered by a government contract or grant. Indeed, some part of the funding which comes in the form of a grant may actually be a now-disguised fee payment for such public service, although this is not recognized either by the organization or the granting agency. Thus, governments need to differentiate their fee-for-public-service contributions from those grants which are meant to endow, foster or preserve. When government contracts for a concert in a prison or a hospital, this exchange is on a fee-for-public-service basis but it does not endow the orchestra. Yet, at least a portion of the regular season of a performance organization is a public service, and governments cannot fulfill their fee-for-public-service responsibilities to the arts simply by contracting for "run out" concerts or other special services. More study is needed in order to be able to estimate this fee component in arts organizations which do not have performance seasons and subscription sales.

Although the aesthetic mission of an arts organization sets its basic direction, organizational management must recognize the multi-market exchange system in which arts activities take place. Management needs to understand the complex interrelationships and interdependencies among these submarkets and to adopt financial plans which make reasonable demands for revenues from each identified market.

Footnotes

[1] Cheung, S. N. S., "Why are better seats underpriced?" *Economic Inquiry*, XV, 513–533, October, 1977.

[2] A reviewer of a draft of this chapter pointed out that the high price of scarce goods does not necessarily result from the desire to exclude others from consumption; rather, the widespread desire to consume something which is scarce leads to its being rationed among a few using price as a basis, and even if wealth were distributed uniformly, scarce items would be higher in price than items that are in plentiful supply. The reviewer conceded, however, that there is perhaps some truth to the idea of the desire to exclude, especially as it applies to the arts, as in the case of "limited editions" of art works or signed versus unsigned lithographs. Space does not permit further development of the topic of the historic, exclusionary relation between art and wealth. The interested reader may refer to: Cooper, L. G., "Implications of the Historic Relations between Art and Wealth." Working paper. Study Center for Cultural Policy and Management in the Arts. Graduate School of Management, University of California, Los Angeles, 1978.

[3] The proper generalization of the single market equilibrium pricing procedure for determining the quantity of products and services of an arts organization would be enormously complex. If there were n_1 products associated with performance, n_2 products associated with merchandizing and n_3 products associated with grants and contributions, then an $(n_1 + n_2 + n_3 + 1)$ dimensional space would be associated with the demand. The problem would then be to find a vector of quantities $(q_1^*, q_2^*, \ldots q^*_{n_1 + n_2 + n_3})$ which corresponds to a vector of prices for products $(p_1^*, p_2^*, \ldots p^*_{n_1 + n_2 + n_3})$ such that total revenue $\left(\sum_{i=1}^{n_1 + n_2 + n_3} p_i^* \times q_i^* \right)$ was maximized. Such an endeavor is beyond the current capability of equilibrium pricing techniques. Further, the cost of gathering the needed information is so high that such an analysis is extremely unlikely to be carried out in the foreseeable future.

[4] Farrell, J., Larrabee, E., and Nelson, C. A., *The Public Service Budget of Arts and Cultural Organizations: A Better Measure of Full Financial Need*. (New York: Associated Councils of the Arts, 1976), p. 2.

[5] Ibid, p. 5.

[6] Ibid, pp. 4–5.

[7] There is a much more complex explanation which is minutely more accurate, but leads to the same conclusion for all practical purposes. It deals with the fact that the delivery of q_2 goods or services might cost more than the sum of area 2 and 3. Figure 2 allocates fixed and variable costs uniformly over each unit of quantity. The reality of most arts organizations is a high cost to open the doors and a relatively lower cost of each additional performance. Until our ability to measure demand increases dramatically, the difference is not worth worrying about.

[8] Newman, D., *Subscribe Now!*, (New York: Theatre Communications Group, 1977).

[9] Obviously, not all arts organizations have a season. But balanced analogies to the proposed revenue pattern may be developed for less traditional arts organizations.

3.9
Federal Government Programs in the Arts, and Their Possible Expansion

Many federal government programs currently provide financial assistance for the arts, normally under legislation with very broad purposes, such as generating employment or fostering education. In these cases, governments or organizations seeking assistance for the arts find themselves in competition with other agencies which have designed programs geared more directly to the objectives of the legislation (such as jobs through public works construction). Still, such federal programs have opened up significant opportunities for public support of the arts. What is particularly important is that by encompassing the arts in these programs, there is now open recognition of the many ways in which the arts can contribute to public purposes.

Study of arts organizations in Los Angeles and of the applications of local governments for financial assistance from the federal government under these programs suggests that knowledge about how such programs might be employed to advance the arts is, as yet, very limited. A review of the programs suggests further possibilities for the arts, and particularly for community arts organizations, which are outlined in the sections that follow, covering the more important of the programs (from the standpoint of the arts).

Department of Commerce— Economic Development Administration

Public Works Impact Projects

Public Works Impact Projects are mandated by the Public Works and Economic Development Act of 1965. Funds are awarded to states and local subdivisions, Indian tribes and private or public nonprofit organizations representing a redevelopment area or economic development center. The federal government provides 80 percent financing of the project, which must demonstrate its positive impact upon the economic development of the community. This program is of special significance for the arts since neighborhood arts organizations, which are for the most part nonprofit and often located in redevelopment areas, could on their own initiative launch a drive to secure a community arts center in their locale. As with CETA programs, neighborhood arts organizations would have to demonstrate a public need and at the same time develop an argument as to how the arts would have an effect on the economic revitalization of the affected redevelopment area. This program would be most appropriate in low-income and minority communities, since most redevelopment areas have significant concentrations of these populations.

State and Local Economic Planning Grants

State and Local Economic Planning Grants are also mandated by the Public Works and Economic Development Act of 1965. The objectives of this program are to assist state and local governments to undertake an economic planning process which can be coordinated with other substate planning activities.

Comprehensive Economic Development Strategy

Comprehensive Economic Development Strategy (CEDS) is a demonstration program being conducted in thirty-seven places. It has introduced an economic development packaging concept regarding program decisions. The concept is place-oriented rather than project-oriented. The strategy ideally includes consideration of all resources (local, state, federal and private) which are directed to priority-ranked projects that suit development objectives.

For example, in Memphis, Tennessee a master plan is under study to redevelop historic Beale Street, that cradle of musical acclaim, as a new focal point in the downtown. An integral part of the plan extends a commercial corridor beyond the historic district to link pedestrian movement with the unkempt, but elegant, Orpheum Theater. As a result the Orpheum, which has recently been reactivated for low-budget concert performances, has a good chance of being restored under a continuing effort of economic and physical revitalization.

Another example of cultural-commercial ties is in San Antonio, Texas. There CEDS is linked to the city's Urban Development Action Grant (UDAG) economic development component. In one instance a UDAG project is being developed that will link the Alamo and the city's unique Riverwalk with a grade-separated pedestrian corridor. The corridor is being considered to link the River- that will offer shopping and dining opportunities to passersby. A similar proposal for a pedestrian corridor is being considered for linking the Riverwalk with the old Lone Star Brewery that was recently converted into a museum. These new axes will give better articulation to the downtown and open up pedestrian traffic along the Riverwalk system to more cultural and commercial opportunities. The cultural facilities have been recognized as important people attractors in planning for downtown revitalization.

CEDS has introduced a place-oriented approach in EDA decision making. The ability to receive EDA funding for cultural facilities can be improved by having these projects as part of a total development plan as presented in a CEDS.

Department of Housing and Urban Development— Housing and Community Development

Community Development Block Grants

The Housing and Community Development Act of 1974 provides for Housing and Community Development Block Grants to states and local governments for community development projects. The purpose of this program is to encourage housing and community development in a coordinated manner. The grants provide for the expansion of community services, particularly for individuals of low and moderate income. Thus, they can be used for the revitalization of deteriorating areas.

Funds are provided to city and county governments based on a formula. Cultural and arts facilities are eligible to receive assistance only if they are "neighborhood facilities," defined as facilities which provide health, social, recreational or similar community services primarily for the neighborhood service area.

Special arts facilities for a city are excluded, but monies can be used for neighborhood centers, senior centers, recreation and park facilities, and centers for the handicapped, which may include performance space, studio and workshop facilities. A redevelopment project consisting of reconstruction of housing and facilities for a community center has the greatest potential for funding. Construction funds must be used for publicly owned facilities; however, they may be used for rehabilitation of privately owned structures provided they are part of a local public development project.

Department of Health, Education and Welfare—U.S. Office of Education

Educationally Deprived Children

Title IV-C of the Elementary and Secondary Education Act (as amended by Public Law 95-961) provides formula grants to state education agencies to help local education agencies to "improve their educational practices". Wide latitude is given to the states to develop their own funding priorities. Programs have often included cultural components and frequently have addressed the problems of children with special needs, e.g., educationally deprived, gifted and talented, and physically handicapped. Schools are encouraged to expand educational activities beyond school buildings and coordination with the programs of community arts organizations is possible.

Emergency School Aid Special Arts Projects

Project grants of up to $100,000 are made to organizations with statewide education responsibilities to support arts education projects. These are limited to desegregated elementary and secondary schools using the arts as a vehicle for interracial and intercultural communication and understanding. Only one of the Special Arts Projects Grants is made per state.

Emergency School Aid Act: Educational Television and Radio

Grants are made to public or private nonprofit agencies to develop radio and television programs which serve to overcome minority group isolation due to educational disadvantage, as in the case of the Special Arts Projects. Applicant organizations must have demonstrated expertise in television and radio programming.

Ethnic Heritage Studies Program

This program is authorized by the Education Amendments of 1972. Proposed projects must have multi-ethnic impact; that is, impact beyond a single ethnic group. No matching requirement is involved. Eligible applicants for the program include public or private nonprofit educational agencies, institutions or ethnic organizations. Project grants are used to provide students with an opportunity to learn about their own cultural heritage and the contributions of other ethnic groups to the nation. Proposed programs must include plans for at least one of the following three activities: (1) development of curriculum materials; (2) dissemination of such materials; (3) provisions for training persons to use these materials. In addition, each project must provide plans for cooperation with organizations having a special interest in the ethnic group under study.

These guidelines provide an opportunity for community arts organizations to develop materials that could be used in the schools and in their own arts education projects.

Community Education Projects

This program was authorized by the Special Projects provisions of the Education Amendments of 1974. Project grants are to meet educational, recreational or cultural needs of the community through the establishment of a community education program in cooperation with community groups. Funds can be used to train persons to plan and operate community education programs. Funds support the administration of community education programs rather than programming costs. Public or private nonprofit organizations are also eligible to receive grants to establish and maintain local community education programs.

State and local educational agencies are eligible to receive grants to establish and maintain local community education programs, while institutions of higher education are eligible for training grants. There are many artists, particularly in low income and minority areas, who are talented but who have not pursued a college education. Training grants to universities could be used to train these artists in the skills needed to operate a local arts education program. Perhaps some type of credential could be awarded upon completion of such a training course, enabling the individual to seek other arts-related employment.

Arts Education Program

As amended by Title III of the 1978 Amendments to the Elementary and Secondary Education Act, this program supports projects meeting community or statewide arts education needs. The revised guidelines designate public or private organizations as eligible applicants along with state and local educational agencies. The program's focus has shifted from supporting individual arts education projects with small grants (seventy-nine were made in 1978) to assisting state- or communitywide comprehensive projects with larger awards. It is estimated that $1.25 million will be available for this project in 1980. The Alliance for Arts Education, located in the Kennedy Center, is funded by the Office of Education to provide technical assistance and information to Arts Education Program applicants. Funds are used to develop, implement and improve arts education programs. Art forms to be addressed are dance, visual arts, music and drama. Funds may be used to reimburse arts groups for their assistance in the planning and development of such programs.

National Endowment for the Arts

The National Endowment for the Arts (NEA) has spearheaded federal involvement in the arts. The NEA was created as an independent federal agency in 1965 to assist the development of the country's cultural resources. In recent years, the NEA's level of spending has been over $100 million. The total fiscal year appropriation for 1979 was $149.4 million.

Expansion Arts

This program assists the arts of diverse cultural groups as well as communities in urban, suburban and rural areas. It supports neighborhood and community arts organizations directed by professionals. Program funds have also been used to provide arts services for traditionally excluded environments, such as hospitals and prisons, and to foster new and innovative art forms. The program has developed a new category, City Arts, to help municipal governments provide community arts projects with financial and technical assistance and to generate private funds for neighborhood efforts.

Design Arts Program

This is a multi-faceted program that provides financial assistance to both individuals and organizations. The individual grants include project fellowships for design students, entering professional designers fellowships, individual project fellowships for exceptionally talented individuals in pursuit of specific design, research or educational projects, and senior-level sabbatical fellowships. Grants are also made available to arts organizations and educational institutions for experimental and innovative design research projects. Under the Design Demonstration program, city agencies, neighborhood organizations and local arts groups are eligible for grants to support community design and planning projects, design competition, design assistance for arts facilities and the like. Design Communication grants are for increasing public awareness about the role and value of design or the consequences of design decisions. Archival and documentary activities are also eligible. All of the organizational grants are made available on a one-to-one matching basis to institutions with nonprofit tax-exempt status.

Office of Partnership

Funds are provided to officially designated state arts agencies. Matching grants are also available to state agencies for the development of community arts agencies.

The Office of Partnership also supports the Artists-in-Schools program which provides accomplished artists with the opportunity to help students develop their own artistic skills. Over the last few years, thousands of performing and visual artists have worked with millions of students under this program.

Strengthening the Federal Contribution to the Arts

A National Endowment for the Arts report, prepared after a review of the various federal government programs affecting the arts in the cities and submitted to the president's Urban and Regional Policy Group in October 1977, urged that "every federal government program designed to aid the cities and their residents should make systematic use of the arts." In order to implement this recommendation, the following actions were suggested:

"A Require a component on the arts in local plans and applications submitted for federal urban funds, especially for economic and physical development.

B State explicitly in federal laws and regulations that program funds should be used for arts activities and products that support program goals.

C Similarly, include the arts in urban research and development or pilot programs, and call upon arts expertise in conducting urban program evaluations.

D Require a showing of significant local private-public cooperation in federally supported arts components of urban programs.

E Provide federal subsidies for nonprofit jobs in the arts located in urban centers.

F Review guidelines and designs for urban construction and public works projects undertaken with federal funds to insure they enhance livability."

An overriding principle is that federal programs, taken together, should be broad enough in scope and flexible enough in administration to be significantly helpful in carrying out local cultural plans. The federal government has supposedly been moving in the direction of gearing its financial assistance to the declared needs of cities and other local entities as implemented through major block grants. It would be in the spirit of this general thrust for the more specialized federal programs and grants to equally help meet the variable local requirements in the arts.

Comprehensive Employment and Training Act (CETA)

What is desirable in this regard can best be specified by illustrating the changes needed in one federal program—CETA. Similar kinds of considerations arise in connection with other major federal programs as well.

While CETA funding has been of immeasurable

short-term value to many arts organizations, limitations and risks are inherent in the nature of this program. Size and duration of funding are dependent both upon the actions of Congress in appropriating money for CETA at the national level and the decisions of prime sponsors (including local legislative bodies) in allocating the available funds at the community level. By necessity, CETA projects are of limited duration, seldom funded for more than a year. Because CETA is primarily designed to provide employment to as many eligible persons as possible, funding for administration and supplies is limited. Furthermore, performance standards and contractual agreements require that high proportions of all CETA enrollees be "transitioned" to unsubsidized jobs during or at the end of the project year or other contract period. If arts organizations fail to meet these standards they may be defunded and, in any case, it is not likely that they will be refunded. Therefore, it remains essential to develop more permanent sources of both public and private employment for artists.

Both CETA and the (earlier) WPA primarily must be classified as job creation programs. The WPA differed from CETA in that it was administered by the federal government and its component arts programs were federal programs (although regional administrators, even under WPA, could play an important role). Those hired under the arts program—theater, music, art and writing projects—were drawn mainly from the relief rolls, but a certain percentage of employees were arts professionals.

It would be difficult to include a WPA-type program within the CETA framework because it violates the concept of decentralization—and decategorization—upon which CETA presumably is based. Prime sponsors strongly resist (though not always successfully) all efforts to mandate at the federal level the types of programs which must be implemented with CETA funds.

It is possible, at least in theory, to implement a national arts program under CETA. This type of program, however, does not fit easily into the general framework of the act—employment or training programs directed to the hard core unemployed or groups with special labor market handicaps (such as youths, migrant workers, or the elderly). It would be possible, of course, to amend the act to add unemployed and/or underemployed artists to the list of groups to be served. Department of Labor administrators, however, usually are not well versed in the specific problems of the arts or the particular needs of artists.

It would appear that separate legislation should be directed to employment in the arts (just as the youth unemployment problem is the subject of special legislation). Whether that program should be administered federally, or at the state or local level, is a matter of debate. There can also be argument over the question of whether the program should primarily be aimed at job creation (permanent or transitional), or should be, in effect, a national theater, e.g., one which employs established professionals. The WPA in a sense combined the two, but it is uncertain whether that is still possible in the context of American society today. The major consideration is that the arts have special requirements of their own. Consequently, it would be desirable if federal programs of significance to the arts would make special provisions and arrangements to assist this very special, and nationally important, set of activities.

National Direction for the Arts

The issue of funding, however important, should not overshadow the necessity of the development of a clear national direction for the arts. Despite the growth of federal involvement in the arts over the past few years, there remains a gap at the highest level of government regarding a national arts policy. The Federal Council on the Arts and the Humanities has been given a greater role than it previously fulfilled in coordinating federal cultural programs and making recommendations on national cultural policy issues. The question remains as to whether there is a need for an effective central body within the federal establishment that monitors overall federal arts participation and is in a position to propose a coherent policy framework.

Perhaps the most obvious place to begin a new thrust of recognition of the growing importance of the arts, and to provide for the development of national policy, is at the White House, the highest level of influence within the federal government. In order to achieve these ends, there should be created within the executive office of the president an office of cultural affairs (as recommended by the American Council for the Arts).

The National Endowment for the Arts and other federal agencies significantly involved with the arts can be expected to continue to play a vital role in the development of the arts through direct funding. They should, in fact, be seen as partners in the overall development of policy. Direct access for the arts within the White House—on an official basis—would add a currently missing ingredient.

3.10
Enhancement of Arts Employment through the Cooperation of Trade Unions and Employers

Because of their key position in the arts, unions can play a significant role in enhancing the strength of the arts within the economy. Currently, unions help to stabilize the industry and serve to control the labor market. Unions frequently have had to act as an adversary against employers and managers. Now, however, there are new possibilities for alliance and mutual aid. An important set of strategies for change to bolster the employment of artists involves cooperative efforts of trade unions and employers.

A New Approach to Collective Bargaining in Nonprofit Organizations

Unions and arts management could strengthen their arts organizations and thus enhance arts employment by uniting to participate in collective bargaining with funding sources. Before discussing this issue, the difference between profit and nonprofit organizations will be discussed in terms of collective bargaining.

Perhaps the most distinctive feature that sets apart the arts as a whole from other industries is the large role of nonprofit organizations. Since profit maximization is not of critical importance in the nonprofit performing arts, the criterion for determining the success of arts organizations for the most part is not the same as in the private sector, where the primary criterion is profit.

Management in both private (for-profit) and nonprofit arts is responsible for the operation of the organization. Unlike private industry, management in the nonprofit arts has little authority over the available funds. The latter is the obligation of the governing board or of other funding sources. In the private sector, a firm's management has the authority to raise prices in order to increase revenues (according to what the market can bear), an option which is generally unavailable to arts management. The division of revenues, the basis of traditional conflict between management and labor and one of the central elements involved in collective bargaining, is therefore not as large an issue in the nonprofit performing arts field.

As for bargaining power, performing arts organizations, unlike many other industries, cannot be operated by supervisory personnel during a strike. Performers have a high degree of bargaining power. The commercial sector and the large nonprofit organizations are highly unionized and a strike can completely paralyze the industry.

Many private employers maintain countervailing powers in collective bargaining. They can group together and lock out employees or they can form mutual aid pacts to pool profits when a union strikes a certain employer. Although it is not illegal for the nonprofit arts employer to lock his employees out or form a mutual aid pact, such practices are shunned in most instances.

Since it represents a nonprofit organization with constant financial problems, arts management often asks unions to reduce or even forego demands for increased wages. Understandably, union leaders claim that their members should not be asked to subsidize nonprofit organizations, since performing artists as a whole already experience fairly low wage levels. This is precisely the dilemma the performing arts confront—increased wage demands in the face of increased financial constraints.

Behind the bargaining process is the continued existence of last year's deficit and the certainty of one next year. Both sides of the bargaining table recognize the deficit and believe it to be the governing board's responsibility to erase it. However, the usual opportunities available to profit-making corporations to issue bonds or stocks to bring in new capital to meet financial needs are not available to nonprofit arts boards. They do not have the financial capacity or access to funds to match sufficiently ever-growing deficits, or "income gaps" as they have come to be known. In essence, the government and foundations must take on a larger role in subsidization—a task formerly performed by individual contributors.

As a result, future collective bargaining in the arts will probably not be between management on one side and the union on the other, but will more likely be management and unions on one side confronting the source of funding on the other.

Furthermore, if the source of funding is no longer the board of trustees, the board will be on the same side as management and the unions. The three parties then will determine what and how to bargain with government or its "proxy," foundations, corporations, or other sources of funds.

Michael Moskow (*Labor Relations in the Performing Arts,* 1969) maintains that the broadened support for performing arts organizations has implications for unions. He asserts that as arts organizations become more like "public organizations," unions will demand a greater role in decision making. For example, it is one thing if a manager tells a union leader that he cannot grant a wage increase because individual donations cannot cover it; however, it is quite another matter if the union leader is told that the increase is not possible because the organization has not been granted a sufficient level of government funds. Though the union leader has little control over fundraising from individuals, he could be encouraged to play a much larger role in obtaining government funds, increasing audience support, and perhaps even making financial contributions to the organization. Furthermore, the unionist in all likelihood would not be content with a simple denial of government funds, but would become an active party in seeking additional funds.

Needless to say, given increased government participation in the arts, this type of collective bargaining merits serious consideration as a viable alternative to existing collective bargaining practices. Numerous implications and possible consequences arise out of this alternative. While the issue warrants a full, in-depth study, certain elements can be briefly summarized:

1. Existing labor laws may have to be amended to allow cooperative bargaining. In their present form, cooperation between management and unions could possibly be seen as collusion.
2. Management, the union and the board would in effect be cooperators rather than adversaries.
3. There would be joint responsibility for the original proposals, for the implementation of the agreements reached, and the joint consequences of any of the provisions.
4. There would be much more emphasis on the artistic character and purposes of arts institutions than is possible today in the adversary type of collective bargaining.
5. The problems of jurisdictional disputes, stronger versus weaker unions, dividing a shrinking financial pie—some of the most troublesome issues in current negotiations—would be minimized or contained within manageable proportions.
6. There may be a greater possibility of management and unions working together to expand the artistic and financial potentialities of the institutions.
7. There may be introduced practical limitations on the right to strike, to close an institution or to reduce its operations or staff—all differing from the present perceptions by each side.
8. Arts institutions would become integrated into the cultural, social, and economic life of the community. The direction of the institution would become a public rather than a private concern.

Such a bargaining framework would help the public institution to meet educational and societal needs. Furthermore, the issue of state support (on the European model) would be more acceptable to the public and legislators. Consequently, the arts would become the concern of all the society and not just an interested few.[1]

Expansion of the Ninety-nine-Seat Waiver Plan

A different form of cooperation between management and the unions to enhance employment in the arts has been worked out by Actors Equity in what has become known as the Ninety-nine-Seat Waiver Plan. The union has encouraged additional employment opportunities for its members by waiving its own work rules in theaters of ninety-nine seats or less. The plan has been in effect in California since 1972 and, after a five-year trial period, was voted by Equity to continue indefinitely. Basically, work rules regarding work conditions, rehearsals, pay, etc., set by Equity to protect actors are waived, with actors in little theaters taking on the responsibilities of governing their own work en vironment. In effect, in certain situations and with some limitations the actor may work under any condition he may desire, regardless of the rules. The same is also true of management.

The Waiver Plan applies to theaters with seating facilities for ninety-nine people or less in the Los Angeles and San Francisco areas covered by the Los Angeles and San Francisco/Bay Area theater contracts. Equity stresses that it has not relinquished its jurisdiction in the area of ninety-nine-seat theaters, but has merely waived certain work rules. The premises of the waiver rest on the assumption that small theaters as a whole are not commercially viable or competitive with unionized theaters by today's economic standards.

The reasons for the growth of small theaters are numerous. Small theaters have been started by groups of actors wanting to practice their craft in order to "maintain shape." This is understandable considering that the unemployment rate for these artists consistently remains at the 75 percent to 80 percent level. Work in a small theater affords them the opportunity to practice and to gain professional experience. Some small theaters emphasize ensemble playing, while others may be interested in innovative and experimental works; still others may perform original works by local playwrights.

The economic situation of small theaters is precarious at best. Like established arts institutions, they too are subject to income gap. Prices for rent, utilities, printing and materials keep on increasing without corresponding increases in revenue. Comparatively speaking, however, small theaters are in worse financial condition because they do not have the diverse financial resources of larger institutions. There are very few circumstances when small theaters are profitable. A study of Los Angeles small theaters by Professor John Cauble of the UCLA Theater Arts Department concluded that even in situations where small theaters did not have to pay salaries, profitable productions were a rarity. Moreover, the individual actors who begin small theater groups may spend their own money to keep their enterprises functioning. If small theaters were subject to the work rules of the Los Angeles-San Francisco/Bay Area theater contracts, they would be unable to manage economically and in all likelihood would be nonexistent.

Actors are aware of the economic realities of working in small theaters. As there is little or no money to be made, there is no danger of being exploited by a producer. Working conditions in small theaters are not the best and they certainly do not compare to production houses. Most small theaters were not designed for that purpose, but are converted storefronts and warehouses and reflect economic constraints and shoestring budgets.

Following the announcement of the Waiver Plan in 1972, small theater activity increased by 66 percent in the 1972–1973 season according to the Cauble study. The announcement spurred many groups into purchasing equipment against anticipated box office revenues, and led to the development of advertising budgets and seasonal programming to develop new audiences.

Although there is little information available to determine whether small theaters compete with established theater, the Cauble study does shed some light on the issue. In an audience survey, the reasons given for attending larger commercial theaters differ from those for small theater attendance. Seventy-seven percent of the small theater audience also attended the large theaters more than once during the year, e.g., the Shubert, Ahmanson, Hartford or the Music Center. More than 60 percent of the group paid top price for seats at commercial houses and did not regard lower prices to be a major reason for attending small theater. Rather, 87 percent attended small theater because of personal recommendation, and 44 percent went because they wanted to see a particular play. Small theater may also cultivate and develop audiences for larger union theaters. As new and larger audiences become accustomed to theatergoing at small theaters, they may accept the extra effort and expense of attending larger theater, thereby stimulating employment at union houses. Obviously, greater in-depth study is needed and would be extremely helpful in determining the exact impact that the Waiver Plan has had on the development of small theater and its effect upon theatergoing and audience development in the Los Angeles area.

The Los Angeles Drama Critics Circle left no doubts about the effectiveness of the Waiver Plan in raising the artistic standards in small theaters. In the 1973–1974 season, four out of six award nominations were from waiver theaters. The waiver situation has made it possible for small theaters to become recognized on their own merits. Equity has taken a step toward making Los Angeles into an exciting, innovative theatrical center spearheaded by the small theater movement.

One of the major factors behind the Waiver Plan was Equity's difficulty in enforcing the work rules at small theaters. Recognizing the small theater as a viable force which meets the need to employ unemployed actors, Equity has, however, maintained the subsidiary rights as the only requirement for the Waiver Plan. These rights entitle actors in an original work to be adequately compensated if it is transferred to a profit-making situation.

Undoubtedly, Equity has done much to assist its membership in having access to valuable training and showcase opportunities; actors and managers universally approve of the Waiver Plan. Equity, though, does not encourage its membership to participate in small theater for fear its existing contracts might be undermined. The union has made it clear that if the Waiver Plan is abused, it has the authority to withdraw it. Despite Equity's uneasiness with the plan, its experiment has continued to prove successful.

Other arts unions could follow Equity's example. Such unions as the American Federation of Musicians might also consider plans to modify its rules in similar cases. While every union and situation is unique, Equity's action could serve as both a valuable precedent and a guide. The result could be a broadening of possibilities for employment in the performing arts.

Proposal for a Performing Arts Trust Fund and Its Effect Upon Unemployment

Another strategy for enhancing employment in the arts is the establishment of a performing arts trust fund, a concept pioneered by the American Federation of Musicians. The fund could be used to employ increased numbers of unemployed artists. Here the focus is on the profit-making sector of the performing arts industry.

The American Federation of Musicians (AFM) Music Performance Trust Fund was begun over thirty years ago in response to the rise in the then-new technologies that permitted the drastic growth of music recordings. This was seen by the union as the cause for the rapid displacement of live music and the decline in employment of musicians. The unemployment situation became so severe that the AFM went on strike against the major recording studios. Finally it negotiated a settlement that included the implementation of the musicians' trust fund. Financed by royalties from the sale of music recordings, the trust fund has used its revenues to employ musicians for live music performances free to the community. Community benefit is one of the major concerns of AFM's policies regarding the use of trust fund monies. The self-perpetuating fund is now the largest single employer of the 275,000 union members. Musicians are paid at full union scale and, while working, accrue benefits under the union's welfare and pension funds.

In effect, the AFM has a self-circulating financial mechanism which not only benefits the community, but also helps to maintain the livelihood of many union members. In Los Angeles, union musicians have performed for schools, charities and inner city audiences, or with community orchestras, and have provided music lessons to low-income youngsters.

The creation of a similar trust fund for other performing arts holds a great deal of potential in promoting new employment possibilities for artists. In much the same way, trust fund monies could be utilized for community benefit and public relations for the arts as well as increased public support.

As it is there are numerous obstacles that would have to be overcome before another performing arts trust fund could get under way. First, there would have to be cooperation among all unions and guilds involved with the performing arts. Secondly, the cooperation of arts producers would be needed to facilitate the effort, since management largely determines the volume of the end product.

There are numerous avenues for financing a trust fund through arts-related sources of revenue and production media. Considering potential scope, they should be increased, with certain percentages of the proceeds going into the trust fund. Programs sold at arts performances are the second largest source of income after ticket sales. A certain percentage of the proceeds could be designated for a fund. There are numerous industries that prosper from the arts but which contribute little or nothing to them. A certain percentage of parking revenues from audiences could also be tapped, since arts industries support neighboring parking industries. Similarly, there are also products (such as T-shirts, souvenirs and posters) which promote the arts that could be an added source for a trust fund.

As an incentive for such a performing arts trust fund and to assist in its early stages, perhaps the California Arts Council, National Endowment for the Arts or even local government could match generated revenues. The benefits are obvious: a new self-sustaining source of revenue and, as a result, new opportunities for unions to establish programs for community benefit and the employment of union members.

A Cooperative Effort of Unions, Employees, and Employers to Establish a United Arts Fund

Fundraising can be an extremely difficult task for arts institutions. A united arts fund drive could be an effective means of generating support. Employees could have employers deduct a small percentage of their earnings which would be accumulated by the fund, much like the United Way. A tripartite cooperative effort of labor unions, employees and employers would be required. The drive could be conducted at unionized industries and businesses throughout Los Angeles. Labor could act as the catalyst; unions are necessary to reach the greatest number of employees. Moreover, the involvement of unions would provide the needed morale and psychological lift that would help such an effort get under way.

Labor and employers would have to agree to implement a payroll deduction; this is, therefore, one of the most crucial elements of the plan. Business and industry are constantly in search of new methods to assist philanthropic causes, and in this case it would be for the support of the arts. Business and industry would partake in the fund drive by matching employee contributions and would generate interest in greater employee cooperation. In effect, both parties would stimulate one another in the development of such an effort, possibly yielding greater revenues than if just one party were involved. At the same time, employers in all likelihood would gain greater visibility due to their direct participation. Numerous surveys have repeatedly provided evidence that the public is willing to support the arts even if it means slightly higher taxes. If this is the case, the plan holds enormous potential and could stimulate employment in the arts.

In return for contributions from the fund drive, lunch-time performances on the premises of cooperating businesses and industries could be given by the arts groups receiving support from the fund. The visibility of such performances might further enhance the development of the fund drive since employees and employers alike could witness an arts experience of which they are a part through their cooperation in the drive. Another possibility would be to provide contributors with vouchers for reduced ticket prices to performances on predesignated dates, or perhaps even a special performance night or matinee for employees from a particular industry or business. These endeavors could also be beneficial for generating new arts audiences.

Disbursements of generated revenues of the united arts fund drive could be handled in a manner similar to the United Way fund drives. Revenues are funnelled into United Way, where the requests of participating member organizations are evaluated based on past budgets and present needs. Funds are then allocated based on these criteria. Similarly, representatives from arts unions, arts institutions, foundations and other arts leaders could form a committee to allocate funds to participating arts organizations of the fund. It would be essential to have representation from all art forms as well as from large and small arts institutions and individual artists.

Footnotes

[1] For an earlier discussion of this concept, see Faine, H., "Unions and the Arts," *American Economic Review*, Vol. LXII, No. 2, May 1972.

3.11
Using the Arts to Beautify, Restore and Revitalize the City: The Enhancement of Employment and Income in Architecture and Building

Traditionally, the central city has been the core of cultural and economic activities. Its concentrated resources have maintained its economic importance while its complex and diverse nature has provided the fundamental freedom critical to the arts. At its best the urban scene, with distinguished buildings, tree-lined streets, fountains and parks, has attracted and stimulated public use, providing the space and symbols of a cultural resource for its citizens.

Place making

Architecture has for thousands of years been considered one of the fine arts. It is in the city where the architect's roles as artist and as builder come together powerfully. For our own day, urban designer Kevin Lynch has defined it well:

> We need an environment which is not simply well organized, but poetic and symbolic as well. It should speak of the individuals and their complex society, of their aspirations and their historical traditions, of the natural setting, and of the complicated functions and movements of the city world...

Architects are very much concerned with this "poetic and symbolic" element of place making.

A significant example of a building that works both as symbol and as community building is the Oakland Museum. Much of its success lies in its form as a building in an urban park setting. "We were confronted with buildings nearby which were not good architecture, but very formidable nevertheless," Kevin Roche, the museum's architect, explained. The problem was to design a space which would attract people and yet create some of the greenery sorely needed in Oakland. "The greenery is an assembly area for outdoor concerts or the like... In a sense, the whole thing comes together as a problem of use and function and city planning and architectural relations." The museum covers one block of property. Its size well accomodates the 15,000 people who came to see it on the first two days and continue to use it in very large numbers. It has become a place where rich and poor alike come to spend Sundays with their families. Although not spectacular in the usual sense, it functions well in creating a cultural facility which attracts the use of its citizens.

Works of art, whether murals, fountains or buildings, help to attract people to areas and define their uniqueness as places. The artwork which embellishes New York's old Rockefeller Center has given the city a unique place of a special and delightful nature; it is a public art understood by everyone. Lawrence Halprin's fountain in Portland is another crowded public gathering place, where water creates all types of spaces for people to relax or to play in. There is no comparison with the standard fountain decoration. Another example is architect Charles Moore's fountain in New Orleans' Piazza d'Italia, a cultural and economic development sponsored by the city of New Orleans and the Italian-American community. The fountain is the focal point of many community activities.

It is important to note the magnitude of these types of projects. The Piazza d'Italia is approximately 90,000 square feet; the Oakland Museum is one city block; Centre Pompidou in Paris is one million square feet. Their size helps attract crowds, making them valuable additions to areas lacking the pedestrian traffic necessary for increased business activity.

Restoration and Adaptive Use

As concern for the quality of the city increases, the idea of preserving and adapting historic buildings becomes important for more than just cultural reasons. Only recently have there been statistics to prove that restoration can often be more economically feasible than new construction; moreover, it can provide a significant job market (because of its labor-intensive nature) for craftspeople and architects.

Adaptive use, the field of greatest interest for the

rebuilding of historic downtown areas, requires unusual skills and attitudes. Needed are both a knowledge of architectural history and a knowledge of codes and innovative design possibilities (which can make an enormous difference in costs, since demolition and structural costs are normally minimal).

The Biltmore Hotel in Los Angeles is a good example of how architectural restoration has proven to be a good investment and an asset to the downtown area. The Los Angeles Biltmore dates back to 1923. In those days, its elegance and artwork outshone even some of the Hollywood personalities who inhabited it; it was the prototypical stage-set building attracting movie stars and "stargazers." The lobby architecture was original art work done by sculptor Giovanni Smeraldi, who had come from Italy in 1889 to assist in the decoration of the White House.

When the Biltmore was sold to the Ridgeway Corporation in 1976, it had a 40 percent occupancy rate. There were problems of deterioration due mainly to poor management and maintenance and under-financing. Fortunately, the deterioration of the hotel had not progressed beyond repair in the opinion of architects Gene Sommers and Phyliss Lambert of the Ridgeway Corporation.

Prior to the acquisition of the Biltmore, the Ridgeway Corporation had won the bidding for a $36 million, 600-room hotel on Bunker Hill but had found difficulty in financing the project. When they bought the Biltmore instead for a cost of $5.4 million and an estimated $16.5 million for the restoration of the 1,072 guest rooms, it was like buying twice as much for half the price, which is equivalent to one-fourth the cost per room. Specifically, the current average cost for the construction of a new hotel room is $60,000 as compared to the $15,000 a room in the renovated hotel.

When the restoration began, workers had to be brought out of retirement because of the scarcity of craftspeople who could do freehand painting, ornamentation and stenciling. Construction crews finished their work in eighteen months and by April 1977, 800 rooms were completed. Hotel employment increased substantially because of the greater occupancy rates and the addition of new facilities. The staff increased from 400 to 600 full-time jobs. New facilities such as the roof garden generated four new full-time gardeners to maintain it and about 100 hotel plants.

The proprietor invited artist Jim Dine to assist in the design of the interiors of the hotel suites as well as in the design and decoration of the hallways. The result is a series of original friezes, prints, lamp bases and tapestries. Dine also worked closely with the architects during the remodeling phases, which resulted in a refreshing and original design well integrated into a theme. This unique feature of the remodeled portions of the hotel far exceeds the design criteria for new hotel construction and adds to the value of the building as well as its ability to recoup investments.

Although the Biltmore is unique in many ways, it typifies the economic benefits of a well-managed hotel. It seems that in this case the restoration alternative has a greater competitive advantage when compared to new construction. A new hotel would have to charge fifty to sixty dollars a night for a room of equivalent quality to the Biltmore, while the Biltmore can charge less (approximately forty dollars a night in comparison). After a year of operation, with the restoration and remodeling almost complete, the Biltmore frequently reaches 100 percent occupancy.

There are many other examples of the economic benefits of older buildings. In Boston, after recycling the Webster House (built in 1872) to an office complex, the occupancy rate is now 100 percent, compared with a citywide average of 85 percent; also, after adapting the Cast Iron Building (built in 1868) for retail (15 percent) and artist's residences (85 percent), the building is now 100 percent occupied.

Private Support

Recognition of the value of architects' contributions to our cities has come from both private clients and government agencies. A splendid example of the efforts of one individual to stimulate the well-being of his community through architecture is J. Irwin Miller in Columbus, Indiana.

Under the direction of Miller's Cummins Engine Foundation, a unique program was developed to improve the quality of Columbus' architecture. According to the program criteria established initially for a school building, the architect must be selected by the school board and chosen from a list of first-rate American architects provided by a panel of two of the country's most distinguished architects. Competition is encouraged. The selected

Restoration of the historic lobby of The Biltmore Hotel in downtown Los Angeles highlights the hand-painted ceiling by Italian artist Giovanni Smeraldi and ornate artwork of the period.

architect has responsibility for the planning and design of the entire building and its surroundings.

This program was expanded later to include all public buildings on request; in addition, several other buildings have been similarly funded through the efforts and donations of the community at large. By providing a strong precedent, the Cummins Engine Foundation has indirectly contributed to numerous capital improvement projects and historic renovations undertaken by individual businesses in the central business district.

Columbus grew 30 percent during the 1960s. Its physical amenities and status attracted three major corporations to maintain international headquarters there. Yet despite its growth, the town was facing the same problems in 1965 that were plaguing other metropolitan areas nationwide: business was migrating to the suburbs. In response to this, the Columbus Redevelopment Agency was created: its original plan included a twelve-acre parcel of land designated a retail shopping center known as the "Superblock."

The Irwin Management Company, under the direction of J. Irwin Miller, contracted Gruen and Associates to develop plans for the shopping area, but soon realized that retail activity alone would not suffice to revitalize the downtown area. As important as retail activity was, it was determined to be more important to return to downtown its symbolic function as the center of government and culture. Downtown needed to re-establish its role as a meeting place and focal point for community activities.

Initially the plan was called "The Civic Mall" and its chief designer, Cesar Pelli, spoke of it as a modern American equivalent of the Italian Piazza. "It is a space designed to attract and be of use for many more occasions than shopping . . . The Civic Mall should become the place to which everybody in Columbus will gravitate," Pelli wrote during the initial planning stages. The enclosed mall would provide an important linkage between two major commercial areas—the new shopping complex and the existing shops—and the civic buildings. The traffic generated by one activity would then prove to be of mutual advantage.

Interior and exterior landscaping were considered critical to the quality of the spaces. The focal point was a large, moving sculpture by Jean Tinguely called *Chaos I* and the park-like atmosphere was reflected in the children's playground, which was covered with astroturf.

The Civic Mall (renamed The Commons later) was a joint venture between the developer, Miller, and the city. Miller donated the funds for its construction and the city provided the property. After its construction, The Commons was to be returned to the city as a public facility and would be operated by a board of directors. Miller agreed to absorb any deficit during its first full year of operation and the city council approved the plan in December of 1971.

The Commons has far exceeded the expectations of everyone. During the first nine months of operation, fifty-one exhibits were displayed and 178 public performances were presented in The Commons. Approximately 90 percent of the resources for these activities came from the community, the financial and physical involvement of which proved, better than anything, the success of The Commons as a public space. The community wants to improve the quality of its art program and in the future hopes to attract funding for the exhibit of nationally-recognized artists as well as continuing to exhibit local artists.

The success of The Commons has awakened further interest in the downtown area for investors. If the city supports it with tax dollars in addition to the income generated by leases, grants and fundraising, it will prove to be a model of how public and private interests can cooperate to create urban spaces which encourage public participation and in turn strengthen the cultural and economic base of the downtown area.

Another example of enlightened support of architecture and building from the corporate sector is provided by some of the activities of the Bank of America. For the past several years, the bank has administered several programs to encourage building, particularly to assist minority populations:

A Minority Business Loan Program and minority development assistance programs.

Minority Purchasing Program: In 1975 the bank began a program which provided $300,000 in architectural construction services to minority vendors. Another $300,000 went for purchase orders to minority vendors for office equipment and supplies.

Support of Displaced Tenants: In 1974, the bank

acquired a site of several blocks in the Los Angeles area to expand its data center and committed $5 million in loans to Los Angeles for the construction of low-cost housing for the displaced tenants.

City Improvement and Restoration Program (CIRP): In 1974, a bank task force determined restoration needs which resulted in the following recommendations: (1) the rehabilitation of existing housing stock; (2) mortgage financing of older homes; (3) construction of low-cost senior citizen housing; (4) business district rehabilitation; and (5) open space acquisition. This program was implemented beginning in 1975. A Community Development Fund was set up to help cities to utilize federal funds for capital improvement in existing housing and to provide below-market interest rates. The Trust for Public Land (TPL), a nonprofit organization, acquires open space using private sector capital which it re-sells to cities and other agencies for public use. Through this program, Bank of America extended a $10 million dollar credit line in 1975. During that year, the organization had acquired 1,200 acres of land in and near urban areas in California at a saving of about $1 million dollars. In addition, in order to improve the housing situation, Bank of America financed various programs for senior citizen housing. Chico City cooperated with the bank to restore run-down housing belonging to elderly and low-income people and California State University students provided the labor. The bank also funded $500,000 to preserve the city of San Francisco's architectural heritage of Victorian houses. At the end of the program, more than $200,000 had been loaned to individual borrowers.

Public Support

In our current society, the extent to which architects can make a contribution to the economic and cultural life of a city depends in large part on government policies and on an educated public as a client.

In this light, the American Institute of Architects has recommended guidelines which would make it easier for architects to become involved in building on the scale necessary to revitalize communities:

1 State and local governments should retrieve sufficient control over local building, zoning and health regulations to insure an adequate supply of land for large site development. Land should be permanently reserved for community use.
2 Since building at the neighborhood scale requires front money equal to at least 40 percent of the total investment with no appreciable return until five to fifteen years later, government supports must be expanded on the federal and state levels both in the areas of public facilities (such as cultural facilities) and housing.
3 Tax incentives should be given for building communities as opposed to only individual profit-centers and speculative buildings; this would involve a reconsideration of the relationship between public and private interests in investing in public facilities such as cultural facilities.
4 To insure that the necessary revision of the property tax system, zoning and building codes be effected for revitalization, revenue-sharing funds should be granted on the condition that these reforms are established.
5 Trust funds such as the highway trust fund could be examined as sources for community redevelopment, providing more monies for the type of revitalization necessary for the effective rebuilding of cities.
6 The possibility of a national development corporation could be examined to coordinate public and private sources of funding. There have been local examples of this, as in New York with revitalization of the Bedford-Stuyvesant area.
7 Special zoning and codes for cultural facilities and historic restoration should be effected to encourage this type of development as critical to the success of a downtown revitalization. This would encourage restoration as an economically viable alternative to new construction and provide jobs for architects.

8   Government grants for construction could provide for design services to increase the employment of architects.

Richard Stein, president of the New York chapter of the American Institute of Architects, noted in his memo to the National AIA, dated February 25, 1977, that under the provisions of the $2 billion federal public works bill, the sector of the construction industry with the highest rate of unemployment—the design professions and architects—cannot benefit from these grants. The provisions state that construction must start (the term used is "shovel in the ground") within ninety days of the date of approval of the project list by Washington; this is to alleviate the 20 percent unemployment in the construction field. However, if the federal public works bill awarded design contracts as necessary to capital construction, with the starting time as "setting pencil to paper" within ninety days after the project has been accepted, then this could mean a substantial gain in employment for architects. If 6 to 10 percent of the total construction work were allocated for design services, then out of New York City's $200 million grant, about $12 million to $20 million would be allocated for design services, providing some 500 man-years of work in the design field.

Art in Public Places

Architecture can join with the other visual arts in the task of revitalizing our cities. At one time, art as sculpture, painting and landscape design had a major role to play in the making of human spaces. Architects, often artists themselves, hired artists to embellish their buildings (as Bertram Goodhue did with the Los Angeles Central Library). Because the art added a human dimension, many government buildings were embellished with friezes, sculpture and ornamental details because it was deemed important for the buildings to look dignified and elegant. It is not economically feasible to build buildings in the same manner today, although there is no reason to exclude art in landscaping or the interiors of lobby areas, for example. Landscaping has become important economically as a capital improvement which increases property values. Private developers are now designing a good portion of their lots as green spaces. Security Pacific Bank in downtown Los Angeles landscaped over 80 percent of its 4.2 acres of plaza and added fountains, sculpture and waterfalls. According to Gene Johnson, vice president in charge of building facilities, this was done for investment purposes. Although in terms of dollars it has no measurable gain, it is important in establishing the bank's image and attracting custormers.

Los Angeles has also finished a two-block civic center mall carefully landscaped with a variety of trees and plants and containing kiosks, fountains and benches. It is a much-needed space and employees are responding enthusiastically by spending their time and money in the mall shops.

Art in and around public buildings need not be in great quantity to have an impact on the general public, but it must be there in a sufficient amount to effect a change in the cultural environment. When it is there in large quantity, such as the work done through the Fine Arts Program of the WPA, when artists produced 1,400 murals and 3,700 sculptures for public buildings during a span of three years, it creates its own demand.

Exposure to the arts in the daily working environment can be an important form of education. One employee at the Security Pacific Bank said that she "didn't understand modern art" but that after working at the Bank for three years, her interest increased to the point that she often goes to museums to see their painting and sculpture exhibits. The lacing of art into the fabric of the daily environment is probably the most underdeveloped area of the arts. It holds enormous potential as an area for future expansion.

When art is placed where people come into contact with it and it becomes a special part of their environment, it can have a positive impact on public attitudes. This was recently demonstrated in Grand Rapids, Michigan. In 1967, the city had installed a controversial Calder sculpture which, despite the arguments against it, had (according to the editor of the *Grand Rapids Press*) "painlessly increased people's interest (in art) without making them self-conscious of having 'culture.' " In 1973 the museum organized a remarkable exhibit for the downtown area. With monies from the National Endowment for the Arts and state and local sources totaling more than $50,000, the museum invited fourteen nationally-recognized artists to design large outdoor artworks which would become the artists' property after the exhibit. The mu-

An exciting building becomes a focal point for activity: Centre Pompidou, Paris, France, Piano and Rogers, Architects. Credit: Richard Rogers.

seum would construct the artworks free of charge to the artists. Thirteen of the artists accepted and seven began construction directly at the downtown site. During the six months it took to construct the various works, public interest and involvement increased. According to museum director Fred Myers, daily exposure to this "museum without walls" has actually increased the popularity of the programs of the traditional museum; museum attendance has steadily increased since the installation of the first piece of sculpture.

"One Percent" Funding

An innovative for of funding art is the "1 percent program." For new buildings the cost of the artwork can be included as part of the total construction cost of the building, which usually amounts to a few pennies extra per square foot. This program started in 1959 in Philadelphia as part of its redevelopment policy and other cities and states soon followed. Seattle began its program because of the 1962 World's Fair and the program was considered important enough economically to be passed into law shortly after with the approval of Seattle businessmen.

When the General Services Administration (GSA) of the federal government began its program in 1972, it was the first nationwide program to incorporate the cost of artwork into the building costs. Although it initially allowed only .5 percent of the construction costs for art (after July 1976, this amount was reduced to .375 percent), within four years it had devoted $1.4 million to works of art.

According to the General Services Administration the responsibility for the type of artworks to be included lies with the architect who proposes it and suggests its purpose; only after the design of the building is complete, approved and put out to bid does GSA allocate the funds. However, this approach has been criticized for its "after the fact" placement of art within the building design; there are many opportunities for the inclusion of the arts and crafts into details of the building.

The critics of the program would like to see a better integration of art into the initial design phase, but this will depend on the willingness of the architect to work more closely with the artists.

Similar to the GSA program, many states have passed legislation allowing a percentage of the construction costs of public buildings to go for art. As of 1979, 37 cities and 15 states have passed 1 percent legislation.

Although Los Angeles does not have any 1 percent legislation, its concern with art in public places dates back to 1903, when the Citizen Committee on Art was appointed by the mayor. Renamed in 1905 the Municipal Arts Commission, it was officially recognized in 1911 and the Department of Municipal Art was created in 1925 by charter to assist the commission in approving both "works of art and certain structures that impinge on city property."

With the philosophy that "beauty is the most valuable asset a community can possess," as declared in the 1911 commission minutes, the department set out to encourage the creation and purchase of the arts. In 1930, the Los Angeles Chamber of Commerce proposed that $100,000 be allocated for the purchase of art products each year. Through the work of this municipal department and the federal Works Progress Administration, by 1940 Los Angeles had added many works of art to its downtown buildings.

In 1963, the Municipal Arts Deparment spearheaded attempts to begin 1 percent programs in various departments of city government; the Board of Public Works adopted a 1 percent policy in 1967. Parks and Recreation does not feel it necessary to provide funding for artwork within its parks, although it will accept donations of artwork. Presently, it does not seem likely that Los Angeles will legislate a general 1 percent program although recently, with the encouragement of the Municipal Arts Department, some citizens have been investigating the possibility. The Community Redevelopment Agency in Los Angeles, however, does require that 1 percent of the construction costs of buildings in redevelopment areas go for art.

The state of California, despite attempts by Assemblyman Alan Sieroty to introduce a 1 percent law, does not fund artwork in public buildings through construction costs. It does allocate art projects on a geographical basis according to its Art in Public Buildings Act, which only requires that the governor include art as an annual budget item. The act proposes use of a public participatory process involving local town councils throughout the state. However, the basis for allocating the funds is the "bio-region," which roughly allocates monies equally to five regions of California, regardless of the size of each region's population.

Thus, the economic benefits of this program are substantially more limited for populous Los Angeles than a 1 percent program. The total amount of monies budgeted for all arts programs for the 1977–1978 fiscal year was only $700,000 for the entire state, with Los Angeles' portion $110,000, and only a portion of this money goes for art in public buildings. The types of buildings that are listed as possible sites by the state architect are state-owned facilities, although future sites can be leased facilities or state parks.

The art and artist selection process could have significant economic and aesthetic benefits according to the selection policies. Art proposals are to be integrated into the building design with maximum visibility to the general public. The aesthetic benefits may therefore extend beyond the building proper and set a high artistic standard for adjacent development to follow. By seeking a variety of artists with diverse social and economic backgrounds, opportunities for low-income minority artists could be significant if the budget allocation is increased to a reasonable level.

A Final Note

For those who are already committed to good architecture in our cities, as for those who are committed to any of the other arts, the situation is clearcut. The general public, as well as the corporate and the public decision makers, must be convinced of the importance of good architecture. But how do we go about creating and furthering a tradition of good architecture in a city that does not already have such a tradition, as do, for example, cities like Chicago and San Francisco? Surely there is no substitute for dedicated political action for getting one's point of view across, a constant struggle to convince federal, state and local executives and legislators, as well as corporate executives. In such campaigns, examples of buildings that have transformed important sections of cities and other success stories generally are valuable, as are significant achievements in the legislative realm (as in the 1 percent legislation for art in and around buildings).

3.12
City Revitalization Through The Redevelopment And Restoration Process: The Special Role Of The Arts

Many large, older cities are losing people and jobs, or just about holding their own. They are obsolete in large sections because they are the product of the industrial age and have not adapted to the post-industrial period.

Obsolescence is not easy to overcome. A truly effective revitalization effort attacks the causes rather than the symptoms of urban decay and blight. Older central city areas can reverse the out-migration of people and business only by competing more successfully than in the recent past with rapidly growing outer suburbs. Merely duplicating what these suburbs do best (developing large office and retail complexes) will not suffice because outlying areas retain the advantage of lower land and development costs and, thus, lower rents. In addition, the suburban office centers have other advantages, such as abundant free parking, less traffic congestion and close proximity to the desirable middle class residential neighborhoods. Older downtown areas simply cannot compete on this basis.

In reaction to this a more sophisticated approach to the redevelopment process has been emerging. Instead of attempting to supply the largest quantity of office space at the lowest feasible rate, the amenities unique to these older areas have become the basis for effectively competing with younger outlying activity centers. These amenities include the centralized location of downtown and the assets and charms of the older buildings and spaces—and the arts.

The centralized location has made the downtown area the traditional center for business, government and culture. Although the greatest part of recent growth has occurred on the outskirts of the metropolitan areas, there usually remains one main cultural center regardless of the extent of urban sprawl. There may be small cultural sub-centers, but they cannot compete with the traditional downtown cultural center. No one suburban center can claim such centralized resources as the traditional downtown, which all sub-centers are partially dependent upon.

Revitalization Through Redevelopment

The redevelopment process and the state laws regulating it are receptive to the financing of cultural facilities. Although its main purpose in the late 1950s was to rid cities of decaying slums, the goals of redevelopment have been expanded to include any project that is of benefit to the entire redevelopment area. This is accomplished by creating a nonprofit redevelopment agency that is not only eligible to receive and spend Community Development Block Grant funds, but is capable of raising its own revenue independent of the local general tax fund (through "tax increment" financing). Revenue from both sources can then be used to entice private investment into the designated redevelopment area by subsidizing the cost of the land and other costs. Land is assembled, cleared and sold below market cost at the expense of the redevelopment agency.

Tax increment financing is of particular interest in large projects. Such financing consists of recycling the incremental increase in property taxes of the project area back into redevelopment activities rather than into the general fund. In effect, the project pays for itself while the general tax base in the area suffers a temporary freeze until the redevelopment (tax increment) authority expires in that area (usually within twenty to thirty years). At completion, the increased property tax revenues revert back to the general fund along with any unspent tax increment revenues (unless these are diverted by the local government for other uses). Any project found by the redevelopment agency and the city council to accelerate the incremental tax increases, and ultimately the entire tax base of the city, theoretically may be considered worthy of redevelopment funds. Thus, to qualify for tax increment financing, cultural facility investment must prove to contribute to the economic viability of the city and not just the quality of life. Measuring the economic benefits of cultural facilities under such terms of reference requires consideration of other factors than projected gross ticket sales revenues. It requires inclusion of the economic "multiplier effect." Experience in various cities of the country suggests that arts facilities and activities, when appropriately and imaginatively developed, can be an economic asset to the local economy. The "multiplier" measurement should be able to capture that.

Economic Benefit of Cultural Facilities

Existing cultural facilities such as the Los Angeles Music Center operate under an expanding "income gap," whereby their expenditures exceed their revenues, requiring substantial private and public subsidization.[1] Yet because arts centers bring both performers and other employees and audiences into an area, they generate a "ripple" or "snowball" effect.

The first cycle of spending is the cultural facility capital and operating expenditures. But more important is what employees and audiences spend for basic needs and services, such as food, clothing, housing and transportation, and for leisure amenities surrounding the cultural events. If these services are supplied locally, additional employment and income is generated from these industries (see Appendix: Multiplier Effects).

The derivation of the multiplier is a function of the number of cycles of spending that an economic entity can support. Theoretically, an extremely self-sufficient community that does not have to import goods and services from elsewhere (and has little saving) might experience a multiplier as much as 7 or 8, in other words seven or eight dollars for each dollar spent originally (actually, an unlikely situation). Contrarily, an extremely import-dependent community might only experience a 1.11 multiplier, or only an 11 per cent increase in revenues above the initial cultural facility income. Self-sufficiency is determined by the extent to which each industry meets a minimum capacity for serving the population.[2]

Because each metropolitan area has a different degree of self-sufficiency, different multiplier effects should be anticipated. However, previous studies suggest that 2.0 may be taken as a reasonable average multiplier for both facility and audience expenditures.[3] For a city as large and industrially diverse as Los Angeles, this represents an extremely conservative estimate. Using an even lesser multiplier of 1.38, the Music Center is estimated to generate as much as $61 million in income and audience sales within the city's economy (see Appendix: Multiplier Effects). This does not include the effects upon property values or the multipliers generated by the influx of businesses in proximity to the cultural facility.

The multiplier effects from tourists or visitors from outside a city are far greater than from local users. In a hypothetical case in Los Angeles, if 10 percent of tourists are estimated to visit cultural facilities, about $85 million is poured into the local economy (see Appendix: Multiplier Effects). This is hypothetical because Los Angeles does not have the appropriate scale of cultural facilities to compete with the more culturally-rich cities nor with its other attractions, such as sports and recreation activities. Despite its central location, downtown Los Angeles is estimated to attract only 5 percent of Los Angeles' total tourist volume. But because of the many new developments, such as the projected Central Library renovation, the People Mover System and proposed luxury hotels, tourism attraction may increase.[4]

Economic Benefits of Mixed-Use Facilities

To maximize the multiplier effects and other economic benefits of cultural facilities, the facility must attract a maximum of local and tourist visitors. Building the facility in a centralized location alone may not be a sufficient generator of visitors. Edward Helfeld, director of the Los Angeles Community Redevelopment Agency, observes, "The Music Center is a great asset to the downtown environment when it is being used. But most of the time it is not being used and is just an empty plaza without human activity." What Helfeld suggests as a remedy for the often empty plazas of cultural facilities in general is a mixture of commercial and cultural uses. This would transform these cultural facilities into activity nodes on a more frequent basis.

The demand for multi-use buildings that combine business with pleasure has been steadily increasing due to the increased competition for office tenants and the reform of obsolete building and zoning codes. Guidelines and examples of innovative codes are discussed in another section. The examples which follow illustrate how cultural and commercial facilities can harmonize for their mutual economic benefit.

The city of Atlanta has an innovative cultural-commercial private development in the Midnight Sun Dinner Theater. It is a $2.5 million facility located on top of a Shopping Gallery in Peachtree Center, located within the downtown area.[5]

The more traditional types of cultural facilities are also being mixed with commercial uses in downtown centers. A branch of the Oklahoma City Arts Center is located on the plaza level of a downtown office building. It includes exhibition space, a small restaurant and an auditorium that presently accommodates popular music performers and lectures on the arts. The Denver Center for the Performing Arts is a diverse consortium of many different types of cultural facilities as well as commercial facilities. It consists of a concert hall, four theaters for live performances, a cinema, an outdoor amphitheater, an office building, parking garage, shops, restaurants and boutiques.[6] Introducing commercial elements into cultural facilities is just as advantageous as introducing cultural elements into commercial facilities.

Multi-purpose cultural centers face the same financial obstacle as that of any multi-use building: developers seem to prefer single-purpose buildings. This is because, until now, single-purpose projects have been easier to finance and manage.[7] In addition, the nonprofit status of cultural institutions seems to inhibit these institutions in affiliating with commercial enterprises. Although the successes of previous examples of mixed cultural-commercial development help to dissolve the stigma surrounding these developments, the problem of securing financing still persists. This problem can be partially remedied by retaining buildings as single-purpose structures, but utilizing common spaces for cultural amenities.

Utilization of Public Spaces

Public spaces utilized for cultural activities are malls, streets, parks and plazas. The most critical aspect of this concept is the management and programming of daily activities. The successful utilization of these sites is also dependent upon the adequacy of the architectural design elements of these places. Regardless of how much space the public or private sector allocates to these cultural amenities, only with proper programming and design can the benefits to the local economy be realized.

Whether outdoors or indoors, malls and plazas require the largest capital expenditures. A classic example of a mall converted from a street is Nicollet Mall in Minneapolis, built in 1967. It was able to capitalize on federal grants for redevelopment and is considered a success because of the multitude of new corporate offices locating adjacent to it and the substantial influxes of private investment.

Enclosed malls create public space in private property but require the greatest capital expenditures of all. Perhaps the greatest inspiration for this extravagant type of development is Rockefeller Center. It consists of a series of malls connected to an outdoor sunken plaza where an extensive cultural program has been implemented. However, this type of development is not exclusive to downtown areas and has been the thrust of some of the competition from the suburbs.

The development of these underground spaces is being complemented by elevated pedestrian sidewalks which allow circulation between buildings without the nuisances and hazards associated with automobile traffic. The Bunker Hill Redevelopment Project in Los Angeles will eventually be linked to the civic-cultural center of the city by a system of pedways. These links will be mutually beneficial to both commercial and cultural facilities because of improved accessibility.

Lower capital expenditures are required for the use of existing public spaces such as streets or parks. Well-administered temporary cultural programs in these settings can attract substantial multitudes of people. Blocked-off streets can be the site of various cultural activities including parades, festivals, food bazaars, street theater, dance and folk music. These temporary cultural activities can be implemented by the use of mobile stage equipment and flexible street furniture. The Greater Cleveland Growth Association sponsors such street fairs every Friday evening in the summers. Parks can also be used for low-cost temporary cultural programs; however, the lack of commercial uses in close proximity usually makes park sites less beneficial to the local economy. The most successful events are those that reflect the local community, focusing on ethnic, racial, religious or historic themes.[8]

The close proximity of ethnic neighborhoods to the central downtown area makes it an ideal site for diversifying streets with cultural amenities. The Community Redevelopment Agency in Los Angeles is contemplating the modification of Broadway Street by temporarily banning auto traffic and creating a transit street for buses only. According to CRA director Helfeld, "This street is more than a place to shop; it is a cultural and social experience."[9] People of Hispanic origin are attracted to the shops, stores and theaters of Broadway. Los Angeles architect Robert Alexander recalls, "The crowds already spill into the streets to see the premieres of popular movies. I've been advocating this for thirty years."[10] Although the typical Broadway shopper is of lower income, the enormous pedestrian traffic on the street generates $140 million in annual sales. Since 1969, retail sales have increased 49 percent for Broadway, which exceeds the rate experienced by the central business district as a whole.[11] Increasing the pedestrian capacity of the street should improve this natural commercial-cultural mix, without economically alienating its low-income users.

Revitalization Through Historic Restoration

One of the most advantageous features of older downtown environments such as Broadway is the fact that they are old! Behind the dirt and deterioration of many of these buildings (and in some instances, whole blocks) is the charm, grace and human scale that seem to have been forgotten in much of our new development. The character and attention to detail of many of these old buildings simply cannot be duplicated anywhere, especially in newly developing suburbs. It is an amenity unique to the downtown environment and an excellent basis upon which to compete with suburban centers.

Unfortunately, financiers of public and private development do not issue loans on the basis of intrinsic cultural value. They are chiefly concerned with evidence that the project, whether a new development or restoration, show a reasonable return on the investment. Up to this time, such evidence was generally lacking and restoration was looked upon as an elitist indulgence.

The economic benefits of restoration as exemplified in actual case studies have provided a track record which makes it easier to secure financing. The original Skid Row (where timber skidded down chutes) in downtown Seattle is an appropriate example of the economic viability of restoration. The cost of renovating the Pioneer Building of 1889 was calculated to be nineteen dollars per square foot. At that time, the cost of constructing a comparable new office building was thirty dollars per square foot. Another cost saving was realized because restoration was faster than constructing a new building. This cut some labor costs, but the most substantial benefit was the ability to lease the renovated space earlier than would have been possible with conventional new construction. The developer concludes, "There are risks that require careful planning to overcome, but the rewards are great—it is very profitable."[12]

The Pioneer Building was only one of the structures to be restored in what became the Pioneer Square Historic District, approximately 150 buildings within twenty-four blocks. The project was approved during Seattle's worst period of unemployment and has been instrumental in the city's economic recovery by increasing the assessed value in the district by 450 percent. In addition, the initial city investment of $200,000 was matched ten times over by state, federal and private sources.

The financial success of the project has benefited the city as well as the individual investors. The key to its success lies in its ability to draw people. The high business density and mixed uses generate large volumes of retail shoppers. Tourists are attracted by the visible ties with the past. Even suburban shoppers are being drawn to this unique facility, reversing the effects of suburban flight.

Although the California State Redevelopment Law permits the use of tax-increment financing for restoration, Los Angeles has in the past chosen not to utilize it. "Both public and private redevelopment have permitted a thoughtless elimination of special older places," remarked Kurt Meyer, chairman of the redevelopment agency.

The Community Redevelopment Agency's commitment to refurbishing the Central Library represents a landmark shift in emphasis toward restoration in downtown Los Angeles. This city has been in dire need of a new Central Library for the past decade. Proposals to build a new one were estimated to cost from $70 to $90 million. In addition, the loss of the old Central Library would mean the demise of one of the most significant works of architecture in the city and a cultural landmark. When it was estimated that expansion and renovation of the old Central Library would be less than one-half the cost of a new building, or $30 million, the city council and the Community Redevelopment Agency concurred that the latter was the most fiscally responsible decision to make.

The CRA has also expressed an interest in restoring large-scale projects even outside the redevelopment area. This includes a Broadway Street project that would convert vacant commercial office space into low/moderate-income housing for the elderly and enhance the physical shopping environment for its continued use by Hispanics. The agency is also contemplating purchasing and potentially restoring an office building on Spring Street for its own use and as an example for private development. Plans are also being formalized for the reinstallation of the historic cultural monument of Angel's Flight near its original location. This vertical trolley car transported passengers from the top of Bunker Hill to its base, but was dismantled in 1969 for safety reasons.

The Cultural Heritage Board of Los Angeles is another agency involved in the restoration process. It is severely limited for lack of funds and has only been able to function as the traditional "museum house" preserver. The designation of Carrol Street in the Silverlake area as a historic district will help to preserve an entire block of Victorian homes. But the small scale of these efforts minimizes the economic benefits to the city's tax base, unlike the extensive programs in other cities, e.g., San Francisco, Seattle and Washington, DC.

The magnitude of the problem suggests that the most effective approach is to involve more private investment in the restoration process. A notable example of this in Los Angeles is the Bradbury Building, built in 1893. The interior court is spanned by a giant skylight-ceiling, creating a unique experience for visitors and employees. Although the building attracts multitudes of tourists as well as local visitors, its predominant usage for office space rather than retail space prevents it from realizing its full multiplier value. But after refurbishment, the owners were able to charge much higher rent—though still less than market rents for new office space downtown—allowing it to compete very successfully in the leasing market.

The redevelopment process is but one way to induce private development into large-scale restoration projects. Sacramento, California was the first city in the nation to use tax-increment financing in the preservation of its historic district. The property tax base at the beginning of the renewal process was $500,000. After twenty years, the property tax base is now over $8 million and is still increasing. (Non-property taxes such as sales taxes have also increased enormously.) Preservation efforts are now reaching a scale where they are revitalizing some cities. In Savannah, Georgia the Historic Savannah Project has saved more than 800 buildings within a three-square-mile area. A combination of private and redevelopment funds of $40 million has increased property values from ten to twelve times. The private sector has also benefited from the multiplier effects of the dramatic increase in tourism from one million to thirty-four million.

There are other indirect methods of inducing private development into restoration investment without incurring massive public debts. Reforming local building code laws to reflect a less stringent standard for older structures would substantially reduce the cost of bringing a historic landmark up to code. Ordinances establishing historic districts insure environmental design controls to protect all of the investors. The registration of landmarks, as done by the Los Angeles Cultural Heritage Board, helps to publicly identify significant structures worth preserving and postpones any plans to destroy such buildings until a restoration strategy can be devised.

Using Special Opportunities to Revitalize the City: The People Mover

Los Angeles was chosen in 1977 as one of the cities to receive federal funding for experimentation in new transportation modes, in this case a "people mover" covering some three miles of the downtown area. The people mover would test the role of a new mode of transportation by tying together key nodes in the downtown area and determining whether this would serve to revitalize downtown.

Given the goal of revitalizing the older sections of the central city, the question arises whether such an opportunity might not be broadened to intensify the impact of the new facility. This can be done by reconceptualizing the facility from a transportation system alone into a joint transportation-communication network that would highlight and amplify the cultural life of the neighborhoods being linked as well as of the city as a whole.

What follows is an elaboration of the latter approach. Its elements are flexible and independent of each other. What is critical to the plan is its freshness, vitality and essential playfulness.

The commercial streets around Broadway, Little Tokyo, Chinatown, as well as Olvera Street, the Los Angeles Public Library, the railroad station, the Convention Center and the Music Center—the focal points of downtown—are now isolated from each other by major streets, open lots and a freeway. There is no pleasant way of walking and meandering from one to the other. Nor are there yet the kinds of activities that foster strolling in the city—galleries, bookshops opening onto the street, cafes, street musicians. The proposed people mover could serve to connect these neighborhoods. In addition, the revitalization objective could be greatly strengthened if along its three miles there were the communication of information, entertainment and culture. This would be done along the route in the carriages, at specially established interchanges opening onto plazas and at a main center.

A basic element of the scheme is the people mover itself with its carriages and three-mile structure. The carriages could have clip-on information boards, audio-visual screens and games; they would be information capsules. The structure would not only support the carriages, but also could be used to store the tents, pneumatic and other simple shelters, and software that will be described later.

The route must be clearly defined. One possibility would be the use of large lighter-than-air balloons that could act as symbolic landmarks, brightly colored and freely shaped. An alternative would be the use of brightly colored banners or other permanent markers. The different symbols could serve much as they did in medieval times, when different standards represented different neighborhoods.

At interchanges, plazas could be developed where more static activities and information would be found. Each would be different, with its contents changing to relate to its surrounding neighborhood. Drawing on popular imagery and advertising techniques as well as complex new forms of information retrieval, we might visualize it as a cross between a computerized museum exhibit and Sunset Strip.

In addition, other activities must be placed on or near the plazas to serve as magnets for attracting a wide range of people. Street fairs, bands and theater groups would add to the life and vitality of the area. At points of pedestrian concentration, open air stalls, cafes, bookstores and galleries will naturally spring up. A center for orientation, as well as a location for activities and performances on a larger scale could be the beautiful, but under-used railway station. Parking for those coming off the freeways could be located here.

As one approaches the people mover, the nature of the information system must depend upon the speed of the vehicle or the pedestrian. Where the freeway comes close to the people mover, one would find fast information, art forms, neon lighting and billboards conveying the major activities to be found in the vicinity as well as traffic and weather reports. Information at appropriate scales would be keyed to street travel, to the parking lots, to sidewalks.

To produce something more than movies, television or concerts, it is important to develop participatory entertainment and cultural activities; theaters, shows, fairgrounds, art exhibits and information retrieval all are possibilities to involve people.

The process and performance of city government and its control could be shown electronically on large screens. We can envision a city operations center showing how a city lives, what is happening in the council chamber, where events are being held; what is on at the cinema or playing in the concert halls; news of the city, the state and the nation.

There are new technological marvels such as screens made of highly polished and focused lenticules which for the first time can be used for showing films in broad daylight. Three different films could be shown simultaneously on the same screen directed to audiences in three different places. Simple light-bulb, computer-controlled systems can also be used for film and information, from simulated horse racing to information on what is actually happening at the track. The centers could have two-way links so one could pick up some of the action on the home tv or telephone; small monitoring sets could be located in various places in the city or along the strips. The communications facilities' support structures can vary from light scaffolding frames put up like simple erector set systems to sophisticated space decks. These frames could be used vertically or horizontally as roofs or walls carrying clip-on screen and other software.

People draw people—what is needed is the right catalyst. Such a system might well attract tens of thousands of travelers a day. The trip in the people mover, the interchanges and plazas, and the information center will be dynamic, lively experiences. They will attract both tourists and residents looking for an enjoyable way to spend the day.

The broader public will develop a heightened awareness of the value of the neighborhoods linked by the system. The communities centered on Broadway, Little Tokyo and Chinatown will find a larger audience for their concerns and a greater market for their goods and services. The older downtown areas will seem more attractive to artists and professionals looking for an urban milieu. Workers in the Bradbury building will find themselves joined by neighbors who also relish the atmosphere of Broadway. And they in turn will enhance the area by making it the center of artistic and sophisticated activity. Through the people-mover-communicator, older areas can be enhanced and their cultural contributions strengthened by making them more visible and accessible to the larger city.

Other cities can be expected to have special opportunities for imaginative downtown development quite different from a people mover. What is important is that any opportunity for downtown development be seen as an opportunity to create interest and vitality in the downtown area so that tourists and residents are attracted in numbers sufficient to revitalize the city economically as well as culturally.

Conclusion

The traditional role of the redevelopment process in revitalizing older downtown areas must be broadened if the outmigration to suburban centers is to be reversed rather than merely postponed. The centralized location of downtowns have made them natural regional centers for government, business and culture which cannot be duplicated in scale or quality by the competing suburban centers. The enhancement of the unique cultural and historical features of these older areas is one way of competing successfully with the suburbs and improving the tax base.

Cultural amenities within or in proximity to redevelopment areas have proven to be economically advantageous. Although these facilities may operate at a deficit, the economic multipliers create increased revenues in the public and private sector. Cultural amenities, whether in a formal, traditional institutional setting, a public space or within a mixed-use development, can improve the local tax base by generating an influx of local visitors and tourists.

Another unique cultural feature of the urban core that allows it to compete successfully with suburban centers is the large stock of historical landmarks and districts. The economic benefits of restoration are now coming to light as evidenced by many examples of reduced construction costs and faster returns on investments when compared to new development. Just as in the redevelopment process, tax-increment funding is now being used as a mechanism for attracting private capital into large-scale restoration efforts. The tax base is enlarged through increased property values and the indirect income generated by visitors and tourists. Large-scale restoration projects have become economic recovery plans for some older metropolitan cities.

Footnotes

[1] Susan Barton, "No Matter Which Way You Slice It," *The Paper Forum,* Issue No. 5, Spring 1977, p. 4.

[2] Richard Mickley, "Preliminary Feasibility Study of the Proposed San Francisco Performing Arts Center" (draft), unpublished, Stanford Research Institute, Menlo Park, California, March 30, 1976, p. 43, 44.

[3] Joint Committee on Cultural Resources, *In Search of a Regional Policy for the Arts: Phase II,* Johns Hopkins University, Center for Metropolitan Planning and Research, 1975, p. 20.

[4] Community Redevelopment Agency of the City of Los Angeles, *Chinatown Study,* May 1977, p. 94.

[5] Ralph Burgard, "Town Square Revisited," unpublished seminar report, Massachusetts Institute of Technol-

ogy, Boston, Massachusetts, January 27–29, 1976, p. 4.

[6] Ralph Burgard, ibid., p. 4.

[7] Raymond Girvigian, *Digest Report of the Conference on Economic Benefits of Preserving Old Buildings*, Seattle, Washington, September 1975, concluding remarks.

[8] Ralph Burgard, op. cit., p. 11.

[9] Edward Helfeld, Administrator, Community Redevelopment Agency of the City of Los Angeles, Interview conducted in Los Angeles, September 1977.

[10] Robert Alexander, Robert Alexander and Associates, FAIA, Interview conducted in Los Angeles, September 1977.

[11] Kurt Meyer, Chairman of the Community Redevelopment Agency, interview conducted in Los Angeles, September 1977.

[12] Raymond Girvigian quoting Earl V. Seaman, op. cit., pp. 5–6.

3.13
Locational Planning For The Arts

The arts, like other urban activities, are affected by public regulations dealing with land use and structures. In certain cases, changes in such regulations can have a favorable impact on the expansion of the arts. It is obvious that there must be some changes in the current zoning laws in many cities if the artist is to be accommodated in the parts of the city where the mixing of studios and living accommodations is now prohibited.

There are two areas of public regulation dealing with the use of land and structures. These involve zoning and the approach to mixing land uses in an unplanned manner. Such regulations were basic to the establishment of zoning as a means of protecting the "sanctity of the home" as they barred all non-residential uses from residential areas in particular. Other regulations, not as frequently observed, restricted the intrusion of residential uses into commercial and industrial areas. The fear of mixing residential and non-residential uses in an unplanned manner caused numerous communities to adopt prohibitions against the extension of the mixed uses and ordinances establishing "exclusive" zones. Changes in the concept of the desirable structure of commercial areas have resulted in some recent reversals of this policy, especially where non-conforming uses had existed on a large scale, and where new techniques of urban design overcame prior objectionable conditions.

The Establishment of Artists' Colonies

In the post-industrial age which we are now entering, when service employment can be expected to be the mainstay of most cities' economies, and when large older cities have to struggle to maintain their economic and financial viability, the creation of artists' enclaves seems particularly appropriate. Arts and cultural activities will inevitably have to be counted on as a significant part of city economy. The artists' enclave may well become an important symbol of the post-industrial city, suggesting the importance of art in its many forms to the economic and residential life of the city.

Some General Principles

Artists have special locational needs; they require large areas of work and storage space for the practice of their art and yet their income is frequently limited. Their hours of work do not correspond necessarily to the normal work patterns of others, often requiring either close proximity of residence and studio or their fusion. Art buyers must be able to come to the studios to acquire the work of the artists. The area should, therefore, be visually attractive and safe to lure potential middle-class art clients.

What seems ideally suited to these special needs is an individual large, substantial building in a preferred location or in an area that is being revitalized. The selection of vacant loft buildings where they exist is best because there is no displacement of persons occupying the space. The building must be substantial and be capable of being used for the intended purpose. It probably should be located in or adjacent to an attractive commercial area.

The main problem is economic. The cost of a building in a central location and of renovations making it suitable for residential purposes as well as for studio activities is great and must be passed on to the occupant. Unless subsidies are available for artists, the district would be of value to a limited number of artists. Such rehabilitated structures become increasingly attractive to others, causing impressive increases in property values.[1] Many artists soon find themselves unable to live in the enclave because of the increased costs. However, in a situation where a central city is concerned about losing taxpaying residents—and many larger central cities are experiencing serious declines—it makes good sense for the city to sponsor such enclaves as a way of helping to revitalize the city. At the same time, through federal assistance it is appropriate to subsidize at least some portion of the rent of artists.[2]

Under such circumstances it would be necessary to define rather carefully who is eligible to receive such assistance. New York City has already begun the task of definition, limiting the "artist" to one "who is regularly engaged in the fine arts, such as painting and sculpture or in the performing or creative arts, including choreography and film making, or in the composition of music on a professional basis, and is so certified by the city department of cultural affairs and/or state council on the arts."[3]

The Situation in Los Angeles[4]

The problem of locating artists' centers has some special features in Los Angeles. As in other parts of the country, the city some years ago set up exclusive residential, commercial and industrial districts. As a result of this action, it was necessary to develop a new zone for mixed occupancies to accommodate artists. The new zone permits residences in commercial or industrial structures. (Excerpts from the ordinance are included in the appendix.)

There are certain areas within the city of Los Angeles which have already attracted groups of artists. These include Mt. Washington and the several canyons leading from Westwood and Beverly Hills to the San Fernando Valley. There is already a cultural appeal associated with these locations and artists compete with affluent individuals for homes in these limited places. In residential zones, the application of the ordinance requires the agreement of the residents of the area.

Insofar as commercial and industrial areas are concerned, there seems to be a better-than-average potential for artist use of specific buildings rather than zones for combined occupancy, especially in the Hollywood area where, while there are no loft buildings as in New York, there are industrial structures that could lend themselves to the development of centers of artistic endeavor.

In downtown Los Angeles, there are vacancies in buildings where the garment industry and banking offices were once located. One or more of these structures might become a center for the arts by renovating the upper floors. Because the cost of bringing the buildings into a habitable condition as a residence might, however, price the accommodations out of the range of artists, rent subsidies might be required. While at present there is limited attraction in being located in the downtown business district of Los Angeles, the restoration and revitalization proposals outlined elsewhere in this book could fundamentally alter this situation. Downtown Los Angeles could become a significant center for artists to live and work.

A Zoning Proposal

What follows is a comprehensive proposal for zoning that draws on features of existing ordinances in New York and Los Angeles. It is designed both to enable artists to practice their professions in a variety of urban settings and to handle in advance the problems this might generate.

Residential Districts

Single family districts would permit the practice of the arts on the following basis: In detached housing, the practice by individuals of crafts (as defined in a "home occupation") would continue without constraint other than that related to a public nuisance or creating conditions dangerous to the general welfare. In detached housing, groups could form an "ensemble" subject to the obtaining of a "C-A" type zone overlay and further subject to the following conditions: (1) that the performance of the art involving the group would not exceed a certain number at any one time, to avoid traffic and parking problems on residential streets; (2) that the hours of group work would be limited to daytime between 10:00 AM and 5:00 PM; (3) that all fire laws and the laws related to sound, vibration and the emission of noxious odors would be respected.

In multiple family districts the practice of the arts would be strictly limited to activities that are quiet and which do not in any way tend to endanger adjoining residents.

In all residential districts the sale of works of art or crafts would be limited to those produced on the premises. The hours of sales would be restricted to the daytime when the use of the streets and parking areas would be minimal.

In commercial districts the practice of the arts is already permitted, subject to the types of art that are consistent with the nature of the district. For example:

In planning shopping centers the display and sale of all forms of the arts could be exercised either within the mall areas or in streets closed off with permission from traffic authorities, or there could be creative activities in the upper levels of multiple-story buildings. Where residential facilities are associated with artists' studios, they should be above the ground floor so as not to interrupt the continuity of the retail sales functions.

In strip commercial areas where vacant stores abound, the store front could be used for a studio and the display and sale of artworks or, as in some cases, performances. Where residential facilities are permitted (as they should be under the following conditions), they would be separate and to the rear of the work-sales area. The residential facilities would have to be in a safe and sanitary condition with all essential services available and usable.

In central business districts the buildings should limit studio-residence to the floors above the ground floor and require that residential accommodations be safe, sanitary and appropriate for residential purposes. The uses could be any that fire laws permit and the space users should be required to have parking facilities related to residential occupancies and additional spaces for potential clients.

Provision of educational and recreational facilities for the families of artists living in the heart of a commercial district would have to be carefully considered or "no children accepted" regulations would have to be applied, thus creating adults-only communities.

Industrial Districts

While it is necessary to limit zoning to exclusive industrial use in many areas, others might allow a planned, compact enclave where artists could practice, provided their activities were not incompatible with industry and would not cause industrial practices to be limited by their presence. There are so many conditions within industrial districts that create an undesirable environment for living that it would appear best that the current practice of excluding residential facilities be continued. There is no reason to exclude the studio itself, only the residential occupancy.

There may be isolated industrial buildings in small industrial zones which were created to provide space for uses that no longer exist. These structures may be located in places where their transformation into studios would be appropriate and where the use would be preferable to current vacancy. Studios in Hollywood, Culver City and in part of Los Angeles might fit this description. Conditional-use permits might then be granted for the conversion of these structures to centers of the arts and related residential facilities.

In zones that permit the mixture of professional offices and residences, as long as artists conduct themselves like other professionals there is no reason for limiting their professional activities. The residential area is a separate and distinct unit from the professional facility.

The types of zoning that might accommodate the various individuals who practice the arts might be viewed as follows:

Individual practice: Where individuals practice the arts, it is possible to accommodate them in residential areas of most cities provided: (1) that their activities are not obnoxious to their neighbors, and (2) that as a home occupation they may merchandise their art or craft products on the premises. In the latter case, the business portion of the activity would be disclosed if the artist required a business telephone and therefore a business license. The level of sound would need to be controlled by some performing artists during hours of practice. The introduction of unusual amounts of traffic in a "school" situation and the consequent parking of excess vehicles could invite neighborhood antagonism and protest.

Group Practice: Whenever there is a large-scale operation, implying more than one artist or pupil, the areas open are generally in the commercial districts, although certain of the districts are reserved at present for highly specialized types of retail services (the neighborhood, district and regional shopping centers where areas are designed and specifically limited to retail sales operations). This does not mean that there could not be precincts in these centers for the practice of the arts, especially on second- or third-floor levels, which are usually not desirable for retail outlets (other than in large department stores).

The potential economic benefits of a genuinely flexible approach to zoning and locational planning for the arts are significant. It would enable artists to live and work in many areas of a city. If zoning changes were linked to the restoration and revitalization of the downtown, artists might choose it as a location for their work. This in turn would greatly enhance the center of the city and contribute to it the excitement and energy of creativity so sorely needed.

Footnotes

[1] The experience of SoHo (an abbreviation for South of Houston) in New York, where an art colony was encour-

aged, is instructive. When the rehabilitated space was offered for rent or lease, the immediate attraction of the project for renters caused rents to skyrocket. Rents originally ranging from 60¢ to $1.60 per square foot escalated up to $3.00 or more a square foot. In addition, people desiring apartments have paid several thousands of dollars as "key money" in order to secure a lease. The people now occupying the facilities are only those who can afford to pay rents at the inflated prices or were able to buy accommodations before the area became glamorous. (Based on information provided by Ms. Adriana R. Kleiman, AIP, principal planner on the staff of the Planning Department of New York City.)

[2] Since there is large-scale unemployment and relatively low annual income for people in the arts, it would seem reasonable that "rent subsidy" programs of HUD would be a potential program.

[3] Assembly Bill 7552-B, signed into law August 8, 1977 (State of New York) Article 7-B, Section 275.

[4] Information provided by Calvin Hamilton, director of planning for the city of Los Angeles, and by members of his staff.

3.14
Strengthening Neighborhood Arts

Neighborhood arts must play a critical role in the rehabilitation of our central cities. This is virtually by definition because neighborhood arts are primarily associated with minority cultures that represent a majority or near-majority of the population in most major cities. However, in contrast to the development of impressive cultural facilities for the traditional arts in most of the cities, neighborhood arts programs have not kept pace.

Support for neighborhood arts does not require an "either-or" decision against the traditional arts. The traditional arts, faced with formidable financial difficulties of their own, also require added support; the presentation of classical music, dance and opera to new and more diverse audiences remains an important goal. A balanced and planned program for the decentralization of arts facilities could meet the needs of both urban and suburban populations by making a diversity of cultural modes readily and freely accessible. These facilities would supplement rather than supplant the existing cultural complexes in downtown areas. The Neighborhood Arts Program in San Francisco has not visibly harmed attendance at events in the San Francisco Opera House or other centralized facilities. By stimulating a more general interest in and appreciation for the arts in a variety of forms, a decentralized arts program could have a long-run impact upon patronage of the arts in both the nonprofit and profit-making sectors.

A Neighborhood Arts Program

What is most needed in Los Angeles, as in other cities, is an organization that can speak for all the neighborhood arts in the city. San Francisco has successfully developed such a broad umbrella agency in the Neighborhood Arts Program, created in 1967 as a service arm of the San Francisco Art Commission. Private, nonprofit arts organizations retain their individual and independent identities, but receive technical assistance and other support from the Neighborhood Arts Program. The Neighborhood Arts Program has a relatively small central staff, but specialized support is given to neighborhood arts through a decentralized "district organizer" system: each designated geographic area "has an organizer and a workshop coordinator who are artists or artist-entrepreneurs known and respected in their respective neighborhoods."[1] Each organizer has control over a modest monthly budget which he or she is free to use in the service of perceived neighborhood needs, without bureaucratic red tape.

The Neighborhood Arts Program office provides technical and production assistance to neighborhood arts organizations: crews to set up stages, sound and lighting systems and other requirements for public presentations; help with publicity and proposal writing; and, above all, the design and printing of flyers and posters announcing cultural events sponsored by local groups. This last service has proven to be of special value to neighborhood arts organizations, which rarely can afford the costs of commercial printing. With this combination of technical services and district organizing, the Neighborhood Arts Program has been able to strengthen and extend the operations of neighborhood groups without undermining their autonomy.

With support from the San Francisco Art Commission and some key politicians, alliances of neighborhood and minority organizations succeeded in the early 1970s in defeating efforts to concentrate arts programs and facilities in the downtown areas. Instead, a $2.5 million Community Cultural Centers Program was adopted, with a commitment to the creation and/or renovation of neighborhood arts buildings in various sections of the city.[2]

The San Francisco Neighborhood Arts Program is distinguished by innovative and diverse programming: the San Francisco Blues Festival, mini-circuses, arts festivals, murals, the Undumbara Theater Dragon Project in Chinatown and elsewhere, dance programs including a dance film project, oral history projects, traveling puppet shows, music and art workshops, poetry readings, concerts by both recognized and developing musicians in jazz and folk music, and gardening and floral design.

It would be misleading, of course, to suggest that San Francisco's program has been without its problems and tensions. At its inception, political and institutional conflicts were common, and even today there are occasional disputes at various levels, notably between neighborhood arts organizations and government officials. Obviously, much of this is inevitable in the political context in which any such program must operate.

Nevertheless, by the mid-1970s the Neighborhood Arts Program was sufficiently entrenched that it could explore hitherto undeveloped sources of governmental support, and the result was a pioneering development of CETA (Comprehensive Employment and Training Act) programs in the arts, with employment of artists on public and other nonprofit projects underwritten by federal funds and administered locally. Initiated early in 1975, by March of that year about 125 artists in San Francisco were at work on CETA-funded projects and by the end of 1976 several thousand artists were employed on CETA projects throughout the nation.

Educational Programs

For the neighborhood arts programs to develop in the long run, there must be educational programs to build future community involvement with the arts. Recent studies indicate that an interest in the arts often is generated by appropriate training and exposure during childhood and adolescence, making it evident that the schools and neighborhood organizations directed to young people have particularly critical roles to play in developing a wider and more permanent audience. Indeed, much of the existing audience is young, and in the case of popular music and dance, teenagers represent a substantial proportion of the market. Often, however, this interest is temporary and ephemeral, diminishing as adulthood is attained and the process of raising a family begins. One task of education is to stimulate an appreciation of the arts as a lifetime experience extending far beyond adolescence, seen as an essential part of the enjoyment of living.

Regrettably, the dominant trend is in the opposite direction. Arts instruction programs are among the first targets of budget-conscious school boards in California and elsewhere, and subjects such as music and art are often regarded as frills rather than as intrinsically valuable studies which can become the direct or indirect basis for careers. The California Arts Council recently funded a special program—Alternatives in Education—which explored the possible role of the arts in the teaching of other academic subjects, and a thorough evaluation of the results of that program might produce findings which will define a new function for arts education. Further, creative skills may be related to a range of career occupations, including many which are outside the arts field, and educational research might well focus on new instructional and counseling techniques for identification and development of this relationship.

Universities in urban areas have the potential capacity to serve artistic needs in minority communities, but with few exceptions, this potential remains undeveloped and even unexplored. In Los Angeles, however, the USC School of Performing Arts has embarked upon a community outreach program which involves residents of the surrounding black and Latino communities through provision of free or low-cost admissions to performances, in-school symphony concerts, liaison with community leaders, and enrollment of minorities both in arts and arts management classes. USC perhaps is uniquely situated because of its location in a designated redevelopment area with a predominantly minority population, but universities in other cities (e.g., the University of Chicago and Columbia University) are similarly situated and even those which are not, like UCLA, have developed linkages with the community through special outreach efforts.

In greater Los Angeles, the presence of experienced and renowned artists—in music, dance, and drama, particularly—as permanent residents affords a special opportunity for educational innovation. With sufficient imagination and administrative flexibility, schools at all levels (from elementary school to college) can draw upon this available reservoir of skill and talent for teaching classes, workshops and clinics in the arts. Many resident jazz musicians, for example, can relate more effectively to minority students and instruct with greater knowledge and realism than can the full-time credentialed teachers.[3] Recently retired professionals in the arts can fulfill many of these part-time instructional functions, with benefit to themselves as well as the students.

Even some oral history techniques could be utilized in the service of community arts and education. Audio and video tapes of interviews with recognized performers interspersed with tapes of actual performances can be valuable as both an educational and entertainment device. Los Angeles artist and theatrical producer Ed Bereal is now in the process of taping such interviews with prominent jazz musicians.

In a related effort, the Los Angeles-based Jazz Heritage Foundation, headed by guitarist Kenny Burrell, prepares materials in the field of jazz for use by public radio and television and educational institutions, develops apprenticeship-type scholarships in composition and arranging, and produces concerts and workshops honoring the contributions of great American musicians. Such programs can stimulate further linkages between education and community arts.

Locke High School in Los Angeles was the site of one of the most effective educational workshops ever given. Partially funded through the Rockefeller Foundation and the California State University at Los Angeles from 1968 until its termination in 1972, the Locke jazz workshop consisted of a rehearsal band and, most important, private instruction of talented students by music professionals who were paid $30 for two visits, each visit lasting from thirty minutes to two hours. The success of the workshop, measured in part by the number of graduates who have since attained professional recognition, illustrates the essential role performed by dedicated teachers who have rapport with students. Some aspects of the workshop have been replicated at other schools, but not the unique element of individual instruction which characterized the Locke experiment.

Interviews with teachers in predominantly black and Chicano schools suggest that such schools often lack the quality of instruments and other equipment which is common in the more affluent areas. Furthermore, children in wealthier households have access to private instruction and may have their own instruments, privileges rarely available to youngsters in the inner-city ghettos and barrios. One knowledgeable teacher estimates that about 40 percent of his students (all of them black) have potential professional talent, but that a much smaller percentage have the necessary self-motivation and self-confidence to translate their potential into realistic careers. One problem is that so many of the youngsters in low-income households have no parental support—often there is only one parent present—and constantly face both economic and emotional difficulties which afflict the more affluent homes much less frequently. This may help to explain the troubling and ironic fact that virtually all-white "high school all-star" jazz orchestras annually appear at the renowned Monterey Jazz Festival, performing music which emerges predominantly from black culture.

These considerations emphasize the need for special instructional programs and improved equipment in low-income minority schools, which at least can partly offset the deficiencies encountered at home as well as in the neighborhoods. There are such programs from time to time, but frequently they depend upon extramural funding which may be only intermittently available.

Title I of the Elementary and Secondary Education Act provides funding for special educational projects directed to low-income areas. One such program in Los Angeles is the Intergroup Cultural Awareness Program (ICAP), which "provides elementary and secondary students with the opportunity to attend performances in their schools presented by performing artists of various ethnic backgrounds in the areas of dance, theater, vocal and instrumental music."

Eligible schools within the district, primarily located in the inner city, are able to "purchase" with their allotted Title I funds a series of performances from an extensive list of options, organized and made available through the ICAP. Musical and dance performances range from classical to jazz, with performers drawn from a wide range of backgrounds and ethnic groups. A Teachers' Guide offers biographies of program participants, annotated bibliographies, glossaries of key terms, and other aids to teaching. A major purpose of the program is to build more positive self-images among youngsters, who can identify with successful performers of their own ethnic group, as well as to acquaint them with the products of other cultures (both minority and the majority).

A somewhat similar ad hoc program, acclaimed by interviewees as particularly well received by students, was the history of jazz series presented in several Los Angeles area schools in 1974. Funded in part by the AFM Music Performance Trust Fund, the series traced, through professional demonstrations, the development of jazz from the New Orleans and ragtime styles to modern and Latin jazz. A comparable CETA-funded program, administered by the Musicians Union, was recently launched in Los Angeles.

Neighborhood Cultural Centers

An especially innovative, but temporary, neighborhood program was developed in 1974 by the director of a Los Angeles city recreation center in cooperation with a private music instructor. Free training in music fundamentals, instrumental music, jazz improvisation, stage band, rhythm techniques, singing and other aspects of music was offered to local youth and adults, mainly black. This eight-week series of workshops and seminars had the added merit of reaching many who might not be currently enrolled in the public schools.

This type of program illustrates the role played by neighborhood recreational and cultural centers which are accessible to and used by local residents. The more formal institutions—schools, museums, art galleries—sometimes lack flexibility and rapport with the minority community and may have an aura of elitism. Every urban area has a multiplicity of localized resources, but often they are ignored or inadequately used as a potential locus for arts events and education. Parks and playgrounds, daycare facilities, shopping malls, post offices and other public buildings, housing projects and other such centers can serve as conduits for both the visual and performing arts.[4]

Thus, art as an integral part of the everyday environment, rather than as an isolated phenomenon on display only in "elite" places, can be enhanced by both corporate and government policies. By including opportunities for artistic events in the planning and construction of business and commercial centers and of major public buildings and parks throughout the country, music, drama, dance and art can be brought directly into the work and recreational settings where many Americans spend the greater part of their lives. In downtown Los Angeles, for example, plazas located in or near major businessses are centers for the presentation of concerts, art exhibits and other cultural happenings. As indicated elsewhere in this book, public housing projects in east Los Angeles have been provided with murals and other artwork designed and implemented locally.

In south Los Angeles, new residential housing has been designed on the principle that artists will be among the residents and will have ready access to performance or art facilities where they can serve both their own needs and those of the community. The arts-focused housing is located in the heart of Watts, sponsored by the Watts Community Housing Corporation (WCHC). A nonprofit corporation, (its board representatives include Studio Watts, the Westminster Neighborhood Association, the Ward AME church, and a community arts council entitled The Meeting at Watts Towers) the WCHC has already constructed a forty-unit senior citizens housing project, and another 104 units of family housing are slated for completion later. Ten percent of these units are reserved for artists and one unit is available for possible use by a designated "artist-in-residence," who can use it as a studio and/or residence.

The project contains a central gallery-workshop for the use of artist residents, an outdoor theater and sculpture garden. Some of the land also is reserved for gardening by the tenants, all of whom are eligible for rental subsidies under Section 236 of the Housing Act. A unique feature of this development is the provision that all income from the project's laundry room, amounting to an estimated $300 a month, is dedicated to the support of arts activities.

The corporation recently obtained CETA funding from the city of Los Angeles for the employment of thirteen unemployed persons as community arts specialists, who worked primarily on a proposed newsletter to inform the surrounding community of the project's artistic programs and served as a linkage with other local resources. One purpose was to build a base of support within the wider community, as well as the political, business and educational structures.

The project's chief founder, artist James M. Woods, comments that a variety of bureaucratic obstacles extended the planning and construction process to seven years (1969–1976)—a much longer time than he considers necessary—and that virtually all of the planning funds had been provided by private foundations. He notes what he regards as a lack of confidence by some key public agencies in the capacity of black-sponsored organizations to administer such projects effectively.

To supplement programs and classes in the public schools and in centralized arts centers such as the County Art Museum, local communities should have publicly supported or subsidized cultural centers with facilities for both the performing and visual arts. Musical instruments, art supplies and other equipment should be available for use by residents, especially young people, in classes and workshops. Construction, staffing and programming of such centers should be a specific element in urban redevelopment planning and in the general plan for the total community.

It is essential, of course, to recognize that this ambitious plan for decentralized arts centers will face opposition within the larger community, or will encounter special problems in implementation. Questions inevitably will be raised in relation to possible cost, conflict with existing institutions or programs, and potential political interference in the arts. Additionally, problems may occur in connection with night-time crime and reluctance of many residents to leave home in some sections of the city.

The problem of cost for an urban community can be somewhat minimized by an approach which makes maximum use of existing facilities, such as parks, playgrounds and schools, and taps the many federal sources of support. Both general revenue sharing and two special measures—the Comprehensive Employment and Training Act (CETA) and the Housing and Community Development Act—provide funds to cities, counties and states under conditions which allow wide local latitude in their usage, and these can be used in the employment of artists and other professionals and in the needed construction and/or renovation of cultural facilities. Local Public Works grants under the Economic Development Administration, Public Works Impact projects under the Public Works and Economic Development Act of 1965, State and Local Economic Planning grants under the same act, and certain other funding sources also are available for the local planning, construction and/or renovation of artistic structures.

School districts can tap funds made available through various sections of the Elementary and Secondary Education Act (ESEA) and other measures administered by HEW, including special programs for educationally-deprived children, the Emergency School Aid Act, the Ethnic Heritage Studies Program, Community Education projects, and the Elementary and Secondary School Education in the Arts Program (these acts and programs are described in detail elsewhere in this book).

It is important that these various grant proposals in the arts be coordinated and integrated within an overall community plan adopted by the appropriate planning agencies. There will be unavoidable political problems as city council members and county supervisors press for additional funding in their respective districts, sometimes without regard for actual need or the special priorities for low-income minority neighborhoods. But this is a continuing and omnipresent difficulty which must be met and overcome in relation to any program.

Both cost and political considerations suggest that duplication with existing agencies, organizations and programs be avoided wherever possible. Where nonprofit arts organizations already exist in neighborhoods and are under competent management, their programs should be assisted and strengthened as part of the community arts plan without construction of new facilities.

The problem of security might be diminished through the proper planning of programs and facilities to minimize risks of crime. For example, shopping malls and other centers which are well-lit and well-policed, with adequate and secure parking areas, are ideal locations for artistic events. Consideration might also be given to the establishment of cultural parks in certain neighborhoods, akin to industrial parks (indeed, in some areas cultural and industrial parks might occupy the same space and facilities), which can encompass these security safeguards as an element in their planning and construction.

The neighborhood arts need support. We recommend the establishment of a neighborhood arts program along the lines of the San Francisco model, the development and enrichment of educational programs, and the creation of decentralized neighborhood cultural centers. Together with a department of cultural affairs in city government, these changes could help to generate the kind of cultural climate in which the neighborhood arts can flourish.

Footnotes

[1] Unless otherwise indicated, quotations and general information on the San Francisco Neighborhood Arts Program are drawn from the biennial report of Neighborhood Arts Program for 1972–74, an unpublished report on the NAP/CETA program by Paul Kleyman and Barbara Winer (1976), and correspondence from Mr. Kleyman (1977). For a further discussion of neighborhood arts, in San Francisco and

elsewhere, see Paul Bullock, *Creative Careers: Minorities in the Arts* (Institute of Industrial Relations, UCLA, 1977).

[2] Nine of these decentralized centers were either in operation or about to open in the fall of 1977.

[3] In the Spring of 1978, the UCLA Center for Afro-American Studies and Council for Educational Development initiated a new class—"Ellingtonia"—on the music and cultural significance of Duke Ellington. The renowned guitarist Kenny Burrell was named as instructor.

[4] A recent example in Los Angeles is the William Grant Still Community Arts Center, dedicated in March 1978 and located in a renovated former fire station. Originally proposed by City Councilman David Cunningham, the building was remodeled with HUD funding and the center is now part of the Municipal Arts Department.

3.15
Organizing to Strengthen the Economic Role of the Arts

Considerations of the role of the arts in the economic life of the city and the possibilities that exist for growth and development constantly encounter the problem of lack of coordination and mechanisms for planning. The need for coordinating units appears at all levels. The traditional arts in the nonprofit sector need a strong council for considering common issues and for advocacy. The community (neighborhood) arts should have their own umbrella agency. At the municipal level, different departments involved in cultural programs should be brought together to achieve maximum effectiveness. There is need also for careful consideration of how best to bring the arts into economic development efforts in the city. And there is a need for cultural planning.

These kinds of needs are common in cities across the nation. Methods of meeting such needs can best be discussed by using the Los Angeles example once again.

Creating a Department of Cultural Affairs

Currently, any cooperation and communication between city arts agencies in Los Angeles are conducted on a haphazard and ad hoc basis. Change is clearly required. A new Department of Cultural Affairs has been proposed by a study group (Mayor's Committee on Cultural Affairs, under the chairmanship of Gordon Davidson) which has examined the situation in Los Angeles. Efforts are currently under way at city hall, with the full support of the mayor, to reorganize the arts programs and agencies along new administrative lines.

The authors of this book endorse the proposal for the creation of a department of cultural affairs and here suggest how such a department might be organized and the responsibilities it should be given. This, we hope, might be suggestive for similar agencies elsewhere.

A unified agency in Los Angeles should combine the Department of Municipal Arts, the Cultural Affairs Division of the Recreation and Parks Department, and the Motion Picture Coordination Section of the Board of Public Works. The new agency must have equal status with other agencies overseeing the essentials of city government and must assume all municipal responsibilities relating to cultural affairs. The Cultural Affairs Department should act as an advocate for all cultural institutions within city government, and should also help to bring the arts into plans for the city's development.

Policy Objectives and Responsibilities

The department should take a strong leadership role in developing and articulating a comprehensive cultural policy, and just as important, have the power to implement it. Broad policy objectives should include:

1 Documenting the financial and economic importance of the arts industry to the city of Los Angeles;
2 Preserving the city's unique cultural heritage by developing a strong cultural awareness of the past and present;
3 Making the city's cultural resources accessible to all residents;
4 Promoting the development and growth of the city's cultural life including enhanced educational activities in the arts;
5 Integrating the arts into the urban planning processes of the city, including redevelopment.

The Department of Cultural Affairs could play an important role in stimulating the development of the arts by:

1 Supervising city aid to cultural institutions;
2 Helping to determine funding allocations;
3 Administering free programs to the public;
4 Providing technical services to cultural organizations, groups and individual artists;
5 Coordinating the efforts of other city agencies that affect cultural activites, as well as cooperating with the county;
6 Developing close relationships with the

arts activities and policies of the Los Angeles Unified School District.

To clarify these objectives and tasks, let us consider a number of them in some depth.

Assessment of Cultural Activity

In an earlier section we tried to give some sense of the range of cultural activities in Los Angeles. However, a full inventory lies beyond the possibilities of this project. The Department of Cultural Affairs should undertake a full study to accurately determine the contribution of the arts to the city. We have provided the schematic outline to guide such an endeavor. By exploring funding sources, audiences, programs and facilities of cultural institutions, gaps or deficiencies in the provision of cultural services can be identified. The information may also provide a basis for developing communications networks with all the city's cultural institutions, including those involved with both traditional and community arts. At the same time, the department can familiarize itself with the obstacles that must be overcome for the continued development of the arts. A composite profile of the arts could also serve to legitimize the need for a coordinated approach to municipal cultural affairs, and in doing so, provide valuable background information for the development of a comprehensive cultural policy.

Coordination of Support Services

Generalized planning implicit in the activities of federal and state agencies should be matched by detailed planning on a local level. The filtering down process of funds from the federal and state levels to cultural institutions in Los Angeles requires that the city understand citywide needs and opportunities. Study of the activities of federal, state and municipal arts agencies should reveal complementary or overlapping areas. Because local agencies have the best capability of understanding the cultural needs of their jurisdictions, they are in the best position to identify activity and funding gaps. Determining these gaps might conceivably provide an avenue for attracting new private and government funding sources.

Existing private and government funds and services are insufficient to meet the growing needs of the city's cultural institutions, particularly with a rapidly changing population structure. The Department of Cultural Affairs should maintain an official liaison with major sources of potential support. The agency would be in an ideal position to coordinate support resources geared to specific program needs.

As a well-informed agency, the department could improve the consistency of support and have a central role in integrating the needs of cultural groups. Cultural Affairs could strengthen its role by providing all cultural groups with information on public and private funding sources as well as technical assistance in the area of grantsmanship. As part of this program, the agency, if properly funded, could develop—in conjunction with the NEA, the California Arts Council and private support groups—a system of grants (or fellowships) to artists and arts organizations for research and development of ideas for innovative projects. Within this context, the agency could also develop financial and other incentives to encourage the Los Angeles Unified School District to bring artists and arts organizations into the public schools as integral parts of the education curriculum.

City and County Participation

The county of Los Angeles is a major contributor to the arts and maintains many facilities within the city of Los Angeles, including museums, theaters and amphitheaters, in addition to many park facilities used for cultural purposes. However, there has been little examination of the relation between city and county cultural agencies. Fear that investigation will disclose duplication of services discourages the likelihood for cooperation. Yet city and county cooperation could create new opportunities and resources for arts activities. One jointly funded city-county program, Shakespeare in the Park, has proven to be enormously successful in providing free theater to county and city residents alike. Obviously, given the abundance of excellent county facilities, there is room for combined activities, provided they are well coordinated and planned sufficiently in advance. Perhaps a first step might be a city-county coordinated effort to provide the use of public sites for exhibition and performing spaces.

The Music and Performing Arts Commission, the county's arts funding agency, and the Cultural Affairs Department should explore joint funding of programs. Cooperation with county government should be an important part of the Department of Cultural Affairs' overall cultural policy.

Historical Districts and Redevelopment

The Cultural Affairs Department should be allowed to play an active role in the development of historical districts and redevelopment projects. Currently in Los Angeles there exist no designated historical districts, only single historical buildings. Cultural Affairs could work with other city agencies in persuading the city to declare an entire area as having historical significance.

Only the city has the authority to provide financial incentives for private development involving the arts. The department could work closely with such agencies as the Planning Department and the Community Redevelopment Agency in overall planning efforts to encourage an arts component, where feasible, in urban development and redevelopment strategies. At present there is no active arts input into these processes, except for the Cultural Heritage Board's designation of historical-cultural landmarks. Provision for the arts must be integrated into plans for physical structures to provide functionally appropriate spaces for retail activities, such as arts-related businesses for galleries, artisans, crafts or theatrical studios, to name a few. The Department of Cultural Affairs should work with other city agencies to include provisions benefiting the arts. As an example of current arts-related activity, the Community Redevelopment Agency is considering the possible development of artists' housing and arts-related industries in vacated, but structurally sound, buildings in Los Angeles' former financial district on Spring Street. Other redevelopment plans are also being formulated for Hollywood, an area rich in cultural history. The arts should be involved in this planning, but no mechanism currently exists to integrate the arts into the planning process.

Development of a Community Arts Division

Community (neighborhood) arts activity helps to meet the artistic urges of thousands of residents who have little or no alternative for creative expression. In a social sense, it also helps neighborhoods to express a sense of community and ethnic pride. The Department of Cultural Affairs should have a Community Arts Division to foster the development of community (neighborhood) arts organizations. Guidance and assistance should run from securing permits for community arts festivals to obtaining major funding for new innovative programs. Information about what is available and aid in determining how to make the most of existing resources are needed by community groups.

The department would have to proceed with caution in developing new, municipal community arts facilities, particularly in areas that are already served by existing independent community arts organizations. The department must avoid destructive competition. An alternative is to explore opportunities for cooperative partnerships in projects of mutual benefit between the city and community art groups. The division could work to facilitate performance and teacher exchange programs between its own programs and community arts organizations.

An important component of the division would be that of providing technical assistance in the area of proposal writing. Workshops on management techniques, perhaps in conjunction with local universities, would also be extremely useful. The division should also provide free or low-cost printing services for publicity for community arts events. The department could also assist community groups with technical services such as mobile lighting, sound systems and stages for community arts festivals. A similar service has been successfully provided by the San Francisco Arts Commission through its Neighborhood Arts Program.

As part of its overall functions, the department should act as a clearinghouse for all arts functions, including those sponsored by the community arts. It should allow use of public and private facilities wherever possible for public performances or exhibitions. As the city agency devoted to the development of traditional and community arts, Cultural Affairs could function to bridge the communication gap between them by designing joint proposals that would bring them together to participate on projects of mutual interest. The Department of Cultural Affairs would be an enormous asset in generating an understanding between traditional and community arts.

Cooperation with For-Profit Arts Firms

The for-profit arts are extremely important in the provision of employment and income for artists and arts-related workers, in stimulating tourism, and in strengthening the economic base of the city. They should, therefore, be of prime interest to the Department of Cultural Affairs as well as to the city agencies directly concerned with economic development.

The department might appropriately be an advocate within the city for the private arts firms. There are helpful public regulations that can be sponsored to meet the needs of these industries (such as the "one-stop" permit arrangement for using public streets and facilities in filmmaking in Los Angeles). There are promotional activities that can be of assistance to both the nonprofit and profit-making arts activities that might well be fostered by the department, such as joint promotions to attract tourists, voucher ticket sales or the setting up of booths for the sale of unsold tickets at a reduced rate.

The department might also help to provide useful information on available training facilities for youthful, unemployed workers, to help them get jobs in for-profit arts activities. This is particularly important for behind-the-scenes workers. In some cases, private firms might be open to assisting in the establishment of training and information facilities. The department should seek this type of cooperation.

Finally, the department should be in a position to press for-profit firms, as well as nonprofit organizations, to meet targets for affirmative action hiring. Given the very high rates of unemployment among minority workers, such activities deserve high priority in Los Angeles, as in other central cities facing the same situation.

Cultural Affairs Foundation

Along with the implementation of a viable Cultural Affairs Department, a mechanism must be developed to expand private support for the arts. Under present guidelines, cultural agencies within the city are really not permitted to raise revenues to expand their own programs. Any funds that are raised, as, for example, through the sales of programs, revert to the city's general fund.

The Municipal Art Gallery, as well as the Cultural Heritage Board, raise funds through the Municipal Art Gallery Associates and the Cultural Heritage Foundation. A Cultural Affairs Foundation could be fashioned along similar lines to facilitate private fundraising efforts from business, foundations and individuals. Monies could then be channeled to activities and institutions in need of city funding. As a necessary incentive, there would have to be a dollar-for-dollar match of city funds. In effect, the foundation would serve as a much needed conduit for private support. Perhaps the foundation might be composed of different committees, each responsible for certain areas, such as the Municipal Gallery or community arts.

Unanswered Questions

Cooperation from other city agencies is needed for the department to become effective. We have not dealt with the jurisdictional problems that must be overcome or the required changes in the city charter to accommodate our suggestions. That is beyond our scope and would require another study. Nor have we dealt with all aspects of the work of a future Department of Cultural Affairs. Further study should be given to its potential relation to the schools (primary, secondary and higher education), corporations which fund artistic programs or install exhibitions, state and local design and architectural organizations, and special employment programs (such as CETA) which employ artists. The concern here has been to suggest the broad dimensions of a coordinated citywide set of activities in the arts.

Including the Arts in Economic Development Efforts

Most large cities, including Los Angeles, have launched substantial efforts to increase jobs and incomes for local residents—particularly the unemployed—and to strengthen the local economy. Such economic development efforts are led by agencies specifically established for such purposes and/or by regular agencies of the city government. (In the case of Los Angeles, there is an Office of Economic Development in the Mayor's Office, and economic development is a major objective of the Community Development Department as well.) In most instances, such economic development activities center on efforts to hold on to manufacturing establishments already in the city and to attract new manufacturing activities. A secondary objective is to try to retain wholesale and retail trade outlets, particularly where such trade activities tend to cluster together (e.g., a jewelry center).

Given the threat of losing substantial manufacturing and trade employment, it is not hard to understand the tendency of such economic development activities to concentrate their efforts in this way. However, at best, this is a holding operation and, in many instances, it is a losing proposition. The larger cities are experiencing tremendous changes. Manufacturing industry, formerly the backbone of local economies, has strong reasons for moving to outlying areas of the metropolitan region. So does much of trade. In the post-industrial era, service activities inevitably must be the major economic support of the city. But service activities have different requirements from traditional manufacturing or trade activities. The individuals who make decisions about the location of such service activities normally find that they have many locational choices. Today, such service activities have a strong tendency to cluster in cities and in parts of cities which are pleasant places in which to work and, for many, to live and play. The same, for that matter, is true today of much of specialized manufacturing and trade. The cities which are successful in retaining existing activities and drawing in new ones are the ones which are found to be attractive for management and labor.

This is where the arts come in. While the suburbs have substantial advantages over the city for many kinds of activities, the city has many important advantages for the arts. For many arts activities, such as symphony, opera, major theater and dance, a central location is an advantage. For visual arts and crafts, the highly unique nature of the individual products recreate many of the marketplace needs which originally contributed to the evolution of urban areas. On the other side, the arts serve to enhance one of the built-in advantages of the city, that of urbanity. Government and the private sector need to recognize the role of artists as dynamic city builders. Innovative ways must be designed for artists to enhance this role through sharing in the economic rewards of appreciated property values.

Thus, there are significant reasons for careful attention to the future of the arts in a major central city. Those who make decisions about local economic development activities have to be convinced of this fact. Just as public-private task forces are organized to try to hold on to a produce market or the garment industry or jewelry exchange, so task forces need to be organized to increase employment in the arts and to magnify the economic impact of arts activities. There are many elements that determine the economic impact of the arts, including: (1) the strength of the tourist industry, since much of the potential economic impact of the arts is by way of the tourist multiplier; (2) the extent to which individuals and families throughout the metropolitan region know about the arts activities in the central city (in the case of Los Angeles, this involves some 10 million people, as against the 2.8 million who live in the city itself); (3) the extent to which arts facilities and activities are included in new urban developments in the city, in urban redevelopment, and in preservation and restoration activities, since here, too, there is a question of the multiplier effect; and, of course, (4) the extent to which support of the arts is strengthened and put on a sustained basis, since employment and income in the arts are determined by the kind of support that is forthcoming. All of these and similar issues should be of concern to those involved with the economic development efforts of the city.

The probability that cities across the country will reorganize their economic development efforts to encompass such concerns would be greatly increased it the federal government's grants for economic development (through the Economic Development Administration of the Department of Commerce and through the Department of Housing and Urban Development) made specific provision for the arts in relation to such grants.

Any city economic development effort which involves the arts must necessarily be much concerned with corporate contributions to the arts. Nationally, corporate contribution to the arts are almost as large as public contributions in total amounts, the former having increased more than ten-fold within a decade. While many objectives are involved in such corporate contributions, the increase in arts employment and income does not seem to have been among them. Corporations interested in the economic viability of the central city might well consider the economic dimension of the arts in making decisions on grants and sponsored arts exhibits and performances. In economic development efforts, city agencies should inform corporate donors about the economic stimulus which the arts can provide, particularly in evolving programs to attract tourists and private investment to the city.

Establishing a Cultural Element in the General Plan for the City, County and Region[1]

The private market generally provides a significant organizing force for private business activities (although sometimes bolstered by public regulation); activities in the public realm require a much higher degree of planning to achieve the key objectives which have been set for them. Services that encompass many separate and disparate organizations, of both a public and private nature, particularly require planning guidance. This has become evident in the health services, where combined public-private planning is strongly supported; for example, there are substantial regional health planning agencies in every part of the country. The arts equally require substantial planning if they are to achieve the objectives which have been set for them, including the objective of making a major contribution to the local economy.

The logical form for such planning is through the introduction of a cultural element in the general plans that are prepared in almost every city and metropolitan region of the country. Such a cultural element would then join the other elements already part of the typical city plan and of many regional plans as well (the various elements normally being mandated by local and state legislation) e.g., elements for land use, housing, transportation, open space and other environmental features, and service and utility systems. The purpose of these elements, individually and taken together, is to provide a framework for specific governmental decisions, that is, an improved basis on which individual decisions by governmental units can achieve the major goals that have been established. Since it can be assumed that a major goal for almost every city and metropolitan region is the strengthening of the local and regional economy, then it can further be assumed that a newly-introduced cultural element would join the other elements in providing a decision framework for strengthening these economies.

An element in a general plan has its own set of requirements if it is to significantly aid in guiding both public and private decisions. Thus, a cultural element would have to do at least the following:

A **Provide basic information about arts activities and about the people involved in them.** This requires a constantly maintained inventory of the arts. Such an inventory alone could make the cultural element a key factor in strengthening the contribution of the arts to the local economy, as well as in achieving other objectives for the arts. Today, all decision makers have "to fly blind" in making decisions about the arts and the relationship of the arts to other public services and facilities and to the local economy. Each city and region needs basic up-to-date information on employment, underemployment and unemployment in the various arts activities for the various worker categories (including minorities, youth, etc.) and, as noted, this will require substantial effort. Also needed is information on audiences for the various arts categories, expenditures and receipts, and, in general, on the income generated by the arts activities, including the "ripple" effect, i.e., the indirect income generated by expenditures on the arts.

B **Make plans for broader and more flexible use of public (and, to some extent, private) facilities for arts activities, experimental arts groups and arts education efforts.** Such planning of facilities use is already being carried out to some extent in many cities through parks and recreation agencies and through arts councils and commissions. However, it is rarely done on a comprehensive basis and as a deliberate way of enlarging the scope for, and the economic impact of, the arts. Effective planning of facilities would require a high level of diplomacy, imagination and skill, since many different kinds of public and private agencies have to be convinced to make their buildings and other facilities available to arts groups, given the many

130

problems of security and insurance costs. Planning and execution with regard to facilities is clearly interlocked; it would be essential for the local and regional planning agencies to work closely with city and county departments of cultural affairs and with the various arts councils and commissions in broadening the base for facility use by arts groups.

C **Probe for ways in which the arts might be tied into the various public services in order to enlarge the scope of arts employment and income.** Some of the most exciting developments in the arts have taken place through the introduction of arts activities into basic public and private services and into facilities and other structures. The use of the arts for the education of those with learning difficulties and for troubled children has opened up new educational vistas, as have such programs as artists-in-residence and artists' performances in the schools on a scheduled basis. In health, art therapy has been employed very successfully in both in-patient and out-patient settings as primary therapy and adjunctive therapy. The display of graphic arts in hospital hallways and patients' rooms, as well as performances for patients, has been well received by both patients and hospital personnel. Cultural activities in parks and recreational areas are, of course, well established. Graphic arts related to transportation, on vehicles, at stations and in publicity, have also received increasing attention. Performances by professional artists in jails and other correctional institutions, as well as arts training in such institutions, have similarly created much interest. Art-in-Public-Buildings programs (including 1 percent arrangements), while still extremely limited in scope, have also opened up new vistas for the arts. The future possibilities of these and similar activities can be greatly enlarged by careful planning and imaginative execution. Substantial cooperation and coordination among individual public agencies, and with the executive and legislative branches of city, county, regional and state governments, are required and can be assisted by a well-designed program of cultural planning.

D **Make plans for the fuller use of the arts in urban development and redevelopment,** including downtown and neighborhood revitalization, preservation and restoration, the building of new-towns-in-town, the building of planned unit developments (PUDs), major landscaping activities, the building of new shopping plazas and centers, and the many other environmental changes in city and region. While this comes closer than the previous three items to traditional physical planning activities of city and regional planning agencies, even this item will call for new approaches in most city, county and regional planning agencies.

All of the following deserve attention in large central cities (and in large older suburbs, for that matter):

A Not only downtown areas but other major employment/activity centers within the city (in Los Angeles, for example, an old center like Hollywood or a new center like Century City) provide rich opportunities for greatly adding to their attractiveness by introducing arts facilities and activities as well as residential units that can serve as art colonies. Public redevelopment projects particularly tend to suffer from an "edifice complex" and high-rise sterility; redevelopment areas urgently need arts facilities and activities to enliven them and increase their attractiveness for living and working (and tourists).

B The preservation and restoration of buildings and districts of historical and architectural significance not only involve high levels of artistry and craftsmanship, but offer opportunities for creating areas of unusual attractiveness in which to live and work. Historical buildings and districts are among a city's greatest economic—and cultural—assets.

C Superior architecture, landscaping and urban design, together with sculpture and other visual art forms associated with environmental design, are themselves sources of urban strength. Business and professional firms, as well as many residents, have demonstrated their strong locational preference for city areas that feature such urban environmental amenities. The creation of such good architectural and other arts features is often a sound investment in the future of the city.

D There are innovative zoning features that can ease the problem of where artists can live and cluster in the city. To attract artists into the city by providing environments in which they can live and work at rent they can afford to pay is another form of investment in the future viability of the city.

Planning that considered all these features would have to extend beyond cultural planning and encompass other elements in the general plan of the city, county and/or region, including housing, transportation, land use, etc. A close interrelationship among elements of a plan is, however, an expected characteristic of comprehensive local planning. In this regard, a newly incorporated cultural element would join the other elements in being one part of a larger whole.

Given the breadth of the cultural planning that is called for, no one agency of local government could encompass the totality. Rather, what is needed is a cooperative set of cultural planning activities among the city, county and regional governments, together with all the communities which are members of the regional organization. For the city itself, the cultural planning tasks must be divided between the central planning agency (in Los Angeles, the Department of Planning and the Los Angeles Planning Commission and the major arts action agency (in the case of Los Angeles, either the existing Municipal Arts Department or the proposed new Department of Cultural Affairs). Other agencies, such as the office of economic development and agencies dealing with parks and playgrounds and urban redevelopment and housing, must also be involved in the cultural planning process. While all this sounds terribly complex, cultural planning can no more avoid the built-in complexities of government than can other kinds of planning.

To those who have not had close contact with city and regional planning operations, it would seem that the evident need for the planning of cultural activities in relation to public decisions would be enough to establish its desirability. But the content and nature of urban planning are not determined by logic alone. These are highly political matters, since they touch on the rights and privileges of mayors, city councilmembers, county supervisors and other politically sensitive individuals. Leaders of arts organizations will normally have to launch a campaign to convince the politicians that such an expansion of city and regional planning is politically desirable as well as economically helpful. And, of course, they will first have to convince themselves that this is actually the case. Arts people have not had much experience with planning. They will have to learn about a new science and art—that of urban planning.

Footnote

[1] A valuable treatment of considerations that enter into the development of a cultural element is provided by Gregg W. Perloff, "Developing a Cultural Element for a City General Plan," Master's Thesis, University of California, Berkeley, 1975.

Appendix A

TABLE A-1: Total Number of Employed Persons in Detailed Artistic Occupations, Los Angeles—Long Beach SMSA[1], 1950, 1960 and 1970, and Percentage Changes

	1950	1960	% Change 50–60	1970	% Change 60–70
Total, All Occupations[2]	1,690,395	2,615,496	54.7%	2,826,565	8.0%
Professional, Technical, Kindred (Total)	207,196	369,582	78.3	481,997	30.4
Actors, Actresses	4,495	3,155	−29.8	2,267	−28.2
Architects	1,399	1,866	33.3	2,815	50.8
Artists, Art Teachers[3]	5,391	8,201	52.1	6,650	−18.9
Authors	2,503	3,943	57.5	2,308	−40.5
Dancers, Dancing Teachers[3]	1,232	1,644	33.4	651	−60.4
Designers	2,664	5,403	102.8	8,298	53.5
Editors, Reporters	4,969	5,255	5.7	6,846	30.2
Musicians, Music Teachers[3]	9,391	9,596	2.1	6,038	−37.0
Photographers	3,281	3,690	12.4	3,846	4.2
Radio, TV Announcers	—	—	—	515	—
PR Men, Publicity Writers	—	2,441	—	4,632	89.7
Entertainers (n.e.c.)	992	846	−14.7	4,899	—
Total Writers, Artists and Entertainers	36,317	46,040	26.7	49,150	6.7
Craftsmen, Foremen, Kindred (Total)	265,659	366,287	37.8	362,748	0.9
Decorators, Window Dressers	2,174	2,968	36.5	3,104	4.5
Jewelers	1,739	1,426	−17.9	1,397	−2.0
Motion Picture Projectionists	1,069	971	−9.1	865	−10.9
Service (Total)	145,125	203,368	40.1	298,546	46.8
Attendants, Recreation and Amusement	1,834	2,238	22.1	3,052	36.3
Ushers, Recreation and Amusement	1,088	932	−14.3	879	−5.6

Notes: 1. 1950 is SMA
       2. 1950 is 14 years + over, 1960 and 1970 is 16 + over
       3. 1970 does not include teachers

Source: U.S. Census of Population 1950 (Table 73), 1960 (Table 121), and 1970 (Table 171)

Table A-2: Total Number of Persons Employed in Detailed Artistic Occupations By Sex, Los Angeles—Long Beach SMSA, 1950, 1960 and 1970

	1950 M	1950 F	1960 M	1960 F	1970 M	1970 F
Total, All Occupations	1,160,620	529,775	1,726,039	889,457	1,727,254	1,099,311
Professional, Technical, Kindred (Total)	134,627	72,569	255,029	114,553	310,414	171,583
Actors	2,944	1,351	2,194	961	1,409	855
Architects	1,342	57	1,811	55	2,723	92
Artists, Teachers	3,435	1,956	5,783	2,418	4,633	2,017
Authors	1,708	795	3,213	730	1,761	547
Dancers, Teachers	420	812	536	1,108	112	539
Designers	1,746	918	4,259	1,144	6,225	2,073
Editors, Reporters	3,670	1,299	4,015	1,240	4,959	1,887
Musicians, Teachers	5,744	3,647	5,246	4,350	4,582	1,456
Photographers	2,821	460	3,356	334	3,482	364
Radio, TV Announcers	—	—	—	—	481	34
PR Men, Publicity Writers	—	—	1,874	567	3,375	1,257
Entertainers (n.e.c.)	721	271	718	128	3,853	1,046
Total Writers, Artists, & Entertainers	24,551	11,766	33,005	13,035	36,453	12,697
Craftsmen, Foremen (Total)	257,074	8,585	353,768	12,519	342,896	19,852
Decorators, Window Dressers	1,452	722	1,741	1,227	1,747	1,357
Jewelers	1,645	94	1,342	84	1,280	117
Motion Picture Projectionists	1,052	17	960	11	829	36
Service (Total)	80,766	64,359	108,495	94,873	148,284	150,262
Attendants, Recreation, and Amusement	1,676	158	1,927	311	2,361	691
Ushers, Recreation and Amusement	554	534	521	411	562	317

Source: U.S. Census of Population, 1950 (Table 73), 1960 (Table 121) and 1970 (Table 171)

Table A-3: Occupation of Experienced Civilian Labor Force by Race and Sex, 1960 and 1970

1960—Male

	Total	Nonwhite	% of Total
Total, All Occupations	1,825,049	150,991	8.2%
Professional, Technical (Total)	263,646	11,648	4.4
Architects	1,824	86	4.7
Artists, Teachers	6,088	297	4.8
Authors, Editors, Reporters	7,810	186	2.3
Designers, Draftsmen	17,087	1,288	7.5
Musicians, Teachers	5,771	440	7.6

1960 Female

	Total	Nonwhite	% of Total
Total, All Occupations	934,314	95,186	10.0%
Professional, Technical (Total)	118,423	8,119	6.8
Artists, Teachers	2,520	109	4.3
Authors, Editors, Reporters	2,126	21	0.9
Designers, Draftsmen	2,190	117	5.3
Musicians, Teachers	4,538	196	4.3
Actors, Dancers, Entertainers (n.e.c.)	3,451	142	4.1

1970—Male

	Total	White	%	Black	%	Sp. Am.	%
Total, All Occupations	1,833,745	1,611,453	87.8%	157,119	8.5%	303,344	16.5%
Professional, Technical (Total)	325,974	297,030	91.1	14,010	4.2	26,829	8.2
Architects	2,794	2,477	88.6	78	2.7	236	8.4
Writers, Artists, Entertainers	41,848	38,518	92.0	1,949	4.6	4,183	9.9

1970—Female

	Total	White	%	Black	%	Sp. Am.	%
Total All Occupations	1,169,798	996,428	85.1%	128,004	10.9%	173,524	14.8%
Professional, Technical (Total)	178,713	153,900	86.1	16,780	9.3	13,178	7.8
Authors, Editors, Reporters	2,749	2,672	97.1	58	2.1	150	5.4
Actors, Dancers, Entertainers, (n.e.c.)	15,531	14,451	93.0	608	3.9	1,221	7.8
Actors, Dancers	2,805	2,556	91.1	208	7.4	155	5.5

Source: U.S. Census of Population, 1960 (Table 122) and 1970 (Table 172).

Table A-4: Median Income and Percent Worked 50–52 Weeks in Previous Year For Artistic Occupations by Sex, Los Angeles—Long Beach SMSA, 1950, 1960 and 1970

Male

	1950		1960		1970	
	Med. Inc.	% worked 50–52 wks.	Med. Inc.	% worked 50–52 wks.	Med. Inc.	% worked 50–52 wks.
Total, All Occupations	$3,239	66.2%	$5,684	68.5%	$8,542	68.6%
Professional Technical	4,313	71.7	7,743	75.2	12,162	72.0
Architects	5,204	81.6	9,169	86.7	13,729	83.4
Artists, Teachers	3,352	58.6	6,663	68.8	—	—
Authors, Editors, Reporters	5,012	68.7	7,798	68.2	—	—
Designers, Draftsmen	3,806	72.4	6,413	75.3	—	—
Musicians, Teachers	3,240	46.4	5,509	41.5	10,428	58.1

Female

	1950		1960		1970	
	Med. Inc.	% worked 50–52 wks.	Med. Inc.	% worked 50–52 wks.	Med. Inc.	% worked 50–52 wks.
Total, All Occupations	$1,891	53.0%	$2,957	49.4%	$4,461	51.6%
Professional, Technical	2,652	45.7	4,279	40.1	6,974	43.6
Actresses, Dancers, Entertainers (n.e.c.)	1,669	18.8	2,764	16.8	—	—
Artists, Teachers	2,073	44.0	4,034	44.1	—	—
Authors, Editors, Reporters	2,397	63.3	4,228	57.9	6,123	20.5
Designers, Draftsmen	2,543	37.0	4,206	59.4	—	—
Musicians, Teachers	1,283	37.0	1,665	28.5	—	—
Writers, Artists, Entertainers	—	—	—	—	4,973	40.5
Actors, Dancers	—	—	—	—	4,641	29.1

Source: U.S. Census of Population, 1950 (Table 78), 1960 (Table 124) and 1970 (Table 174).

Table A-5: Number of Persons Employed in Detailed Arts Related Industries, Los Angeles—Long Beach SMSA, 1950, 1960 and 1970

	1950			1960			1970		
	Total	% Male	% Female	Total	% Male	% Female	Total	% Male	% Female
Total, All Industries	1,690,395	69%	31%	2,615,496	66%	34%	2,826,565	61%	39%
Telecommunications/ Communications	27,081	43	57	43,009	50	50	51,913	49	51
Radio, TV	4,703	73	27	5,410	75	25	6,636	76	24
Business, Repair Services	61,097	83	17	102,617	75	25	138,820	70	30
Advertising	5,568	71	29	7,527	64	36	7,832	60	40
Entertainment, Recreation Services	50,594	75	25	50,742	72	28	54,528	70	30
Theaters, Motion Pictures	31,210	74	26	31,131	74	26	32,932	70	30
Bowling Alleys, Billiard, Pool	1,875	89	11	3,898	65	35	2,513	60	40
Miscellaneous	12,806	76	24	15,634	70	30	13,621	68	32
Professional, Related Services	164,634	42	58	304,244	42	58	—	—	—
Engineering, Architecture	4,526	86	14	—	—	—	15,017	82	18
Museums, Art Galleries, Zoos	—	—	—	—	—	—	1,470	64	36

Source: U.S. Census of Population, 1950 (Table 79), 1960 (Table 127) and 1970 (Table 184).

Table A-6: Number of Persons Employed in Arts Related Industries by Race and Sex, Los Angeles—Long Beach SMSA, 1950 and 1960

Male

	1950			1960		
	White	Black	Other	White	Black	Other
Total	1,089,127	50,159	18,334	1,588,693	99,777	37,569
Communications	11,437	181	29	20,971	477	151
Business, Repair Services	48,152	2,271	502	70,285	5,454	1,380
Entertainment, Recreation Services	36,690	1,138	187	34,644	1,502	429
Professional Related Services	65,914	3,313	775	117,907	7,733	2,870

Female

	1950			1960		
	White	Black	Other	White	Black	Other
Total	486,918	35,517	7,340	802,034	68,130	19,293
Communications	15,333	70	31	20,665	603	142
Business, Repair Services	9,909	184	79	23,706	1,308	452
Entertainment, Recreation Services	12,295	251	33	13,703	333	127
Professional Related Services	89,527	4,346	759	160,168	12,490	3,076

Source: U.S. Census of Population, 1950 (Table 83) and 1960 (Table 129).

Table A-7: Number of Establishments and Employees in Arts Related Services, Los Angeles City, 1972

	Establishments Number	Establishments w/payroll	Paid Employees Workweek of Mar. 12
Photographic studios (portrait)	884	93	983
Advertising	1,070	425	5,309
Commercial art, photography	—	260	1,457
Graphics, related design	—	—	—
Commercial photography	—	106	462
Commercial art	—	47	202
Other	—	107	793
Interior design	—	53	250
Architectural services	—	251	3,084
Amusement, recreation service, motion pictures (total)	4,732	1,837	28,093
Motion picture production, distribution, services	1,517	868	16,333
Production, ex. for TV	—	279	7,043
Production for TV	—	203	3,220
Services allied to production	—	245	4,336
Film exchanges	—	96	1,286
Distribution for TV	—	25	180
Services allied to distribution	—	20	268
Motion picture theaters	—	157	2,442
Theaters	—	141	2,147
Drive-ins	—	16	299
Producers, orchestras, entertainers	—	462	4,158
Dance bands, orchestras	—	78	1,069
Symphonies, other classical dance & music	—	13	320
Other entertain/present. (incl. variety)	—	195	1,407
Producers—legit. theater	—	37	490
Producers—radio, TV	—	41	381
Theatrical Services	—	98	491
Managers, agents	—	60	299
Other	—	38	194
Other amusement, recreation services	—	286	4,126
Dance halls, studios, schools	—	42	337
Public dance halls	—	8	180
Schools (child and professional)	—	34	157
Commercial sports	—	24	669
Amusement parks	—	7	(D)*

*(D) = Withheld to avoid disclosure
Source: U.S. Census of Selected Services, 1972.

Appendix B
Data Sources Used in California Employment Development Department Projections[1]

1. Employment Development Department (EDD) records of employers covered under the California Unemployment Insurance Code.

2. EDD's Current Employment Statistics (CES) sample.

3. Special tabulations of employment for detailed industries and occupations by class of worker, from the 1970 census.

4. National multiple jobholder and unpaid absence factors supplied by the Bureau of Labor Statistics (BLS).

5. Occupational change factors in California, supplied by BLS, which incorporate changes in industry staffing patterns into the model.

6. BLS labor force separation rates for California occupations.

---

[1] From California Employment Development Department, *Los Angeles County Manpower 1975–1980*, Feb. 1976. p. 71.

Table B-1: Projected Employment in Detailed Artistic Occupations, Los Angeles County, 1975–1980

	1975	1980	% Change
Total, all occupations	3,331,500	3,608,900	8.3%
Art, Drama, Music Teachers	1,513	1,642	8.5
Writers, Artists, Entertainers	64,945	71,886	10.6
Actors	3,376	3,557	5.3
Athletes, Kindred	2,897	3,272	12.9
Authors	2,593	2,863	10.4
Dancers	955	1,020	6.8
Designers	10,912	12,039	10.3
Editors, Reporters	8,735	9,521	8.9
Musicians, Composers	9,308	9,933	6.7
Painters, Sculptors	7,878	8,989	14.1
Photographers	4,425	4,768	7.7
PR Men, Writers	6,273	6,991	11.4
Radio, TV Announcers	682	742	8.7
Writers, Artists and Entertainers (n.e.c.)	6,912	8,192	18.5
Architects	3,739	4,140	10.7
Archivists, Curators	246	284	15.4
Engravers, exc. Photoengravers	405	424	4.6
Photoengravers, Lithographers	1,916	2,221	15.9
Decorators, Window Dressers	3,755	3,781	0.6
Jewelers, Watchmakers	1,686	1,696	0.5
Motion Picture Projectionists	1,247	1,241	−0.4

Source: California Employment Development Department, *Los Angeles County Manpower 1975–1980,* Feb. 1976, Table 3.

Table B-2: Projected Job Opportunities in Artistic Occupations Due to Industry Change and Replacement Needs, Los Angeles County, 1975–1980

	Net demand from industrial change	Replacement needs due to labor force separations	Total job opportunities 1975–1980	Average annual job opportunities
Total, all occupations	277,439	610,757	888,196	177,639
Art, Drama, Music Teachers	130	229	359	72
Writers, Artists, Entertainers	6,940	9,977	16,917	3,383
Actors	181	542	723	145
Athletes, Kindred	374	433	807	161
Authors	270	428	698	140
Dancers	65	389	454	91
Designers	1,128	1,443	2,571	514
Editors, Reporters	785	1,454	2,239	448
Musicians, Composers	625	1,388	2,013	403
Painters, Sculptors	1,111	1,252	2,363	473
Photographers	344	502	846	169
PR Men, Writers	718	1,055	1,773	355
Radio, TV Announcers	60	43	103	21
Writers, Artists, Entertainers (n.e.c.)	1,279	1,048	2,327	465
Architects	401	355	756	151
Archivists, Curators	38	43	81	16
Engravers, exc. Photoengravers	20	77	97	19
Photoengravers, Lithographers	305	225	530	106
Decorators, Window Dressers	36	742	778	156
Jewelers	11	347	358	72
Motion Picture Projectionists	−6	281	275	55

Source: California Employment Development Department, *Los Angeles County Manpower 1975–1980,* Feb. 1976, Table 4.

Appendix C

The multiplier process refers to the effect of one economic activity on the entire economy. It is commonly used by economists to estimate the effect of government policies upon the national economy. In the following cases, multiplier effects are calculated to estimate the local effect of spending generated by cultural facilities, although other types of facilities have similar effects.

The multiplier effect is considered an indirect or induced economic benefit. It is created by the recycling of a proportion of the purchases of goods and services by the cultural institutions, their employees, and their audiences or users into the local economic base.

The portion of a dollar spent by a resident employee or a resident member of the audience is spent either on goods or services originating from local businesses or from out of town businesses. The portion spent locally is represented by the *marginal propensity to consume locally* (MPC). The "leakage" of business external to the local economic base is represented by (1-MPC). The multiplier varies directly with the local expenditures and inversely with the out-of-town expenditures represented by the following formula:[1]

$$\frac{1}{1-MPC}$$

The largest multiplier effects can be anticipated when the MPC is at a maximum. This occurs when the local economic base is large and diverse enough to supply the greatest proportion of the goods and services demanded.

The most accurate method of calculating the value of the multiplier is by direct observation of the money flow of the art institutions, employees and audiences. This would require surveys and data retrieval and analysis.

To date perhaps the study that most accurately calculated the multiplier effect was the Baltimore case study.[2] A model consisting of thirty equations was developed to estimate the total impact of the arts on the economic base of Baltimore. Five of these equations included a multiplier value, as explained below:

1      $BP = (m_p - 1)(E)$
       BP = Purchases by local businesses from local sources in support of institution-related expenditures in the local economy
       m_p = Repurchase coefficient (1.818) for the local business sector (multiplier effects)
       E = Institution-related direct expenditure in the local community (expenditures by employees, local and tourist audiences, and the institution itself)

2      $BV = (.45)(E)(m_i - 1)$
       BV = Local business volume stimulated by institution-related income spent by local business employees
       m_i = Re-spending coefficient (2.857) for individuals (multiplier value)

  E = Institution-related direct expenditures in the local community

3 J = Emps + x (E + OC)
  J = Number of local jobs resulting from institution-related direct effects on the local business sector and government
 Emps = Total number of employees
  x = Marginal employment requirement (.000065) of an additional dollar's worth of local spending (multiplier value)
  E = Institution-related direct expenditure in the local community
  OC = Operating cost of government-provided municipal and public school services attributable to the institution and its employee households

4 PY = W + $_p$ (E + OC)
  PY = Total local personal income due to institution-related direct effects on the local business sector and government
  W = Gross compensation (including withholding taxes and retirement funds
  p = Profit and payrolls per dollar (.457) of institution-related expenditures (multiplier effect)
  E = Institution-related direct expenditures in the local community
  OC = Operating cost of government-provided municipal and public school services attributable to the institution and its employee households

5 DG = k (PY)
  DG = Durable goods purchases attributable to institution-related increases in total personal income
  k = Proportion of personal income (.031) devoted to purchases of durable goods (multiplier value)
  PY = Total local personal income due to instituion-related direct effects on the local business sector and government

 The multiplier values were interpolated from national data for various U.S. cities on the basis of the market size. For example, the multiplier for submodel 1, m_p, was interpolated as 1.818 for Baltimore although the range for these values for American cities was between 1.15 and 2.50. The remaining variables are determined by institution, employee and audience surveys.

 The extensive data retrieval required to apply this model is beyond the scope of most studies encompassing a large metropolitan area. For this reason other methods have been developed that may be less accurate but can still approximate the effects upon the local economic base. If certain assumptions are made concerning the multiplier values, a metropolitan-wide survey can be achieved with a minimum of data.

 The submodels could be easily combined by assuming that the multiplier values are equal for all equations. Major differences in values should be compensated for by simply not accounting for the economic activity in question, thus yielding a more conservative type of estimation. The percentage of error can also be minimized by examining only one type of facility, such as theaters, rather than the entire spectrum of cultural facilities. In addition, the multiplier value should be derived for each individual market area, that is, a different multiplier for each city.

The most unique example of an approximation of the multiplier effects of cultural facilities occurred in New York City.[3] The opportunity for a near-controlled experiment was created when the Broadway musical theaters closed because of a strike by the musicians union. The loss in local businesses during this period was then assumed to be a measure of the local economy's dependence upon theater activity. These figures were then adjusted for seasonal variations and multiplied by 1.6 to obtain the multiplier effects on the local economy. Other metropolitan areas can use this method by simply deriving their own multiplier as follows:

$$\text{Multiplier Value (M)} = \frac{\text{Population of subject metropolitan area}}{\text{Population of New York metropolitan area}} \times 1.6$$

Example:

$$M = \frac{\text{L. A. population (County)}}{\text{N.Y. population (5 Boroughs)}} \times 1.6$$

$$= \frac{7.6 \text{ million}}{8.8 \text{ million}} \times 1.6$$

$$= 1.38$$

Without conducting extensive employee or audience surveys, a minimum ancillary expenditures (restaurants, taxi, etc.) estimate is derived by multiplying 1.6 by the total gross ticket sales of the facilities under study. By making these crude, but very conservative assumptions, an approximate measurement of economic benefits can be made without extensive data retrieval efforts. Using this technique the economic benefits to the local Los Angeles economy of the Music Center is estimated to be $52.6 million. This is a very conservative estimate because most studies in other cities have used a 2.0 multiplier rather than a 1.38 multiplier.[4]

The homogeneity of audiences within similar types of facilities permits a more universal application of multipliers.[5] For this reason the 1.6 multiplier has been aplied in other metropolitan regions much smaller than New York.[6] Using this rationale, the economic contribution of the Music Center on Los Angeles may actually be as great as $61 million.

A more scientifically based multiplier estimate has been developed for a feasibility report for the San Francisco Performing Arts Center.[7] A multiplier value is determined according to a self-sufficiency index for a given metropolitan area. The self-sufficiency aspect of the local economy is determined by the minimum requirements method.[8] For example, the San Francisco region is estimated to be 55 percent self-sufficient, yielding a 2.22 multiplier for the appropriate new income items generated by the proposed facility and users. Using this method, a proposed concert hall that incurs a net annual cost of $61,400 per year to the city will generate $5,500,000 per year to the local economic base.

The assumptions that must be made in multiplier effect studies are considered highly debatable by proponents of decentralized community cultural facilities and some economists. For example, it is assumed that money spent at or around a cultural center would be recycled within the local economic base rather than in some other city. If there is a high percentage of out-of-town users and suburban employees, much of this money may indeed be spent outside of the local economic base. Money that is spent locally may be considered beneficial to the local economic base, but can also be viewed as a geographic raid whereby one area is just draining the potential benefits of another local economy.[9]

Most of the studies concerning indirect benefits of cultural facilities do not attempt to estimate the effects of tourism generated by the arts. This is because the data from the visitors' bureaus does not separate tourism generated by the arts from that by other amenities such as recreation. The tourist multipliers are generally greater since their expenditures for housing, food and transportation are greater.

Metropolitan areas such as New York and San Francisco are most likely to derive the greatest indirect benefits from tourism generated by cultural facilities. This is because audience surveys have documented a large percentage of out-of-towners at cultural events. For example, in San Francisco the De Young Museum attracted 35 percent San Franciscans, 27 percent other Bay Area residents and 38 percent out-of-state or foreign tourists[10] and the Opera House attendees consisted of 55 percent out-of-towners.[11] Making the assumption that most of the ancillary expenses (mostly hotels and restaurants) occur within the vicinity of these facilities, the multiplier effects are far greater than in the case of the resident audience.

According to the U.S. Department of Commerce, in some cases the multiplier value may be as high as 5.0; however, a more recent study by the National Tourism Resources Review Commission estimates the minimum multiplier effect at only .75.[12] Considering the volume of tourists in large cities, even a low multiplier has a substantial effect.

Los Angeles' cultural facilities do not attract a substantial tourist trade for several reasons. Most tickets for theater are sold to local annual subscribers with only a limited amount of tickets for sale to the general public. There is no attempt to promote existing cultural facilities beyond the local community. And even if such efforts were made, the scale of Los Angeles' present facilities cannot accommodate the increased volume of attendance from tourism. Hypothetically, if the arts would generate only 10 percent of the city's tourism, the local benefits (using a .75 multiplier) would exceed $84 million annually (using the spending pattern recommended by the Southern California Visitors Council).

Footnotes

[1] Charles Tiebout, *The Community Economic Base Study,* Committee for Economic Development, New York, NY, Supplementary Paper No. 16, December 1962, pp. 59–61.

[2] David Cwi and Katherine Lyall, Center for Metropolitan Planning and Research, Johns Hopkins University, *Local Economic Impacts of Art Institutions: A Model for Assessment and a Case Study in Baltimore,* National Endowment for the Arts, Washington, DC, 1978.

[3] Mathtech, *The Impact of the Broadway Theater on the Economy of New York City,* The League of New York Theaters and Producers, Inc., New York, NY, February 22, 1977, p. 44.

[4] Joint Committee on Cultural Resources, *In Search of a Regional Policy for the Arts: Phase II,* Johns Hopkins University, Metropolitan Planning and Research, 1975, p. 20.

[5] William J. Baumol and William G. Bowen, *Performing Arts—The Economic Dilemma,* MIT Press, Cambridge, MA, January 1967, pp. 71–98.

[6] Raymond J. Richardson and John F. Maxwell, "Lake Placid Center for Music, Drama, and Art," New York State Council on the Arts, unpublished, 1974.

[7] Richard Mickley, "Preliminary Feasibility Study of the Proposed San Francisco Performing Arts Center" (Draft), unpublished, Stanford Research Institute, Stanford, CA, March 30, 1976.

[8] Edward L. Ullman, *The Economic Base of American Cities,* University of Washington Press, Seattle, WA, 1969.

[9] Cecelia Brimaggi, *San Francisco Civic Arts Funding: Who Pays? Who Benefits?,* Intersection Center, San Francisco, CA, 1977, p. 9.

[10] De Young Museum, "Audience Survey," conducted March 1975.

[11] Richard Mickley, op. cit., p. 4.

[12] National Tourism Resources Review Commission, *Destination USA,* Vol. 1, Summary Report, U.S. Government Printing Office, Washington, DC, June 1973, p. 13.

Appendix D

Excerpts from New York City Zoning Ordinance, 1-1-77

Section 12-10 Definitions

Joint Living-Working Quarters for Artists

A "joint living-working quarter for artists" consists of one or more rooms in a non-residential building, on one or more floors, which are arranged and designed for use by, and are used by, not more than four non-related artists, or an artist and his family maintaining a common household, with lawful cooking space and sanitary facilities including the requirements of the Housing Maintenance code, and including adequate working space reserved for the artist or artists residing therein. AN ARTIST IS A PERSON SO CERTIFIED BY THE NEW YORK CITY DEPARTMENT OF CULTURAL AFFAIRS. . . .

Note: The ordinance lists an extensive group of industrial uses, but in Section 42-14, Use Group 17, it is implied that only those uses which limit their impact on adjacent residential areas would be a suitable environment for the mixed living-working quarters for artists.

Section 42-14-D Special Uses in Certain Industrial Areas

Joint living-working quarters for artists in buildings in MI-5A and MI-5B industrial districts, provided:

a Building erected prior to 1951.
b Lot coverage by building does not exceed 5,000 square feet. Can be in a building with more than 5,000 square feet of lot area if the entire building was held in cooperative ownership by ARTISTS on September 15, 1970.
c In MI-5B districts in buildings occupying *less than 3,600 square feet* of lot area, joint living-working quarters for artists may not be located below the floor level of the second story unless modified by the Planning Commission.
d In buildings occupying *more* than 3,600 square feet of lot area the joint living-working quarters for artists may not be located below the floor level of the third story unless modified by the Planning Commission.

Section 42-141 Modifications

The restrictions in the MI-5A and MI-5B districts may be modified:

4 When the Commission finds that the space below the floor level of the second story is required by the artist whom the Department of Cultural Affairs has certified as working on a heavy or bulky medium which is not easily transported to the upper floors.

Section 43-17 Special Provisions

In the MI-5A and MI-5B districts no building containing joint living-working quarters for artists shall be enlarged, except that mezzanines are allowed within individual quarters, provided that they do not exceed 33 1/3 percent of the gross floor area of such quarters.

In the districts indicated, no building containing joint living-working quarters for artists shall be subdivided into quarters of less than 1,200 square feet except when no story contains more than one joint living-working quarter for artists.

Section 74-77 Artists Centers in the C6-1, C6-2, C6-3 and C6-4 Commercial Districts

The City Planning Commission may permit residential and non-residential uses to be arranged within a building to be occupied as living and working quarters by artists engaged in the visual or performing arts, with or without related community studio space.

As a condition precedent to the grant of such special permit the Planning Commission shall make the following findings:
a That the location, design and construction of such building particularly suit it to the use as an artists' center, and that full realization of these advantages requires modification of the regulations controlling arrangement of residential and non-residential uses within the building. . . .
b That an organization has been established for assuring that the dwelling units will be occupied by persons who qualify as artists.

Section 74-78 Modifications by Special Permit

In MI-5A and MI-5B Districts the Planning Commission may, after public notice and hearing and subject to Board of Estimate approval, permit modifications provided that:

> The commission finds that the owner of the space has made a good faith effort to rent such space to a mandated use at fair market rentals. . . . Such effort shall have been actively pursued for a period of not less than six months for buildings under 3,600 square feet and for one year for buildings over 3,600 square feet, prior to the date of the application for a Special Permit.

Excerpts from Los Angeles City Zoning Ordinance as Amended 1-6-75

Section 13.06 Commercial and Artcraft District

Purpose—To create enclaves whereby artisan segments of the population may live, create, and market their artifacts. Artcraft activities, combined with commercial and residential uses, will be permitted in those areas appropriate for the establishment of a "C-A" District.

Requirements—Each application for the establishment of a "C-A" District shall include the signature of 75 percent of the owners or lessees of property of an area not less than 3 acres in total size, or by resolution of the Commission or Council. The area shall be computed by contiguous parcels of land which may be separated by public streets, ways, or alleys.

Conditions—Regulations must promote optimal conditions for art and craft functions while maintaining adequate protection against obnoxious pollutants for the adjacent properties.

Production Techniques—The creating, assembling, compounding or treatment of articles shall be accomplished by hand to the extent practical for a particular artifact.

Only those art products which are made by the artisan or his employees from raw materials can be sold. Mass-produced parts may be used if incidental. In those techniques which necessitate the use of a kiln, the total volume of kiln space shall not exceed 24 cubic feet and no individual kiln shall exceed 8 cubic feet.

Power tools shall be limited to electrically operated motors of not more than one horsepower.

Certain art and craft activities shall be restricted to either indoor or outdoor manufacturing.

Paid helpers shall be limited to no more than 3 persons other than members of the immediate family occupying the dwelling on such premises.

Limited artcraft instruction shall be permitted—classes not more than 2 days a week nor more than 3 hours a day—with not more than 15 persons in each class. All classes to be held on the first floor of the building.

Residential Uses—In "R" zones, the residential regulations as required in the underlying zone shall apply. (Note: See Home Occupation Provisions.)

In the "C" and "M" zones residential uses shall be permitted in connection with the main commercial, industrial or artcraft uses.

Home Occupation shall mean any use customarily conducted entirely within a dwelling and carried on by the inhabitants thereof, which use is clearly incidental and secondary to the use of the structure for dwelling purposes and which use does not change the character therefore or does not adversely affect the uses permitted in the district of which it is a part and wherein no products are sold on the premises other than those produced thereon, no signs are displayed except as permitted by this Ordinance, no persons are employed other than domestic help and no mechanical equipment is used other than that necessary or convenient for domestic purposes.